Making News at
The New York Times

Joseph Turow
SERIES EDITOR

THE NEW MEDIA WORLD

Broadcasting, Voice, and Accountability: A Public Interest
Approach to Policy, Law, and Regulation
*Steve Buckley, Kreszentia Duer, Toby Mendel, and Seán Ó Siochrú,
with Monroe E. Price and Marc Raboy*

Owning the Olympics: Narratives of the New China
Monroe E. Price and Daniel Dayan, editors

The Hyperlinked Society: Questioning Connections in the Digital Age
Joseph Turow and Lokman Tsui, editors

When Media Are New: Understanding the Dynamics of
New Media Adoption and Use
John Carey and Martin C. J. Elton

Making News at *The New York Times*
Nikki Usher

DIGITALCULTUREBOOKS, an imprint of the University of Michigan Press,
is dedicated to publishing work in new media studies and the emerging
field of digital humanities.

Making News at
The New York Times

Nikki Usher

The University of Michigan Press
Ann Arbor

Published in the United States of America by
The University of Michigan Press
Manufactured in the United States of America
⊗ Printed on acid-free paper

2017   2016   2015   2014   4   3   2   1

A CIP catalog record for this book is available from the British Library.

ISBN 978-0-472-11936-3 (cloth : alk. paper)
ISBN 978-0-472-03596-0 (paper : alk. paper)
ISBN 978-0-472-12049-9 (e-book)

To Herbert Gans,
for his invaluable advice, wit, and wisdom
and for inspiring me to begin a journey
into the changing newsroom

Contents

Acknowledgments

This project would have been impossible without the unconditional support I received at the University of Southern California's Annenberg School of Communication and Journalism and at the George Washington University's School of Media and Public Affairs. I extend my deepest gratitude to my advisor, Larry Gross, for his support, advice, and critique. I also want to thank my dissertation committee, Henry Jenkins, Geneva Overholser, and Patti Riley, for their feedback and willingness to let me write a "book" instead of a traditional dissertation. Larry had me change hands and sent me to Joe Turow, a fantastic scholar, editor, and author at Annenberg East—the University of Pennsylvania's Annenberg School. Joe took this manuscript for his ambitious new series with the University of Michigan Press and provided incredible insight, editing, and trenchant support to get it into shape. I am incredibly lucky to have had him at my side. I also have been fortunate to have had the kind support of Tom Dwyer, past executive editor at the University of Michigan Press, who has been steadfastly supportive of my potential as a junior scholar.

I would also like to thank all of the many senior scholars who have helped me from graduate school to this point. In addition, having the chance to engage with Herbert Gans through years' worth of emails and far too few in-person meetings has been humbling and challenging. My cohort of junior scholars engaged in similar work have been astoundingly supportive, considering that we could be jealously at heads with each other. I particularly want to thank C.W. Anderson for our friendship and his collegiality, and I would be at a loss without Matt Carlson, Seth Lewis, and Matt Powers and our regular email banter. The George Washington University's School of Media and Public Affairs has been encouraging throughout this process as I have moved from dissertation to book. I want to thank all my colleagues, especially Kim Gross, Frank Sesno, Steven Livingston, Bob Entman, and Catie Bailard. Kim, Frank, Silvio Waisbord, and Matt Hindman read various drafts of this book; Bob provided amazing advice about the publishing process, Silvio a chill pill. Matt challenged me and helped me think through some serious blocks, and I am lucky he was working on a new book as I began mine. Our colleague emeritus Jerry Manheim read much of this manuscript. All of my colleagues deserve thanks, and I expect our ties to deepen over the coming years. My dutiful research assistant Todd Kominiak read every word and formatted the document. And of course, deep gratitude goes to those who helped make sure I was housed and fed, and properly funded and reimbursed: Christine Lloreda at Annenberg and Maria Jackson at GWU.

Finally, special thanks to *The New York Times* and the business desk in particular. Larry Ingrassia and Bill Schmidt let me into the newsroom, and Kevin McKenna guided me while I was there—and answered any and all possible questions I might have. Special thanks to a few *Times* staffers who made my work so much fun: Tanzina Vega, Michael J. de la Merced, Mark Getzfred, Brian Stelter, Javier Hernandez, Eric Dash, and Kelly Couturier. Liz Alderman was the crucial link in my *International Herald Tribune* knowledge and in a visit to Paris, which was truly amazing. Many at *The Times* helped in so many ways, though of course all errors here are my own.

Thanks to all of my friends outside the walls of academia who have helped me through this process—both with the manuscript and with your kind support. And special thanks to my wife, Shelly Layser, who continues to be my inspiration. I couldn't ask for anything more in a life partner.

Introduction

THE TIMES IN THE DIGITAL AGE

The new *New York Times* building that stands blocks away from its namesake Times Square is a fifty-two-story, Renzo Piano-designed office tower between Fortieth and Forty-first streets on Eighth Avenue. The ground floor of the building is dedicated to a *New York Times* auditorium, rented out for events and used by *The Times* for "Times Talks," where New Yorkers have the chance to meet their favorite *Times* critic or other public intellectual—or in some cases, a baseball player for the Yankees. The building itself is, as the leasing office proclaims, the first "high rise curtain wall with ceramic sunscreen to be built in the United States."[1] Practically, what this means is that the glass-walled building has light-sensitive blinds that open and shut of their own accord, based on passing clouds or bright afternoon sunlight. The magic of this system wore off quickly for many of the staffers inside, who learned to look up when the loud flaps move and promptly reconfigure the blinds to their liking.

The new building is a great contrast to the paper's home since 1913 on West Forty-third Street. The old building was a dour, sparsely windowed gray stone edifice hidden on a side street away from the bustle of Times Square. Known to generations of journalists as "the factory," it surely contributed to the paper's image as the "Gray Lady" of American journalism. The new home of *The New York Times* for the digital age, though, is smack-dab in the middle of its audience. You almost *have* to pass the building to get between the Port Authority and the Times Square subway stop. Journalists who happen to be eating lunch in the fourteenth-floor cafeteria, or simply looking out the window, can see the city in endless motion.

This new building is the symbol of a collection of promises: the start of *The Times* as a fully integrated Web newsroom; *The Times* as a shining glass beacon for innovation in news; *The Times* as a stamp upon the New York skyline, marking its continued relevance. And it is, at the same time, a symbol of the challenge inherent in achieving each of those aspirations.

The architecture itself tries to embody these hopes. Over each of the three entrances to the building hangs a *The New York Times* sign in the distinctive font that has been the legendary banner of the newspaper for decades. Each sign is bold enough to inspire tourists to take photos, but the entrances are not foreboding; in fact, each one is open to the public. People are invited inside the sun-soaked lobby to admire the public art and the glass atrium, though of course they are stopped by security should they try to go inside the elevators leading to the actual newsroom. All the glass, all the open space—the entire interior look of the newsroom is intended to signal a new era for the newspaper in the digital age.

Inside, the three main floors of the newsroom are all connected by red, painted stairways with a big, wide gap for everyone on the fourth floor to peer down at people working on the second and third floors. The most important seats in the house are on the third floor. Here, *The Times* has deliberately tried to place the people charged with deciding the most important print stories of the day directly next to the people who make the up-to-the-minute decisions about what goes on the Web page. The top brass—the executive editor and two managing editors—sit next to the two most prominent members of the online staff.

Gathered in a few cubicles located in the center of the newsroom is the locus of production for the home page and the hub of the Web operations. The cubicles, a medium wood, are situated low enough to make it easy for people to have conversations with each other. This cluster is home to the continuous news desk editor,[2] the domestic and global home page editors, and the Web photo editors. The Web operation, then, is supposed to be a centerpiece of the newsroom, and symbolically, it is also close to the powerful people charged with setting the entire editorial strategy of the newsroom.

But seating plans and architecture do not mean that people will actually talk to each other. During my five months immersed in the newsroom, the activities of the home page editor were generally ignored by executive and managing editors, who, at least on a daily basis, remained preoccupied by deciding what would go on Page One—the front of the physical print paper. Yet just one of these rotating Web producers was responsible at any given time for what more than thirty million unique vistors would see each month.

Those in the newsroom justified the "noninterference" between print and online—a polite way of saying lack of engagement—this way: "These people are chosen because they have great news judgment, are great copy editors, can work quickly, and rarely make mistakes."[3]

The relationship between print and online is bundled with contradictions: the new reality of online work in the digital age at *The New York Times* simply doesn't mesh with the essential character of the daily, print newspaper. It has only been since 1996 that *The Times* has had a Web site of its own, a blip in its 160-plus-year history, and print still pays the bills and builds egos. On the other hand, "traditional" print journalists do write for the Web—in fact, almost everything they will write appears online. They are accustomed to writing breaking news stories on tempo with the latest developments. Their long-form features appear online, often with multimedia complements. Top editors routinely proclaim in missives to the newsroom and to the public that nytimes.com is the newsroom's future.

The challenges facing *The Times* in 2010 were more than just about the relationship between print and online news. In a 24/7 news environment, *The Times* tried to produce and display a rapid stream of content online while still hoping to set an agenda and have a final say. The newspaper was also caught up in the process of trying to build multimedia and interactive graphics, both as new forms of storytelling and as ways to keep readers on the page longer—another way to build clicks and then dollars. And as social media flourished across the Web, *The Times* as an organization tried to capitalize on the momentum, while journalists debated whether to add another tool (or obligation) to their jobs. The question before *The Times* and its journalists was one bound up in the new realities of economic pressure, changes to professional practices, and technological innovation: Just how should *The Times* create content for the Web when simply pasting text online was not enough? What should the process and the values defining news production be in this new era?

In practice, the answer proffered by the nation's premier news organization in 2010 was a bit like the buffet at a Las Vegas casino, with editors, executives, and journalists trying to make *The Times* offer everything to everyone. The print paper would continue to set the agenda, but the Web site would be continually updated, and reporters on deadline would write for that immediate push. The Web site would be filled with interactive and multimedia content, and the newspaper would aggressively pursue a social media strategy. But as one journalist put it to me, "We can't keep doing all this shit—blogging, videos, and writing for the paper. We can't be great at everything." Still another journalist, however, editor Susan Edgerley, told me, "We will succeed in the digital age because *The New York Times* likes to be the best. At everything."[4] Herein lies the great tension at *The Times*: the reality of what journalists were able to do versus the larger aspirations of the newspaper—the quest to be the best online, as it felt like it was in print. Though this book is history now, in an ever-evolving story of newsroom change, it offers a step back to consider *The New York Times* and its story in 2010, caught in one moment between the legacy of its past and what it saw as its future. At the time, *The New York Times* was arguably the most influential journalism outlet in the United States, and it had the most-trafficked newspaper Web site on the entire Web. But stats tell us one thing about the newsroom, and what was happening inside the newsroom tells us another story—about an institution and its journalists adjusting to digital change.

The purpose of this book is to provide an inside portrait of *The Times* that shows how journalists attempted to negotiate the challenges of creating online and print content according to emergent online journalism values: immediacy, interactivity, and participation. This window into *The Times,* between January and June 2010, comes from the five months and over seven hundred hours I spent inside the newsroom (principally stationed at the business desk). In this book, you will see how journalists tried to negotiate the challenges of working in an on-demand, instant news world, attempting to iron out routines that would make it possible to keep up with the pressure of constantly feeding a Web site that was ever-hungry for fresh content. You will see the opportunities and challenges journalists faced as they encountered new demands for interactive content, from video to online graphics. This book also documents how journalists reckoned (or didn't) with a now-active audience able to talk back and create content, thanks to social media. From my experience inside the newsroom, I saw how these three core values of online journalism—immediacy, interactivity, and participation—emerged as points of tension and change. This book, then, offers an analysis and chronicle of how *The New York Times* dealt with these three values.

My key argument is this: there are new values orienting journalism practice in an online journalism world. Journalists must reckon with how to adjust to the demands of a 24/7 news cycle, an environment of interactive engagement, and a world where one-to-many has been upended. The result has been a restructuring of news routines, albeit in a contested way, which has led to the emergence of new news values: immediacy, interactivity, and participation. In turn, these values are ordering news work and professional practice. The "old" news values, ones that also emerge out of routines and internal and external forces, are still present. Objectivity is still a strategic ritual and a vaunted professional aspiration, for instance. But front and center, journalists are now adjusting the ways they incorporate their workflow and professional aspirations in an entirely different working environment from the past.

This work, then, shows the puzzling battles being fought over the front lines as journalists were caught between tradition and change. The austere Gray Lady, where journalists fought to be one of the five most important stories of the day and strove to be on Page One, also had to be nytimes.com, the leader in the world of newspapers online. This meant that journalists struggled to embrace new imperatives in their work: getting fresh content out on the Web while still working for those Page One victories, making the Web site for users to explore stories beyond text, and reaching out to readers across social media platforms. These "musts" became the new reality; whether journalists liked it or not, these values were emerging to order newswork and set standards for journalism at *The Times*. Whether these values were *liked* is less important than whether they *functionally signified* a reorientation of journalism. What we see here is this battle over the meaning of these values, and their place in the newsroom, through the daily lives of journalists in the newsroom.

These values of immediacy, interactivity, and participation emerge from the routines that were (or were not) in place at *The Times*, and they are overarching terms that help categorize the new priorities, goals, and felt imperatives organizing news production at this time. In turn, these values shape the structure of the book and help us interpret the underlying dynamics at work inside the newsroom. The values are embodied by journalists as they attempt to structure their understandings of what news ought to be—and how it ought to be made. They map onto the relationship between print and online, the drive for multimedia, and the push for social media engagement. I also use these terms because they are resonant with a legacy of theoretical work on both the networked digital environment and scholarship about journalism. With immediacy, interactivity, and participation as a backdrop, a study of *The New York Times* in 2010 can also be placed in dialogue with many of challenges facing other newsrooms at the time. However, before moving forward to introduce these values in the context of *The Times* and journalism more generally, I offer some reasons why studying this particular case offers important insights for journalism studies as a whole.

Why *The Times*?

The Times is a pivotal institution in American democracy. Since 1851, it has shaped the contours of elite political discussion and provided substantive reporting from across the world and the nation. Though it is not a perfect paper and can be judged for many failures throughout its history, the Gray Lady continues to retain its gravitas. There are a number of jokes one can make about the future of the news industry; one says that there are two rules: First, all discussions about it must reference *The New York Times*. Second, anyone invested in the larger project of changing journalism ought to stop with *The New York Times* obsession. But here we have an account of *The New York Times* as it underwent a period of digital change—not a remarkable disjuncture marked by organizational overhaul, but rather the fine-tuning of adjustments to the pace of news in 2010. This story about the future of the news is already an account of the past, but it deserves to be recorded because it shows how this tremendous institution grappled with the pressures of doing newswork under social, economic, technological, and professional pressures unique to this moment in journalism.

So why should we care about *The Times*? Fundamentally, *The New York Times* is a special place; its stature, its size, its place in the public imagination, and maybe even its sense of its own importance make its transition to the digital age notable. It has won more Pulitzer Prizes than any other newspaper (over one hundred and ten and counting). And at least for now, publisher Arthur Ochs Sulzberger Jr., though controversial for his lack of business acumen,[5] remains devoted to keeping the newspaper inside the family trust. Despite claims by *New York Magazine* that the Sulzberger children of the fifth generation will sell out to corporate interests,[6] the two-tiered stock structure that keeps the Sulzberger family in control of the newspaper's direction means that there has been at least some insulation from layoffs. Sulzberger's willingness to spend money on journalism that ostensibly does not make the newspaper a profit (e.g., covering Iraq and Afghanistan) was seen as proof to some that he remained committed to an ideal of public service journalism.

There have been some pretty terrible moments for *The New York Times* in recent memory; two such moments, in particular, tarnished the newspaper's image. One was the Judith Miller scandal, where the reporter's erroneous reporting on weapons of mass destruction may have played a significant role in leading the United States into the war in Iraq—or at least pushing the Bush administration's claims to the top of the news agenda at the time.[7] Prior to this, reporter Jayson Blair fabricated enough stories to merit a fourteen-thousand-word public "mea culpa" in the Sunday *Times*.[8] But I am not alone in arguing that

The New York Times is a formidable institution with tremendous journalism muscle that has staying power, as well as the eyes and ears of decision makers, the elite, and increasingly the ordinary public.

Reams have been written about *The New York Times* as an institution. Much of it has personified the people and publishers who have led the newspaper, noting how their visions shaped *Times* coverage. For instance, consider Gay Talese's *The Kingdom and the Power*, where he reminisces that Eisenhower once asked of the top editor at the newspaper, "Who the hell does Reston think he is, telling me how to run the country?"[9] Chroniclers Susan E. Tifft and Alex S. Jones, in *The Trust,* offer a different perspective—how *The Times* owners, "America's most powerful family"—created a global imprimatur for the newspaper. [10]

Even for critics, *The New York Times* remains the most important newspaper in the United States. In fact, William McGowan's *Gray Lady Down: What the Decline and Fall of "The New York Times" Means for America* chronicles how an institution beset by credibility problems and a penchant for more tabloid journalism may destroy the very watchdog fabric of quality journalism that is necessary for a strong democracy.[11]

Thus, *The New York Times* is special in many ways—its size, its publisher (for better or worse), its reputation, its ego. At the same time, *The Times* is facing the same kinds of challenges faced by all newspapers: how to create and inform users in a networked information environment. For this reason, the values that I suggest are influencing newswork at *The Times*—immediacy, interactivity, and participation—are also found elsewhere. But what happens as the journalists who work there adjust to these new values and change their practices has profound consequences because of the stature of *The New York Times.* Thus, it is important to take a closer look at each of these values in the context of *The Times*, as well as in the context of larger debates and observations about journalism generally.

Immediacy: *The Times* and Beyond

At any one point from my main vantage spot on the business desk at *The Times,* a variety of news production processes were happening all at once. The business desk was spread over nearly half a floor, with about one hundred journalists at work. At any one moment, journalists could be writing for the daily paper, thinking about long-term news series, blogging, or continuously updating content for the Web. Immediacy reigned, even when the 24/7 pressure didn't seem to be staring down journalists. On January 20, 2010, Diana B. Henriques had a daily deadline to work on a big story about an FBI sting and big businesses that had been bribed to sell guns to presumed African warlords. The story was headed for A1, and she was free to spend the day pursuing it without worrying about the Web. Yet the next morning, when a source called to ask where the story was on the Web site, Henriques couldn't find it without some dedicated searching; on nytimes.com, it had vanished into the netherworld of small headlines on the business and national pages of the Web site. Her story had fallen victim to the constant churn of demand for new news on the home page.

Other journalists were entirely dominated by the forces of the Web. Online editor Mark Getzfred remained so glued to his computer refreshing the Web site with new content that he barely had time for a single morning meeting. His days were generally spent with this kind of constant intensity: looking for stories from the AP and from *Times* journalists that would respond to the imperatives of more, now, new to feed the hungry Web. He kept the business Web page filled with updated content, even if it meant that, early in the morning, he might be promoting a minor story from Europe or an obscure development with the US Federal Reserve. Only at four p.m., when he got ready for the massive email blast of the day's top stories, which was sent out to *Times* readers, would he sit down to gather his thoughts about the most significant stories of the day.

Within the newspaper were many conflicting rhythms and routines for creating news in the Web world. Immediacy—or "fresh" and "freshness," as *Times* journalists called it—took on a heightened level of prominence whenever the Web was involved. The dynamics for creating Web content for an ASAP world were grueling and unyielding. Though *The Times* prided itself on avoiding the production of commodity news, or news that everyone else would have, and instead hoped to find "value-added" content that only *Times* journalists could provide, the reality was often more complicated.

To journalists, immediacy may actually be considered a core, defining value of news—not just now, but always. Scholar Mark Deuze notes that "from its earliest days, journalism has relied on certain forms, archetypes, themes and routines enabling its practitioners to manage an ever-increasing volume of information within the confounds [*sic*] of continuous deadlines."[12] Immediacy has a legacy in the long history of news: the Romans and Han Chinese can be credited with pioneering daily news. The printing press allowed for the rapid dissemination of what were then called newsbooks and later pamphlets, which recorded major events like earthquakes and voyages to the New World. By the 1600s, European merchants had begun publishing weekly newspapers. Even then, the demands of content and speed wore upon journalists. One Venetian publisher complained that he simply couldn't keep up with the demand for fresh news on this weekly basis.[13]

More recent history continues to tell the story of journalists' collective relationship with immediacy. With the telegraph, for instance, we saw the rise and development of the Associated Press, as well as the first reliable and speedy wartime correspondence, during the Civil War. The advent of the telephone made it possible for journalists to relay detail-heavy stories to editors and also to reach people beyond geographical boundaries, opening up the potential for new information gathering and stories with greater breadth for readers. To remain commercially viable and relevant, the form of news (and news organizations) simply had to adapt to changing technological conditions for the spread and distribution of information.[14]

Radio brought the capacity for instant mass communication into people's homes for the first time, perhaps best illustrated by the Munich Crisis in 1938. For the first time, people got live broadcasts of news as it was happening, or at least as fast as journalists on the scene had time to process it. Newspapers responded to radio by continuing to publish multiple editions throughout the day, but they struggled for differentiation from this new medium.[15] Multiple deadlines and multiple editions helped newspapers compete, but this was ultimately unsustainable, as distribution outside of the suburbs became more complicated. In fact, the afternoon paper, once a way to respond to the day's news, all but died with the rise of the evening news broadcast, local TV news, and a changing suburban landscape.

Morning newspapers then hoped to retain their position of authority based on the sheer number of correspondents and the advantage of a longer news cycle to provide more comprehensive coverage. Immediacy (or timeliness) for newspapers took on a different meaning: newspapers were the place to go for the historical record and the big story, and, hopefully, this edge in reporting muscle would lead to the scoop. The rise of event-driven cable news signified two things: the demand and desire for immediate news and the special function newspapers now fulfilled as a way to provide context and depth beyond all of the noise on cable (and network) TV. Each medium had its own deadlines and purpose, as well as its own sense of time.

But all of this changed with the fundamental revolution in Internet communication technology and the rise of the networked information environment. Manuel Castells, a scholar of global flows, argues that the emergence of high-speech communication technology has brought about a tremendous change in the speed and exchange of information. The monetary value of instant information alone is significant. Bound up in this technological revolution are the spheres of commerce, social life, politics, and the like. Theoretically, anyone who has access to this networked information environment can demand access to information at all times.

The changes, then, were quite significant: The deadlines for ALL news organizations became NOW! As all news organizations had Web sites, the question became one of differentiation. What made any one news outlet different from any other news outlet? And increasingly, social media sites became not just places to congregate and discuss news events, but the very sources of breaking news. In short, news organizations themselves were now part of the culture of the immediacy of the networked information environment. And audience demands about immediacy were not just imagined but actually had significant impact upon the potential revenue of a news organization.

Thus, at the dawn of the 2000s, something new was added to the idea of immediacy for journalists—this was now going to be an overarching, defining feature of online journalism, a value that would define and orient journalism practice; it would reverberate among the profession and among consumers. By 2010, one of the implications of the speed of online news was that journalists were constantly producing online journalism. The result is that the process of journalism was laid bare, mistakes and all: news items were published before they were ready in their final print- or broadcast form, and there was radically diminished time between the production and the consumption of news.[16]

Immediacy has become part of the normative culture of online journalists, whether they like it or not. In an overview of scholarly studies on journalists' perceptions of immediacy, Swedish scholar Michael Karlsson notes, "A somewhat divided conclusion from these studies is that immediacy is an important and sometimes esteemed trait of the online journalist."[17] In American journalism, journalists have resisted an occupational value that seems forced upon the newsroom. At the heart of this frustration lies a larger comment about the idea of journalistic authority and autonomy—whether journalists still have the ability to tell the story and shape the narrative or whether the pace of the story and the felt demand for constant churn destroy journalists' control.

Life in newsrooms obsessed with immediacy has been compared to that of hamsters—the "hamsterization of journalism." As Dean Starkman of *The Columbia Journalism Review* put it, journalists had become little more than hamsters running on a wheel: "The Hamster Wheel isn't speed; it's motion for motion's sake. The Hamster Wheel is volume without thought. It is news panic, a lack of discipline, an inability to say no."[18]

The emphasis on getting more news out faster and faster had the effect, as one editor put it, of "everyone running around like rats."[19] The hamster wheel is a metaphor for news production in the digital age, where speed is more important than fact checking, and quantity is more important than quality. The Federal Communications Commission (FCC) noted the impact of immediacy on news production in one of its quadrennial reports, suggesting that instead of reporting quality stories, journalists were responding to constant, rolling deadlines.[20]

In many newsrooms, Starkman argued, this "news panic" resulted from the compulsion that journalists felt to work faster and harder, lest they risk economic failure. Writing more stories with faster turnaround had financial rewards: bumps in Web traffic that could then prove the case for higher rates for online ads. Newsrooms were thus rewarding work that was generating bumps in Web traffic, rather than the kind of substantial reporting once found on Page One or in investigative features.[21] Generally, journalists at *The Times* were not obsessed with economic failure in the same way that plagued other newsrooms, but, at times, they certainly did appear to be running around like the hamsters Starkman and others have described. At the same time, these journalists also had to reconcile their work with their simultaneous desire to have the final say and be the final authority on the daily news cycle—both manifested in the guise of the print paper. Immediacy oriented and motivated news production at *The Times* in conflicting ways, signaling a larger debate about the importance of first and fresh versus the authority of the journalist, the quality of news, and the enduring news story.

Interactivity: *The Times* and Beyond

Sewell Chan was hard at work on *The Times'* first big profile of Federal Reserve chairman Ben Bernanke in May 2010. In fact, the interview with Bernanke had been the first long interview Chan had been able to have with the chairman since starting the beat earlier in the year. But as part of putting together that week's Sunday business profile, Chan was also doing something other than massaging text—he was digging around for material for an interactive timeline of Bernanke's life to accompany the story. In fact, he had actually managed to find the Fed chairman's high school and college yearbooks. Along with Web producer Danielle Belopotosky and a few others, Chan, a straight-up traditional reporter, worked to craft "A Fed Chairman's Life" to bring pictures (and bad moustaches), dates, anecdotes, and context to the otherwise serious story.[22] For journalists like Chan, it was additional work—work he didn't mind, but extra work nonetheless—and for Belopotosky, it was a pretty serious undertaking to accomplish in about a week's time. The Monday after the story ran, she acknowledged to the other Web producers that she was exhausted.

This effort was the sign of another imperative in the newsroom: an avowed focus on interactives, including multimedia, interactive graphics, photo slideshows, and audio. For every story that required serious planning, someone, either a Web producer assigned to the business desk or journalists on bigger teams with more resources like the programming whizzes and documentary film experts, was likely to be involved. Each potential Pulitzer story ("special project") for the year involved a sit-down meeting not just with the reporter, top editors, individual editors, and the photo and graphics desks, but with people from desks with names like multimedia, interactives, and video. They would help the story come alive on the Web in ways beyond words.

From an editorial perspective, interactivity emerged as a contested value, one that structured, ordered, and influenced newswork and journalists' role perceptions. Traditional journalists saw the importance and, generally, the value of interactive journalism, but they were conflicted by the changes to their old routines. And aside from Pulitzer projects, there was little clarity about who these "new people" in the newsroom were and what the process was for creating a Web interactive.

Though none of the lower-ranking journalists I spoke with talked about the business merits of interactivity, top management did. For top newsroom executives and people on the business staff, *Times* interactive journalism was about "engagement." By this, they meant that people not only got a richer experience of a story but also stayed on the page longer. And time spent on a page is an important measure for Web metrics, one that can be fed to online advertisers as justification for higher rates.

Though newspapers have used photography since 1855, dating back to its first major appearance in reports on the Crimean War, photography online has the capacity to be something different. For example, in the case of an online audio slide show, there is something that is distinct from broadcast, both visually and as an auditory experience. The user sets the pace, generally, and the distinct media of sound and photography complement each other. While newspapers have also used infographics in print for decades, with an interactive online graphic, the user can have a multilevel experience of a dynamic graphic that responds to the pace he or she chooses. Multimedia, then, offers a variety of ways to tell stories with the user central to the experience of controlling and directing his or her way through content.

Interactivity has meaning for online journalism far beyond *The Times*. Interactivity has long been a part of the way people think about online content. Before there even were Web browsers, in the dawn of the early Internet, Ithiel de Sola Pool hypothesized that electronic publishing would be

> more and more like an electronic game, permeated by lights and sound along with words. The players will initiate and the machine will answer back, in an interactive conversational process. It may be for fun, for management, for daily life, or for work.[23]

de Sola Pool accurately predicted a world of online video, audio, and multimedia content.

And as interactivity became part of the online journalism world, a cultural change was taking place that manifested itself on many levels. Entirely new forms of journalism would be created. Journalists could (and would) be compelled to think about news as moving beyond simple text. Nontraditional journalists with skills in Web design, programming, video, and photography would be elevated to greater importance in the newsroom—as they were at *The Times* with the creation of the multimedia desk in 2005 and the interactive news desk in 2009.

The term *interactivity*, though, is pretty muddy. It can mean interactive experiences between users, or it can mean interactive experiences between the user and the computer. When I talk about interactivity in the newsroom, I mean this user-computer interaction. The definition I use comes from Erik Bucy, who writes that interactivity is "the control that users exercise over the selection and presentation of online content, whether story text, audiovisuals, or multimedia, and other aspects of the interface."[24] While users might have the sense that they are, indeed, participating in a two-way exchange, they may never actually achieve control over the content or perform an observable communication behavior with online computer interaction, as Bucy points out. This is very different from both user-to-user communication and actual content creation, activities that are encompassed much more directly by the term (and underlying journalism value of) *participation.*

Some scholars also agree with the more practical notion that interactivity is constitutive of design on the Web—that it is embedded as a property of multimedia. In fact, interactivity is a core value of Web design and creation now, as Web guru Jesse James Garrett notes prolifically across the Web.[25] If you look in any of the Web programming or user interface textbooks starting from around 2000, you will see that the idea of user experience is fundamentally oriented around giving people a reactive and immersive environment. This is moderated by two concerns common to journalism: getting content to users immediately and keeping users on a site. Journalists largely talk about interactivity as "multimedia." However, describing the normative value that emerges from their focus on this work as interactivity encompasses the growing depth and sophistication of storytelling techniques, the presence and rise of programmers and so-called interactive news designers, and the focus from the top on the idea of "engagement" (keeping users on the site).

In contrast to immediacy, interactivity suggests a different set of routines and practices. As Steen Steensen, a Norwegian journalism studies scholar, points out, work on interactive projects forces newsrooms to pause from their 24/7 routines to focus on something "more creative, even more agential."[26] Here, people theoretically have time to experiment, to play, and to create new types of newswork. However, one can also see these spaces for creating interactivity as an institutionalized routine for experimentation—in part, because it takes on the mythical status of a site of innovation.

In the past, though, most observers have argued that newsrooms have largely failed in their efforts to implement multimedia journalism into their daily workflow. In fact, interactivity has been called an "uncomfortable myth" of online journalism.[27] Studies in the United States, Germany, Belgium, and Ireland have all suggested that there is a gap between the perceived opportunity of interactivity and its actual use and implementation.[28] However, this work has noted that interactive journalism influences role perceptions, job descriptions, and work routines. Internal pressures from editors, and more external pressures like corporate demands, influence a drive toward interactivity in US newsrooms.

At *The Times*, the manifestation of interactivity in newswork remains contested, as some journalists see its value, while others view it as an imposition. In another vein, interactivity has a way of both flattening hierarchy and enforcing top-down mandates. And the contrast between interactivity and immediacy became clear in my research at *The Times*: interactivity was simply so much harder to do—from planning to process—that it was largely reserved for off-deadline stories. At *The Times*, we will see how some journalists make interactivity part and parcel of their daily work, document the rise of these interactive journalists (multimedia, Web, and interactive specialists), and look at the variable nature of work routines associated with interactivity. But to be sure, interactivity is coupled with another important value: participation, or the experience of actually creating content and communicating with other users.

Participation: *The Times* and Beyond

Micheline Maynard, or @MickiMaynard, could—and would—tweet every ten or fifteen minutes during the news day. Stationed in Detroit, Maynard put out a regular stream of tweets about the car industry and her airline beat, as well as news about her beloved Detroit sports teams. For her followers on Twitter (about ten thousand), she could leverage her tight network of sources in the airline industry to let them know about a flight delay even before an airline would announce it formally. As she put it: "With Twitter, now I think: How's that [news] going to be my thought on Twitter? . . . What a great way to promote links to stories to these people following you and interested in what you are saying. One of the interesting things about the airline beat is that with snowstorms, I can give them information about delays where a blog post might take hours. And some of the personality of tweeting is kind of fun."[29]

Not everyone shared the same impressions of Twitter, Facebook, and other forms of social media. Bill Keller, then executive editor of *The Times*, had a Twitter account, but despite having almost fifty thousand followers, he had only tweeted 205 times on his own—and even then, there was little commentary or personality with his tweets, which generally offered links to *Times* articles.[30] Publisher Arthur Ochs Sulzberger Jr. didn't practice what he preached about getting journalists onto social media platforms: he wasn't on Twitter, and if he was on Facebook, his profile was blocked from public search.

There is a powerful recalibration, at least in theory, happening between the journalist and the audience. Thanks to the affordances of Web 2.0, a philosophical and technical vision of the Web that provides ordinary people with the capacity to produce their own content and share it across social networks, journalists are dealing with the "people formerly known as the audience," as scholar Jay Rosen noted in 2006.[31] The discussion in journalism about participation mirrors a much larger discussion about the rise of social media, the importance of the "writeable web," as Yochai Benkler puts it, and the potential redistribution of actors from a hub-and-spoke model of content distribution to a more networked model of information content creation and sharing.[32]

With smartphones, Facebook, and Twitter, ordinary people have captured dramatic moments, from the landing of a commercial airline on the Hudson River, to gripping scenes from Iran's "Green Revolution," to the wide-ranging efforts across social media platforms surrounding the Arab Spring. These "acts of journalism," as Clay Shirky calls them,[33] suggest that there is a public ready to engage in covering news. A "participatory logic," in Seth Lewis' terms, suggests that media creation is "unregulated, distributed and outside the bounds of institutional control"—and that, in fact, participation has actually become a fundamental value of online journalism.[34]

Participation challenges the traditional norms of journalism by suggesting that anyone, at any time, could become a reporter. Journalistic authority is transformed, as both journalists and users are now creating media content that may be equally newsworthy. Some note the promise of this fusion: as London School of Economics professor Charlie Beckett imagines, "professionals and amateurs [are] working together to get the real story, linking to each other across brands and old boundaries to share facts, questions, answers, ideas, perspectives."[35]

So what should journalists do to address the fact that not only are their audiences consuming more news online than ever before, but they are also creating, engaging, and talking about news content with each other? The mantra inside newsrooms has been to get journalists on these social media platforms reaching out to audiences. Poynter, the central news-industry non-profit educational institution, ran a social media blog that offered such advice articles as "The Problem with Retweets and How Journalists Can Solve it."[36] The organization also provided training modules with courses on "Facebook for Reporting and Storytelling" as part of the for-pay "Social Media Webinar Series."[37] Journalism schools at Columbia University, the University of Missouri, and the University of California, Berkeley, have offered crash courses to journalists hoping to get up to date on social media as quickly as possible.[38] There were talks of coming up with a social media Pulitzer for Andy Carvin, the NPR social media strategist who verified citizen tweets and retweeted throughout the Arab Spring.[39]

Similarly, news organizations got lots of attention from journoblogs for announcing "social media editors," whose primary purpose had been deemed to integrate social media into the newsroom workflow. In 2009, three news organizations appointed the first set of social media editors: *The New York Times*, NPR, and Toronto's *Globe and Mail*. These new editors were hailed as the first "brave souls" in the industry to tackle this newsroom challenge, according to PBS's *MediaShift* blog.[40] Then, *The Washington Post* and *The Wall Street Journal* quickly followed, adding social media editors to their rosters. *USA Today* and Reuters only established the position in 2011, realizing that their own social media efforts were far behind those of other news organizations. However, most of these news organizations reached an important conclusion: no single editor could be an adequate force to encourage participation in a newsroom—widespread cultural buy-in was necessary to accept participation.

Similarly, news organizations had begun to promote participation via social media as a key to their success. Al Jazeera English had widely touted its institution-wide social media training just before the Arab

Spring as being crucial to its acclaimed coverage of the subsequent events.[41] The BBC had a full team of journalists devoted just to addressing the needs of the BBC's many Twitter feeds—from @BBCWorldservice to @BBCbooks. This was in addition to a full team dedicated to monitoring user input via social media and the BBC's own user-generated content prompts. Notably, in each of these cases, user contributions were seen as being for the benefit of the news organization—users were collaborators, insofar as the information they provided was both accurate and aided in the development of news stories.

However, as with interactivity, the utopian discourse about participation gives way to the economic reality behind news. Participation also addresses underlying concerns with how to raise revenue and increase brand loyalty. Newsrooms like *The Washington Post, The Guardian*, and *The Wall Street Journal* have experimented with actually placing a mini-newspaper of sorts, or a "social reader" as *The Post* called it, on Facebook. Users could read this content on Facebook or be directed back to the main Web site. At the time, the average American spent seven hours a month on Facebook, versus fourteen minutes a month on news Web sites.[42] Thus, by trying experiments to create content on Facebook, news organizations were hoping to leverage some of that time, at least into traffic and users.

Similarly, the utopian discourse around user-as-producer and "networked journalism" was far from the reality at *The Times*. Inside the newsroom, participation was contested in a variety of ways. Many journalists acknowledged this supposedly new relationship with the audience but did not deem it worth their time. I want to stress that inside *The Times*, participation was almost entirely understood as engagement on social media platforms, not as commenting, not as blogging, not as live-chats, not as emails, and not as user-generated content. But perhaps more significantly, the actual implementation of participation as a value *at work* in the newsroom suggested that journalists did have far more power than the ordinary person to contribute to creating and shaping the conversation. Journalists at *The Times*, at least, weren't too sold on this two-way conversation. The conversation was for *them*, not for us.

News Routines and Values:
From the Analog to the Digital Age

In the digital era, new values operate as constraints, guidelines, and conflicting principles—in addition to older values that have shaped news production for decades. The ones I have identified—immediacy, interactivity, and participation—build on a discussion of new news values in the digital age. I am not the first to argue that these values in the digital age are changing news production, but this study further explicates them by showing them at work within the nation's most prominent newsroom. This process of understanding news values from going inside the newsroom has a long and established history. Through newsroom ethnography, scholars have entered the newsroom to explore how various newsroom routines shape and pattern what makes news. Understanding these routines is important, because values are defined, created, and established out of the routines of everyday work practices and the resulting internal, external, professional, technological, and other influences on these routines.

We have many, many studies on the content that comes out of newsrooms, but less understanding of the motivations, decision making, and processes behind the creation of that content. Ethnography is especially useful for a number of reasons, because it helps elucidate these elements of newswork.

The foundation for this work comes out of a body of newsroom sociology research that emerged in full force in the 1970s, sometimes called the "first wave" or the "golden age" of newsroom ethnography. The scholarship remained mostly dormant until about the mid-2000s, when newsroom scholars began a "second wave"[43] that looked into the widespread transformations of news routines in the digital age.

The early ethnographies were concerned with examining the larger routines of the news organization, and they spent less time focusing on the experiences of individual journalists. The scholarship tended to emphasize routine, predictability, and order over disorder as a way to create generalizable descriptions. Ironically, the scholarship from this era—a time when TV reigned on three channels and the daily newspaper was not yet seen to be in great decline—has stood the test of time because these works so accurately identify forces that still order news-work. The other reason these works loom so large is that few scholars today have come close to replicating studies of their scale and significance in the digital age.

To provide a brief review, the tradition begins perhaps in the 1950s, with two studies emphasizing how professional ideology influences news production in many ways, from the socialization of journalists, to newsroom policy, to the very stories that journalists choose to put in the day's papers (or "gatekeeping").[44] Later, Herbert Gans spent ten years on and off at *CBS Evening News, NBC Nightly News, Newsweek,* and *Time,* analyzing the constraints placed upon journalists in perhaps the most influential study of newsrooms thus far. He noted that a combination of internal pressures, from professional socialization to the need for predictable content, as well as external pressures like source relationships and economic factors, influenced how journalists were able to do their work.

Gaye Tuchman, who did her work on newspapers and TV stations in "Seaboard City," a major metropolitan area, argued that newsrooms organized work along strategic rituals designed to make sure that there was a reliable flow of content to the news organization; even the vaunted idea of objectivity was to protect journalists from critique and ensure a continued flow of news from sources. Managing the unexpected was the goal—and the necessity for newsrooms to function.[45] Other scholars emphasized that economic forces constrained the news, that news worked according to a stopwatch culture, that newsrooms were bureaucratically organized (e.g., the beat structure), and that source-reporter relationships constrained what and how journalists could report.[46] And generally, this work does a good job of helping us understand—at least at the organizational level—the forces that constrain and order newswork.

But the economic, political, technological, and social conditions for making news have changed since the golden age of news ethnography in the 1960s–80s. The stakes are higher now than they were in the analog (or perhaps the pre-CNN) age: journalists don't just need to fill broadcast or print deadlines; they also have to feed the constant flow of the Web, playing to an audience that reads or watches whenever it wants to because the content never goes off the air. Similarly, these news organizations are now battling to survive in an increasingly complex and sophisticated economic and technological landscape. A look at newsmaking in the digital age is a reminder that, at *The New York Times,* no one has quite figured out what it means to do newswork predictably or comfortably and that new news routines are still being crafted.

The earlier constraints upon news remain quite on point today, but there are new challenges: creating news in a digital world requires adjusting to the rapid flow of information in a networked information environment. In fact, when sociologist Eric Klinenberg made an appeal for more media sociology in this time of change, he did so noting how technology had dramatically altered the practices and experiences of the journalists he observed.[47] He argued that journalists were staring down a twenty-four-hour "news cyclone" of Web, TV, and print, expected to do it all—and with the understanding that fickle news consumers wanted new news on demand, on their own schedules.

Northwestern sociologist Pablo Boczkowski has made perhaps the most significant contributions to date in the more recent literature on newsrooms changing in the digital age. In his first book, which looked at newsrooms in the late 1990s, he argued that newsroom innovation was contingent on a variety of forces, motivated in part by the individual and organizational flexibilities of the newsroom. In fact, he went to *The New York Times* in 1998, looking at the proto-*Times* online: *CyberTimes,* an outpost of technology coverage publishing only original articles that was later shut down to become—believe it or not—a print section. His more recent book on newsrooms in Argentina notes the dangers of homogenization in an immediate news environment, chronicling two competing newspapers that have become obsessed with copying each other and have prioritized speed over depth.

Two recent book-length interventions about American journalism are important additions that hopefully build on the missing legacy of substantial work on newsroom ethnography. The first project is David Ryfe's 2012 account of three midsized regional newspapers across the country, where he spent about two and a half years doing research.

He played the role of intern to understand the pressures journalists faced—from adjusting to the demands of online news to dealing with economic pressure.[48] At every newsroom he visited, new innovations were introduced, only to fail. His overarching conclusion was that innovation in newsrooms was simply impossible—quite a dark finding. Nonetheless, he agrees that the same pressures observed by the earlier ethnographers do, in fact, still impact journalism.

C.W. Anderson's account of The *Philadelphia Inquirer* and the *Philadelphia Daily News* shows these organizations in their death throes, trying to survive as their circulations plummeted and as editors and reporters were struggling to respond to these economic conditions. More comprehensively, though, he recognizes that newspapers are no longer the central focal point of the news ecology in a city and also looks at bloggers, radical media producers, foundations, computer hackers, and social media experts. Like my investigation here, his work in *Rebuilding the News* argues that journalists are struggling within a "web of institutional, economic, and cultural constraints" that will indeed impact the future of news, though his work is more explicitly focused on the challenges facing metropolitan journalism.[49] Both of these books deal with the reality of producing news in a new media environment, and Anderson's suggests a way to reconceptualize how news makes its way through a community.

There have been dozens and dozens of new journal articles and book collections written on news production in print, TV, and radio newsrooms—and these are quite valuable. These studies highlight the intensity of the challenges that traditional journalists face, as well as the points of contestation in newsrooms. I think their findings can be broken into two core themes: studies that describe the contested nature of professional journalism and professional identity, and work that articulates the difficulties and successes of incorporating new technology into organizational workflow. Traditional journalists have been threatened by new types of journalists, from online journalists to multimedia specialists, who challenge their assessment of authoritative storytelling. Participatory content and blogging have only further forced journalists to assert their relevance as specialists in the new media environment. Similarly, new technology has created a larger conversation about change in news practices. New technology can be seen as external influence (e.g., the Web moves faster) or internal influence (e.g., we should have more reporters writing for the Web), and the affordances of new technology have created a larger discourse around the notions of immediacy, interactivity, and participation in online news.

My project builds on these developments about the constraints, pressures, and challenges of journalism identified by these scholars. What I offer is an analysis of how new online journalism values impact the daily workflows of journalists as sites of obligation, admiration, and contestation. I do so through an ethnographic exploration of *The New York Times* that spanned five months during which I spent between three and five days a week in the newsroom (more often five). I shadowed more than thirty journalists across the newsroom hierarchy and types of positions, watching them go through their days; I interviewed over eighty people; and I generally attended at least three news meetings a day, depending on whom I shadowed— and on a few rare occasions, I spent all day and night at *The Times* to watch the twenty-four-hour news cycle. Over the course of this book, I take a nod from journalism and use people's real names attached to dates. But when people did have negative things to say, unless they really wanted their name to be used, I've left those quotations anonymous and omitted the date associated with the comments to avoid any potential retribution.

Here, I capture one snapshot of a particular moment in the biggest newsroom in the United States, at arguably the most influential paper in the country, during a time of technological change. The period that I studied, January–June 2010, represents a moment of digital change for both news and *The Times* during an uncertain time for newsroom economics and newsroom routines. However, *The Times* is not a static place, and if I tried to chronicle all of the changes at *The Times*, I would never stop researching; I'd be chasing a moving target. Acknowledging that the subject is fluid actually adds analytical strength to my work: these themes will continue to evolve, and what I offer here is an analytical and empirical lens through which to understand and compare change (see Methods).

The focus here is on documenting the emergent values that I

could see from the practices of individual journalists and their collective experiences in the newsroom. Nonetheless, these values of online journalism—whether thought of as logics, frameworks, pressures, constraints, and so on—are likely at the heart of newsrooms elsewhere. Not only have other journalism scholars suggested their influence, but the wide-ranging reports and accounts from journalists in the trenches suggest their influence is well-founded. Thus, while the setting is unique, and the resources and even the worries of the journalists in this study are different, some fundamental similarities are nonetheless quite possible. The rest of the book makes clear how these values of immediacy, interactivity, and participation are framed and understood within the daily lives of newsworkers—accounting for the challenges and the opportunities that they face.

Outline of the Book

In a brief first chapter, I will relate and highlight some of the major dilemmas facing journalism, and particularly newspapers during the time of my research. This book is not a "newspapers are dying" book, nor is it a serenade for the new partnership between user and producer. But it is important to provide some context for the present discussion and the external factors that influence newswork. Another backstory is important as well: the state of *The New York Times*. This is part Web history of the newspaper and part financial history, but it lays the groundwork for the rest of the chapters. The newspaper's journey online is instructive for understanding some of the more recent tensions. Similarly, the state of the newspaper's finances helps ground the economic reasons for why this particular moment at the paper was so important.

The heart of the ethnography begins with Chapter 2. I document three days in the lives of journalists at *The Times*. This close look at three journalists—all of whom have different goals and daily work patterns—offers some insight into the way immediacy, interactivity, and participation are experienced in the newsroom. The first vignette shows the experience of a reporter on a breaking news story;

the second a day spent with a reporter who isn't on deadline but who has an entirely different rhythm, as well as some particular and rather forward-thinking views on multimedia work; and the third a day with a blogger during the unveiling of the iPad (the very first one). These are slices of life inside the newsroom, not full representations of how each value is manifest and contested as a whole—I leave that to the other chapters. Rather, the intention of this chapter is to zoom in on what it was like to be a journalist at *The Times* in 2010, and these anecdotes set the stage for larger debates along the way.

Chapter 3 focuses on immediacy. This is the first of two chapters on that topic, and it is focused on how the news organization as a whole understands (or contests) immediacy in a digital age. We get a sense of the "old" immediacy: the print world, where immediacy equals to-day's news for tomorrow. We see the kind of calculated, rational decision making, the system of meetings, and the planning processes that journalists undertake to prepare stories for each day's print newspaper. We'll be careful to note the kinds of conversations that unfold and the vaunted status with which journalists understand Page One. This is not the rhythm or process behind the creation of journalism for the Web. On the Web, immediacy means now, ASAP journalism. The goal is to keep the Web site looking "fresh," with new content, so that an audience perceived as hungry for different content will keep coming back for more or stay on the page. Chapter 3, then, underscores how the print world lives in almost complete opposition to its online counter-part.

In Chapter 4, we learn more about the impact of immediacy in news production on the traditional journalist, who is caught between serving two masters: print and online. The two different sets of necessities native to each medium produce competing demands of timing and story creation, among others. We see how a story, when produced under ASAP pressure, may actually be *wrong* at first in the rush for speed. Journalists are often asked to write a "second-day story," or a magazine-style take-out, in the same day they have written incremental updates for a breaking news story. We learn how this can be an exhausting process for many journalists. To better understand ASAP journalism, we take a closer look at when a scoop is a scoop in the digital age: As journalists rush to churn out stories faster than anyone else, is anyone counting who gets the story first?

While the focus is on immediacy in both Chapter 3 and Chapter 4, it would be misleading to note that the entire *New York Times* functions according to a breaking news mantra; it does not. Journalists at *The Times* do have the leisure to write longer stories (in fact, this is how they may begin to think about interactivity). *The Times* difference means that some journalists, some of the time, are insulated from the demands of the Web. However, immediacy is increasingly a part of the daily reality of journalism at *The Times*, and fending off the needs of the Web can be difficult, as we will see.

Chapter 5 focuses on interactivity, or the evolution of news content presented via sound, visuals, browsing, and navigation or any kind of complex layering of multimedia. We see how interactivity is a contested value, as journalists explore what it means to create this new form of content. There are economic reasons for pushing forward the creation of interactive content, as top management promotes an agenda of hiring new people and stirring up newsroom initiatives to promote this kind of content. Interactivity can be monetized; more time spent on the page is a valuable advertising metric. But most journalists don't think about interactivity this way. The chapter offers an overview of the new faces in the newsroom and how they talk about online journalism, and then it shows various top-down and bottom-up attempts at interactivity. Throughout, you will see that the meaning and importance of interactivity in online journalism remain contested in the news creation process.

In a world of participatory action via YouTube, Facebook, Twitter, and other forms of social media, Chapter 6 tries to unpack what the idea of participation means inside the newsroom. With a nod to some of the utopian discourse around participation discussed earlier, this chapter illustrates that practice is far from this aspiration of user-as-producer, or redistribution from one to many. For journalists, participation means engagement on a social media platform, but the significance of participation and the way that it will influence their lives are the subject of debate. Top-down management seems to have a strategy, with real economic stakes, yet the top editors have not bought in, and most journalists aren't thinking about economics.

The result is a wide range for experimentation—there isn't even a stable code of ethics, for better or worse. While some journalists seem to spend their entire waking lives on Twitter, developing personal brands and experimenting with reporting techniques, others shy away from the platform out of protest, confusion, or concern. We see instances of journalists learning from each other about social media, but what tends to be emphasized is a one-to-many relationship with the audience, not the engagement that theorists promote. The chapter explores the contested nature of participation at the newspaper, and it sheds some light on the working definition of what this value means to journalists—even those who embrace it.

In Chapter 7, I will bring all of these threads together and make some predictions about the future. *The New York Times* began a Web site in 1996, but it is still struggling to figure out how to balance the demands of working in a dual print/online world. How is it possible that this culture clash still exists? And what does it mean for the future of *The New York Times* that its front page is not the front page for most of its readers? What will happen as the newspaper continues to find ways to personalize and create a more interactive, "sticky" experience for consumers? And how will journalists fare?

These are the stakes: as of 2010, *The New York Times* was in, at best, a hazy experimental stage with much of its online news creation and production. But without a clear sense of purpose and identity, as well as true investment from text journalists who believe in the newspaper as a digital edition, the newspaper could, at some point in the future, likely find that the bulk of its internal values and practices have moved it closer and closer to irrelevancy—or its focus on being the best could mean that it emerges as a change-leader for the industry. The Times liked to think those thirty million unique visitors were coming to *The New York Times* each month because it was the best newspaper site online. However, without true cohesion between past and present mindsets at *The New York Times*, one wonders when the glass will crack. And that brings us back to Renzo Piano's towering metaphor on Eighth Avenue. Thus, after we review the context and temporal setting for this study in the next brief chapter, in Chapter 2, we'll take our first steps into the lobby of the newspaper and beyond.

Chapter 1

Setting

NEWS ABOUT THE NEWS:
THE TIMES IN 2010

What was remarkably different about *The Times* in 2010 is that reporters were not, on a day-to-day level, concerned with losing their jobs or seeing the paper go out of print, unlike those at many other major newspapers.[1] As Bill Keller said on Pulitzer Day in 2010, when the newspaper took home three prizes, "We are here to take note that the death of journalism has been greatly exaggerated. It is alive and well and feisty, especially at The New York Times."[2] And then a celebration began, complete with champagne in plastic cups, as the newsroom stepped back in a moment that reveled in the collaboration among print, online, and digital innovation. This was not a newsroom consumed with self-pity, fear, or concern about its fate in the future. Occasional jokes were made about the dismal price of Times Co. stock (actually, people were excited when it climbed back above twelve dollars, down from a past high in recent memory of fifty-one dollars in 2002, and up from its extreme low of four dollars in 2009). As journalist Jennifer Anderson told me:

> It's popular when I'm at dinner parties for people to ask me how it feels to work when journalism is dying. I don't think about it. I just do my job every day. I don't have time to think about it. And I don't think that's the case here.[3]

The Times still has resources unlike any other newspaper in the country, with over one thousand people on its editorial staff. This fact alone brings comfort to many journalists I spoke with. Thus, my fieldwork tells a story principally about digital change, rather than one about journalists coping with economic desperation.

However, it is important to provide the appropriate setting and context for this study of *The Times*. Why 2010? Why this moment in journalism? Thus, this chapter offers a brief review of what many observers of journalism know too well—a tale of the decline of traditional newspapers. But this is not one more "death of news" story, though there are certainly potential economic costs and benefits associated with *The Times* being able to adapt to the digital age—and with how immediacy, interactivity, and participation become part and parcel of newswork. Thus, to ground the book as a whole, it is important to give you a sense of the economic state of *The Times* when I entered the newsroom, though unlike most other newsrooms, journalists were largely oblivious to management objectives.

But how did *The Times* even get to this point in 2010? There has been no real Web history of the news organization; it remains a scattered story, with bits and pieces held by various members of the newsroom. When conducting final research on the Web history, I had a few questions, but after a round of thirty buyouts in 2013, I was told that a lot of institutional memory had just walked out the door. Thus, I preserve in one place what we know about *The Times*' transition to the digital age as a jumping-off point for the larger study.

The Dark Times for News and New Chances for Innovation

Newsrooms, particularly those of print newspapers, are in serious trouble. Print circulations have been declining for decades, but the acceleration has increased to the point where the newspaper industry has seen circulation dips ranging from .7 percent to seven percent in the past half-dozen years. On one level, this is just an economic problem facing news. On another level, this is a serious problem for the state of American democracy. When newspapers lose circulation, they not only lose subscribers, but are also forced to charge less for advertising. The decline in profits reverberates to the very core of the capacity of newspapers to do original news reporting. With less money in, there's less to spend on the kind of public service journalism that takes time, effort, labor, and resources.

News organizations thought they could make up print declines through online advertising, but this is a strategy that has proven remarkably unstable. The online ad numbers we see now, which go up and down each quarter, are misleading. Online ads are often bundled with print ads, and once those print ads go, the online ads go as well. Online, advertisers know exactly how many people are paying attention to their ads, thanks to being able to track clicks. In the print newspaper, advertisers really can't track who is seeing what ad; if you get the paper, you presumably are counted as seeing the ad. Perhaps worse for newspapers is the fact that advertisers have realized they don't *need* newspapers to reach customers: they can reach consumers directly online. The middleman—the news organization—is then left out of the picture.

The recessions of the 2000s—the first blip at the beginning of the decade and then the second, more crushing recession following the 2007-8 financial crisis—have been particularly harsh for newspapers. Advertisers had less to spend and were less willing to experiment with online ads, and as a result, newsrooms (like many other industries) have suffered a great deal. The difference between the news industry and other industries is that the problem does not go away when the economy gets better; rather, there's a systemic problem with the core financial model of print newspapers. Print newspapers are running out of time, as *Times* media reporter David Carr notes:

> Between operational fiascos and flailing attempts to slash costs on the fly, it's clear that the print newspaper business, which has been fretting over a looming crisis for the last 15 years, is struggling to stay afloat. There are smart people trying to innovate, and tons of great journalism is published daily, but the financial distress is more visible by the week.[4]

Leaders from across the news industry, academics, and those concerned with civic affairs—from big-name billionaires to tech entrepreneurs—are deeply worried about the future of news. Academics like Paul Starr of Princeton have pointed out that our "civic alarm systems" are in great danger, given the steady erosion of local, state, national, and international reporting.[5] Major reports have noted the decline of newspapers, long seen as the source of the bulk of original news reporting.[6] The top twenty-five American newspapers have all seen declines in circulation for consecutive years; even *The Wall Street Journal,* which added paid online subscribers to its circulation numbers, has seen a small dip.[7]

Newspaper newsrooms are 30 percent smaller than they were in 2000, according to the Pew Research Center's State of the News Media Report. One industry analyst, Ken Doctor, estimates that, with all the newsroom layoffs, journalists are producing something like eight hundred thousand fewer stories a year.[8] News stories themselves have pointed out even more jarring details: A *Times* story reported that, over the course of 2009, the *San Francisco Chronicle* had lost 20.6 percent of its circulation.[9] It was not uncommon for former journalists like Alex Jones, now of the Shorenstein Center at Harvard, to mourn the loss of the "iron core" of investigative reporting—a core that has faded as newsrooms have tried to do more with less and appeal to readers with softer, tabloid-style news.[10]

And as C.W. Anderson, Emily Bell, and Clay Shirky write in their report *Post-Industrial Journalism* (referencing the fact that we have now entered a stage where the old "industrial" model is now finished):

> The effect of the current changes in the news ecosystem has
> already been a reduction in the quality of news in the United
> States. On present evidence, we are convinced that journalism
> in this country will get worse before it gets better, and, in some
> places (principally midsize and small cities with no daily paper)
> it will get markedly worse.[11]

Despite all we might say about the problems with traditional news—from journalists being too close to sources, to journalists writing with too much (or too little) regard for objectivity, to a lack of interest in and coverage of a myriad of social and economic issues—traditional news outlets are still important. Newspapers continue to provide the bedrock of original news coverage for most communities, the source for the more highly watched local TV news. Wire reporting from the AP offers some distinctive, useful work, but a steady supply of specific, local-interest reporting has never been its strength.

Thus, it is significant that the number of reporters at state houses and in Washington, in particular, has been downsized by newsroom chains looking to save money. The journalists at The *San Diego Union-Tribune* who won a Pulitzer Prize for National Reporting covering US Representative Randy "Duke" Cunningham's trail of corruption no longer have a Washington bureau. The number of journalists covering New Jersey's state capitol of Trenton has declined from thirty-five in 2003 to just fifteen in 2009. In Texas, state house reporters dropped from twenty-eight to eighteen; in Georgia, from fourteen to six.[12] With fewer eyes representing local communities to pay attention to the actions of those in power, Starr is right to sound an alarm about failure to catch corruption.

There's also a graveyard of newspapers—some closed, others bankrupt, still others anemic shells of their former selves. The two sorriest tales might be the 2009 deaths of the print dailies the *Rocky Mountain News* in Denver and the *Seattle Post-Intelligencer*.[13] The *P-I* signed off after 146 years (and is now only online).[14] These, at least, were in two-newspaper towns. The *Philadelphia Inquirer*, after being sold following the breakup of Knight-Ridder newspapers, has been bankrupt and passed along through four owners over the course of five years.[15] Great newspaper chains have collapsed: the Tribune Company, sold in December 2007 for $8.2 billion to real estate tycoon Sam Zell, went bankrupt amid mismanagement and poor economic fortunes.[16] Still, not all is lost, and journalists are still able to do some amazing work at these places. In 2012, *The Philadelphia Inquirer* managed to take home top honors from the Pulitzer committee with the prestigious prize for public service for its work on Philadelphia public schools.

The disturbing part about all of these stories of decline is that no one seems to have any answers for how to fix the traditional journalism model, though these businesses are trying. Newspapers that were once dailies have cut back to publishing three times a week or just online-only to save costs. In a move that prompted outcry from em-

ployees (two hundred of whom have since lost their jobs) and community members, Advance Publications made the decision to cut the
still-profitable *The Times-Picayune* (New Orleans) to a three-day-a-
week print paper.[17] In this, Advance was following the path set first by
the *Detroit Free Press. The Christian Science Monitor* and *The Capital
Times* in Wisconsin have both pioneered an online-only publishing
strategy. Whether any of these moves were cost saving or destructive is
hard to tell. Newspapers get most of their revenue, still, from the print
newspaper advertising and subscription base, but print also constitutes
a tremendous expenditure of capital resources.

As I write this book, we are at the dawn of the "new" paywall era in
news organizations—sites where you have to pay to access content. *The
Wall Street Journal* has always had an online paywall—in part because
it could reliably target a class of business professionals (who could
likely expense their subscriptions). But until recently, few general-
interest newspapers had tried the experiment. *The New York Times* had
an aborted effort from 2005-07 with TimesSelect, a for-pay subscription to read columnists online, along with some other features. They
canned it, according to a letter to readers, as an effort to preserve the
news ecology's demand for debate and discourse.[18]

The Times was considered fairly revolutionary when it introduced
what was called the "metered paywall" on March 17, 2011. Each visitor would be given twenty free articles a month (reduced in 2012 to
ten), and then asked to pay for a digital subscription (which could be
coupled cheaply with a print subscription). The paywall was intention-
ally porous: articles sent via social networks were free and didn't count
toward this number. As *The Times'* spokesperson Eileen Murphy put it,
this was so *The Times* could remain "open to all and an integral part of
the social Web."[19] *The Times* has been able to gain subscribers in print
and digital. Other organizations have followed suit, although with different models: Gannett newspapers (with the exception of *USA Today*), the *Los Angeles Times,* and *The Boston Globe* all employ some
hybrid paid model for their online content. Since I studied *The Times,*
450 American newsrooms out of 1,380 dailes have launched paywall
editions.[20]

However, early reports back on paywalls suggest that only the largest news organizations are likely to see gains from them. A number of different models exist, from *The Times'* incredibly porous model to the *Arkansas Democrat-Gazette's* paywall (in place since 2002), where readers are charged to read anything that appeared in print in the newspaper. For some local news sites, this may stop the slow but inevitable bleed as their newspapers decline. Ryan Chittum has declared in the *Columbia Journalism Review* that the paywall is over, suggesting that there is no evidence that it will work and that newspapers are unlikely to gain additional revenue.[21] The *Star Tribune* (Minneapolis) has reported that only a small percentage of its readers have subscribed to the paywall.

These changes to the news industry were set in a time of both economic collapse and incredible innovation. The year 2010 brought with it the birth of the iPad, which revolutionized tablet computing. The social Web continued to grow, as Facebook expanded its membership to include approximately one-sixth of the world's population, going "public" in a functional sense long before it did so as an investment vehicle. Broadband expansion continued to boom, and wireless and mobile communication was cheaper than ever before (though data storage had become an increasing problem). Search, aggregation, and peer-produced content had made information increasingly accessible.

And amid all these sorrowful tales of foundering traditional news outlets, there were also exciting areas of news innovation. We are seeing the results now, as online news organizations are reaching bigger audiences than ever before on sites like Buzzfeed, which, despite regular streams of animal photo slideshows, has embarked on a massive hiring spree to boost original content. *The Huffington Post* won a Pulitzer Prize for National Reporting in 2012 for a ten-part series on severely wounded veterans. The site leverages a combination of celebrity news and commentary with original content for massive traffic. Niche online content is also doing well. *Politico,* which does have a print newspaper, offers a select, for-pay version of political news. *Talking Points Memo,* which began as a start-up blog, provides leftist political coverage, and its blend of political news and opinion keeps the site able to provide in-depth coverage of national politics. *The Atlantic* is touting *Quartz,* a

Web-native site, attracting journalists from *The Times, The Wall Street Journal,* and elsewhere to participate in the experiment. Other niche blogs, like *SCOTUSblog,* which monitors the Supreme Court, have gained avid followings.

Foundation-supported newsrooms have begun to supplement the news ecosystem, at least in some ways. *The Texas Tribune,* an outfit funded by a venture capitalist that has now attracted corporate sponsors, provides detailed news about Texas, tackling subjects from politics to immigration. Its work appears not only online but also in *The New York Times,* among other partners. *ProPublica,* first financed by the Sandler family with a $10 million grant, operates much the same way. It, too, has won Pulitzers and has made crowdsourcing public documents a regular part of its reporting. Smaller nonprofit ventures like the *MinnPost* and the *Voice of San Diego* are supported by philanthropic institutions like the Knight Foundation, memberships, events and other revenue streams but still lack backers offering major funding for the moment. Their impact, while widely touted among the news-about-the-news community, remains small within the general audience for news. Matthew Hindman has noted that traffic to these sites is so small that it does not even register on sites that measure Internet traffic.[22]

Participation, as value and practice, fuels other types of news start-ups. A number of news start-ups aim to give users the chance to organize their own stories, rather than rely on journalists to do it for them.[23] Storify is probably the best known; it gives users the ability to aggregate tweets into an organized story. There is even a venture capital accelerator called Matter, whose tagline is "where the values of public media meet the mindsets of Silicon Valley entrepreneurship."[24] Similarly, the Knight News Challenge has pumped millions of dollars into news start-ups, emphasizing that entries likely to win will take on the spirit of participatory journalism and entrepreneurship.[25]

Hackers, too, have begun to explore journalism as an exciting playground. Journalism presents a "new problem space," as Mozilla executive director Mark Surman pointed out.[26] Hackers are working outside newsrooms to create apps that allow for participatory engagement in news creation. Other hackers are working inside newsrooms as programmers, developing interactive graphics, tools that help journalists do their work, and public-facing apps. This collaboration between hackers and journalism has been welcomed with excitement by tech giants like Google and Mozilla and by news foundations like Knight.

So, is this the darkest time for news? There are reasons to be fearful about the traditional state of journalism. All the participatory work of citizens and the supplementary offerings of online journalism may be unable to replace what Anderson, Bell, and Shirky distill quite eloquently as the core function of a traditional, professional journalist:

> Getting key bits of descriptive information out of an eyewitness, aggressively challenging the verbal responses of a seasoned government bureaucrat, knowing exactly where to find a key document, or navigating the routines and idiosyncrasies of complex modern organizations is a non-trivial intellectual endeavor, and a public good to boot. In many instances, the most important aspects of individual journalistic work remain what they've always been at their best: interviewing, making direct observations and analyzing individual documents.[27]

Thus, there are reasons to be hopeful about journalism, as well as reasons to be deeply concerned. This book is not about the death of American journalism, nor does it attempt to prognosticate about its future. But it is important to provide a context to understand the landscape that *The Times* found itself in during 2010.

The State of *The Times*

I was almost kicked out of *The Times* even before I started this research, in part because the newspaper had experienced "staff reductions" of one hundred people in December 2009, and some editors felt that it was still a fairly sensitive time for the paper. In the end, though, in a newsroom of approximately eleven hundred people when I entered the building in January, people made only a few passing references to the layoffs and buyouts and generally went on with their work. Its size, resources, and commitment to public service from its publisher meant that *The New York Times* was in a slightly different place than most other newspapers at the time. Yet it was far from immune to the deepening challenges facing the news industry.

When I arrived at *The Times*, it was undoubtedly the leading online newspaper in the world. It was the fifth most popular news site in the world after Yahoo!, MSN, CNN, and the BBC, and it saw thirty million unique visitors a month. *The Times* had one of the most nimble, quick, stable, and interactive news sites in the world, thanks to the bevy of talented designers and software folks who decided to work in journalism instead of going to Silicon Valley. As publisher Arthur Ochs Sulzberger, Jr. bragged to an audience at the London School of Economics, *The Times* was the "most social" company in the world—the company with the largest social media presence, even bigger than Apple and Google.[28]

Yet if you looked around at the newspaper's financial situation, though better than most, things were still unstable. In 2009, Michael Hirschorn predicted the death of *The Times* within six months.[29] Journalist Seth Mnookin has chronicled the paper's changing fortunes across a variety of magazines.[30] From his work, it becomes clear how precarious *The New York Times'* situation has been at moments. In January 2009, the New York Times Co. took a loan from Mexican telecom mogul Carlos Slim for $250 million. Two months later, the newspaper raised money against its own headquarters for another $225 million. Between 2009 and 2012, *The Times* lost about one hundred thousand print subscribers a year for three straight years.

But a few things have happened to reverse this downward spiral: doubling the print newsstand price hasn't caused anyone to flinch, and the digital subscription plan looks promising. By summer 2011, *The Times* had paid back the Slim loan. However, some uncertainty still existed at the top. Key departures in rapid succession stunned many media observers: in 2011, CEO Janet Robinson stepped down, reportedly because of faltering Times Co. performance,[31] as did Martin Nisenholtz, senior vice president of digital operations, who will not be replaced. We will hear more about Nisenholtz's "engagement" strategy for *Times* digital content later in the book. As of 2012, *The Times* has remained remarkably mum about its paywall operation, except to boast of $100 million in revenue. It has not been specific about advertising-revenue declines due to traffic losses.[32]

The situation remained somewhat ambiguous while I finished this book. *Times* guild members interrupted an afternoon Page One meeting on February 29, 2012, to protest cuts in salaries and medical benefits and weakening retirement security. According to the nyguild. org write-up, more than 250 *Times* employees took part, with many wearing stickers that said "without us, it's just white space." This protest came on the heels of the Robinson exit package, valued at more than $21 million.[33] In 2012, *The Times* again offered buyout packages to thirty employees. The buyouts were placed in the context of declining ad sales. Sulzberger, Jr. noted in a statement: "These are financially challenging times. . . . While our digital subscription plan has been highly successful, the advertising climate remains volatile and we don't see this changing in the near future."[34]

Nevertheless, Sulzberger, Jr. has vaunted aspirations for his newspaper. Again and again, he has commented on *The New York Times* as a standard-bearer for news—consider this interview snippet: "It's an international paper now. I mean, important. Important. Between *The New York Times* and *The International Herald Tribune*, which carries *New York Times* journalism—right?—in print and on the Web, we are an international paper."[35] And as he put *The New York Times*' challenge in a speech at the London School of Economics in 2011, "Our content distinguishes us. Now, we are also challenged to deliver it in ways that draws in readers who are one click away from a dizzying array of other options."[36] The online journalism values I outline here—immediacy, interactivity, and participation—underscore the challenges facing the newspaper, as well as the whole news industry in the 2010s. At *The Times*, we can see how these values offer opportunities for contestation and celebration. But before moving forward to explore these values at work, it is important to explain the brief history of *The Times* on the Web. This history is helpful, because it foreshadows some of the tensions in the newsroom, and it situates the initiatives present at *The Times* during my study.

A Brief Web History of *The Times*

Staff memory offers some institutional perspective on *The Times'* on-line evolution. In the 1980s, *The Times* was one of the most popular electronically delivered newspapers—by fax.[37] The four to six pages of news, features, and editorials were ultimately not commercially viable, however, and the project lost support from the main newsroom. The newspaper also used a technology popular with other leading news-rooms called videotext to deliver news electronically to hotels and businesses on machines that looked a lot like the present personal computer. Another initiative, called *The New York Pulse,* did, in fact, deliver content via the early Internet through dial-up to some of the earliest personal computers.

Between 1983 and 1986, *The Times* had about twenty-five editorial staff and a dozen tech staff working on *The New York Pulse,* though it ultimately reached only 200–250 paid subscribers. *The New York Pulse* was housed out of a building in Union Square, though staff members would occasionally make the trek uptown.[38] This electronic version had its own original content, particularly about New York restaurants, and it contained a comprehensive compilation of *Times* archives. In addition, readers could get the next day's paper on *The New York Pulse* as soon as it hit the street, as Susan Jacobson, a former copy editor at *The New York Pulse,* recalled. However, the project ran up against the recession of the late 1980s, and since it was primarily viewed as an R&D cost and not a scalable project, it didn't have much newsroom support for survival. So in 1986, *The New York Pulse* came to a sudden close.

It took almost ten years for *The Times* to reenter the Internet news market. The first major *Times* initiative to take hold on the Internet was on America Online. The site was called @times, and it launched in mid-1994, at a point when many Americans were getting their first home computers. It featured little original content, though it did include user forums where readers could discuss news. Consultant Rich Meislin, former editor-in-chief of the New York Times Electronic Media Company (as it was then called) from 1998 to 2001, noted that the site was viewed more as a marketing opportunity than as an avenue for growth. The editorial side of the newsroom had virtually "no participation at all."[39]

By the summer of 1995, people from the newsroom began to get involved in thinking about strategy and content for the Web site. But the Web site was an "after-thought, if it was thought of at all," to most people in the newsroom, according to Bernard Gwertzman, who became one of the first editors of the Web site.[40] The Web site operated in a different building from the rest of *The Times*. The physical separation of the *Times* Web site from the print newsroom continued until 2007, when *The Times* moved into its new building.

The official Web site launch at the www.nytimes.com domain was on Monday, January 22, 1996. *The Times* had done a test run in early October 1995 to cover the visit of Pope John Paul II to America, according to Kevin McKenna, who was editorial director of the Web site at the time. The site included most of the paper online—what some would refer to as "shovelware," because it repurposed the paper's print content exactly. But the site also included original articles designed to appeal to the Web audience.

CyberTimes,[41] created in 1996, was *The Times'* first extensive foray into original online content. As John Haskins, one of the former editors of *CyberTimes*, explained:

> Most of the people on the Web at that time were early adopters, so we put together a section about tech culture. We would write technology articles, about one to two a day about the Internet, and have about four to five columns. There was even a news feature that would go something like, "Camping is easier because you can book your tent on the Internet."[42]

In addition to columnists, *CyberTimes* also featured twelve freelancers who wrote about everything from legal issues to education to e-commerce trends. *CyberTimes* was eventually folded into the general NYTimes.com technology section in 1998. As Pablo Boczkowski documents, the creation of *CyberTimes* signaled a break from traditional print routines; the newsroom was now in the business of creating content for the World Wide Web.[43]

Another step forward for the newspaper was the creation of the continuous news desk in 1999, an effort to bring together the print and Web newsrooms. According to associate managing editor Jim Roberts, the goal of the "CND" was to:

> manag[e] a news report on the Web that would extend past the simple print cycle. The need was to update the Web, and the desire was to do it in a way that didn't overtax the print reporting staff. . . . It was done in a very gentle way [so as] to shield reporters from the Web site.[44]

CND's function was to update content for the Web with wires and some original reporting, while other reporters worked on the main story for print. At that time, reporters really didn't want to be writing for the Web; the perception was that writing for the Web took away from the deep analysis required for full-scale reporting (and this idea still endures, to a certain extent). The idea was to have a handful of reporters updating breaking news, leaving print reporters to focus on the print story.

The September 11, 2001, attacks demonstrated the utility of the CND, according to Roberts. Reporters could call into the desk and get their material instantly on the Web. However, the dramatic front page on September 12, 2001, with the bold headline "U.S. Attacked" and a shot of the Two Towers, still standing but engulfed in flames, seemed to epitomize the iconic importance of print, even at a time when instant updates seemed incredibly important. Notably, *The Times* Web site was able to handle the massive amount of traffic on September 11, 2001, a day when cell phones were jammed and other Web sites failed. But there was still friction between reporters and editors who did not see the online newsroom as part of their role, even after the importance of immediate updates had been made clear. Online was still distinct from the print newsroom, with "those online people over there [in that building]," according to one Web producer.

Getting journalists to write for the Web, rather than relying on CND, was a slow process, as many journalists resisted the idea that they should write online. The ethos in the newsroom was to save the best stuff for the print run of the paper. Journalists wanted to keep the Web site looking just like the paper, as a way to ensure that both products would have similar standards. However, around 2002, foreign correspondents and business journalists saw the utility of writing for the Web with their own bylines and labor, rather than relying on the CND, according to assistant managing editor Susan Edgerley.[45] Foreign desk journalists wanted to see their work online, mostly because they couldn't get their work in print in, say, Afghanistan or Uzbekistan or Kenya. Business journalists saw the importance of timeliness, as they wanted to be competitive with *The Journal* and other business news outlets, including the business wires.

Len Apcar, who had become the editor of nytimes.com in 2002, began sharing with the newsroom what could be done online. He held regular brown bag lunches where journalists would say to other journalists, "'I have seen the light' and stand up and give their testimony," or evangelize to other journalists about the benefits of online.[46] He recalled one particular session when political reporter Kit Seelye described live-blogging a 2004 presidential debate. "At the time, a lot of people thought this was heresy," he said, reflecting that writing about something *while* it happened with limited editing and reflection seemed to run counter to the very core ethos of *The Times*. In another step forward, Apcar forced the Web staff and print staff to meet: he brought Web producers to the different desks and introduced them to people in order to explain what Web producers actually did.

However, perhaps the seminal moment for change came when executive editor Bill Keller announced that the print and online newsrooms would merge; his buzzword for it was "integration." Print people would eventually take on the responsibilities of Web tasks, but some others would still be principally devoted to the production of the Web site and its associated activities. By 2005, however, the cultural change was not one that could come just from Keller and other key management. Journalists also had to buy into the change. They quickly saw that online was part of the future of their survival in the industry, according to multiple people I spoke with about the transition to a unified newsroom with online and print working together.

At this point, *The Times* was experimenting as an organization with a variety of new online forms; live-blogging was still a new way to cover events as they unfolded. Blog after blog sprouted up. But perhaps the most significant example of experimentation was the *City Room* blog, which began in 2007. The blog was dedicated to up-to-the-minute coverage of New York's metro news. Specific reporters were assigned to be just *City Room* bloggers; Sewell Chan (the business reporter mentioned in the introduction) was the first *City Room* editor. *City Room* was a place for experimentation with multimedia and user comments.

Contrary to *Times* fashion at the time, *City Room* linked beyond *The Times* to other Web sites, including those competitors. The goal was to make *City Room* a New Yorker's primary destination for news about the city. *City Room*'s style was novel for *The Times*, with short briefs written in a more casual style. *City Room* also took up lighter fare that more serious metro stories might ignore and focused on original content that would not be in the paper.

Keller explained how internal rewards and examples such as *City Room* helped the integration process: "People would look at what this kid [Chan] was doing and saw that it was really neat. We were leading by example in the newsroom. And when someone did something really great, we let other people know about it."[47]

Jonathan Landman, the "integration czar," would go through the newsroom telling people about the benefits of the Web. He wrote more than one hundred memo emails from 2007 to 2009 (about one per week) chronicling *The Times'* progress and development on the Web. All of them could still be found on *The Times* intranet in 2010. His goal was to show people what could happen online. He said in 2010:

> I was like the guy in the white coat. If you wanted to start a blog, you could. You didn't have to have meetings or much of anything. I tried to find enthusiasts and cajole different people, and, yes, there was technical development, but presto, there would be blogs.[48]

Still, as in any newsroom, there were resistors: people who simply didn't want to write online and never saw it as their duty to do so. But as Edgerley explained, "Anyone who still thinks like that has to be on their way out. That's just not a sustainable way to think around here anymore."

According to most people I interviewed or shadowed, the biggest change in terms of integrating what were seen as the "two newsrooms" was the physical movement of *The New York Times* in 2007 into the new offices on Eighth Avenue. Web producers actually sat with each desk, and Web production became a visible process. As reporter Diana Henriques told me, "I could actually see who these people were. If I had a problem, I could go talk to them."[49]

Keller described the changes this way:

> Integrating was more than a matter of administration and getting us all in same building. A lot of it was psychological and cultural, impressing upon people who thought that what they were trying to do was write a story for the front page of the newspaper to think more in terms of home page of [the] Web site and to appreciate the value of blogging, to look at video and audio and slide shows and interactive graphics, not as something someone else did to decorate journalism but as really journalism in [its] own right. I don't claim on any front, administration, jurisdictionally, culturally, psychologically, that we are one big, happy family, but we are a lot closer than we were.[50]

But the reality of journalism also helped, in his view:

> In a funny way, the euphemism [of] the "challenging" economic environment in [the] newspaper business helped motivate people to [change]. [People realized that] a lot of [the] Web is the future, and print is in trouble, [so] "I better get with program, I better figure this out and see if there are skills that I should learn." There was some small element of professional insecurity that helped stir people into embrace the Web more fully.[51]

Notably, during the period of integration that Keller and others spoke about, the primary motive driving integration was not one that clearly imagined the audience as the newly participatory readers that theorists predicted. Instead, competition, survival, and internal reward were more important to encouraging integration.

Keller has vacillated on the extent to which the newsroom has achieved integration. *The Times* allowed Landman to step down from his integration role to become culture editor in 2009. The article announcing the change noted that the period of integration was over:

> In a memo to the staff making the announcement, Mr. Keller said that with the integration that had been achieved, there might be no equivalent to that role [i.e., Landman's] in the future, as other top editors take more responsibility for Internet operations.[52]

But when I asked Keller to reflect on whether integration was indeed complete in 2010, he noted, "Five years later, I try to resist saying we have an integrated newsroom."[53] Keller's ambivalence offers a good preview of what is to come in this book: a newsroom where print and online had two completely different rhythms, as well as contrasting visions of immediacy. Still, journalists seem to be able to live in this somewhat integrated world in a way they were unable to ten or even just five years ago. They write unquestioningly for the Web. People see their section's Web producers, who sit right by the desks of main editors. Web editors sit on every desk. The 24/7 newsroom is in place.

As we will see in the next chapter, there is far more to this story than just Web versus print. The early tensions in the newspaper's online history were compounded by the reality of journalism at *The Times* in 2010. By 2010, *all* journalists had to negotiate with the competing tempos of the ASAP online world and the demands of the print paper. Similarly, journalists had to be prepared to work in an environment that was not just about creating pure text content for the Web, but instead involved collaborating to create interactive news stories using video, audio, and features that invited audience engagement through new forms. Traditional journalists felt compelled to take on new responsibilities as they faced the reality of the social media world before them. The rules for engaging in this conversation were uncertain—in fact, the newspaper didn't even have set guidelines, but journalists felt they needed to get on the bandwagon.

Journalists in the trenches rarely spent time thinking about the economic future of *The Times*. Even on the day the paywall was publicly announced for the first time, journalists on the business desk made a few cracks and jokes, asked about how it would work, and then went about their days. And while *Times* journalists were, to some degree, insulated from larger industry-wide extremes, journalists' ability to reconcile the sometimes conflicting demands of immediacy, interactivity, and participation *did* have consequences for the newspaper's economic fortunes. As this book proceeds, we will see how journalists grappled with these new values of online journalism on a day-to-day basis, but we will also see the possible economic implications of their practices for *The Times* (particularly concerning interactivity and participation).

In the next chapter, though, I offer a close look at the competing biorhythms and demands of journalism at *The Times* in 2010. Small details that appear in this chapter, from a reporter's freedom to book an airline ticket without asking permission to the existence of an R&D department, illustrate *The Times*' unique place within the news industry. At the same time, like any news organization, it was adjusting to newswork in an on-demand world in an industry that had no certain business plan for survival.

As we will see, journalists at *The Times* were negotiating the demands of creating content in an online journalism environment. New values were beginning to order routines and professional perceptions, albeit not without protest. As we see here, and throughout the book, immediacy, interactivity, and participation in the online world emerged as values that were fundamentally restructuring the way journalists were thinking about their work and their priorities in the newsroom. These values did not yet have stable meanings themselves, and they were being defined through practice. Each value, but most specifically interactivity and participation, had clear connections to an economic strategy. However, most journalists simply felt pressure to adapt to the digital age, not for economic reasons, but out of a felt demand to keep up or be left behind as *The Times* moved ahead online.

Chapter 2

Three Days in the Lives of
New York Times Journalists

Graham Bowley, financial reporter, was ready to tackle a task he knew would feed the ire of the American public: revealing just how much money Goldman Sachs had managed to earn in 2010. In the aftermath of the financial collapse, Goldman was a stand-in for all that was wrong with the big banks. Not only was it the largest bank to survive, but in fact, it had prospered. And in front of a congressional panel that year, bankers, led by Goldman's CEO Lloyd Blankfein, had stood firm and blamed the American public, rather than assume accountability for any errors during the financial crisis. But, as the public would later learn, Goldman had knowingly shorted the bubbling housing market as it advised their own clients to pour money into it.

Bowley's specific assignment was to cover the Goldman earnings report, a humdrum task when the economy was hopping along just fine, simply a prescheduled story that could be reliably counted upon for content in the next day's paper. But this was the Great Recession—while the Dow had rebounded from a March 2009 low of 6,443.27 to about 11,000 points in 2010, recovery wasn't being felt elsewhere across the United States. Lenders had just finished a record year of 3.8 million new home foreclosures.[1] Unemployment was still hovering just below 10 percent. Banking had become one of the most-disliked industries in the country; the Gallup poll charting industry favorability among Americans showed a 17 percent drop for bankers over the course of the prior year.[2]

The environment in the newsroom right before the earnings release was tense. These earnings, and just what *The Times* made out of them, would likely become political fodder. The editors also thought there was a good chance of making a lot of ordinary *Times* readers pretty angry, even though a few years ago, they might not have even known what Goldman was. Editors assumed the story was likely to generate massive traffic on the Web.

The significance of this daily assignment meant that Bowley would be filing quick Web updates whenever he had new information about Goldman throughout the day. So, when Bowley came to work at 7:30 a.m., he was ready for an intense day of reporting that editors said could wind up on the front page. He had the drill for writing this kind of breaking Web story down, and he was ready to go.

Bowley's day, which I will review in depth, offers an example of a reporter dealing with what immediacy means in the online world at *The New York Times*. In this chapter, I offer a look at Bowley and two other journalists as they went about a day in their work at *The New York Times*. While journalists often chronicle their experiences in books, here I anatomize their experiences in the form of a single day with the perspective of an outsider looking in, charting patterns and processes. The three days I have chosen highlight the different routines that were emerging at *The Times* as journalists adapted to the myriad of challenges and opportunities of working in a digital on-demand news environment. Each day demonstrates the ways that immediacy, interactivity, and participation are (or are not) manifest in the work routines of journalists. Though this chapter wraps these values into daily narratives, these snapshots, in turn, set in place the later chapters that focus on these core values of online journalism at *The Times*.

Graham Bowley is a financial reporter whose story demonstrates what it is like to be on a 24/7 deadline. Then you will meet Andrew Martin, also a financial reporter, but one who is more focused on consumer affairs and whose story shows an off-deadline day. Finally, you will meet Nick Bilton, a blogger for the *Bits* technology blog, hosted out of the business desk, on the day the first iPad was announced and the newsroom experimented with a variety of ways to report. I could have chosen any of the many days that I observed traditional and non-traditional journalists working from morning to evening, but these three days epitomize the core tensions that emerge in the newsroom over immediacy, interactivity, and participation. These terms are used by scholars, as noted in the first chapter, and rarely by journalists. But framing their days in the context of these emergent values provides a normative dimension to the on-the-ground experiences of journalists.

Bowley's day principally offers a tale about the pressures journalists face in coping with immediacy, though his day also offers some insight into interactivity and participation. He had to deal with the rush of getting a breaking story up on the site, only to write it again for the print paper, showing some of the conflicting ways journalists had to negotiate the constant demands of the Web in relation to more traditional patterns. His brief interlude with a video team hoping to do a quick shoot for the Web shows the confusing and jarring shock to his text-based day—and some of the artificiality of the process is almost amusing (he was asked to do an interview about his story for video with someone on the business desk who wasn't even his editor or working with him on the story). This experience with multimedia underscores the experience many journalists had—interactivity as disruption. Bowley's day doesn't touch on participation much, but his views of the audience are indicative of those of many in the newsroom: the audience was not worth his time.

Martin's day is, in many ways, the opposite of Bowley's. Martin shows the life of an off-deadline reporter who was principally concerned with producing enterprise or investigative work. He was focused on news that was ostensibly unique to *The Times* and that other outlets would hopefully not report, and his work was not slated to a particular date. This doesn't mean that Martin never wrote for 24/7 immediate Web deadlines. In fact, he covered Bank of America, and in much the same way that Bowley went through the exercise of writing up the Goldman report, on another occasion, Martin spent a frenetic day accounting for Bank of America's quarterly earnings.

But life at *The Times* is not always about the now, and it is important to remember this competing drive that requires time to report and to shape story angles. Martin's day also highlights interactivity from a very different perspective: he was all about creating interactive content for his work. But he shows the lack of established patterns and processes for doing so: he had an ad-hoc meeting with his favorite videographer and didn't tell his editor (or the business desk Web editors) what he was thinking. The way he integrated interactivity into his workflow is distinct from most journalists at *The Times*.

Bilton's day, on the other hand, shows how a nontraditional journalist (a blogger) handled a pretty out-of-the ordinary story: the announcement of the first iPad. This was big news to the newsroom—expected in the sense that reporters knew Steve Jobs had planned a big unveiling, but unexpected because they had no idea what the product would be and what it could do. Bilton's day chronicles the pressures of immediacy and trying to report using nontraditional platforms: checking competing blogs and Twitter, and running the nytimes.com "live blog" and other experiments. His attempts to create graphics and content for the event showcase the varying levels of importance and facility that journalists felt toward interactivity. And his work on social media platforms underscores an important theme we will see later in the book, that when journalists do participate online, they use the Web for reporting and to broadcast their views or to talk to other established people. With rare exceptions, participation remains a one-to-many experience, with few voices from the audience heard.

Throughout the book, we'll see many different types of journalists in action, from Web producers to interactive news journalists, but here, I've focused on journalists who highlight the relationship between "tradition and change"[3] in the newsroom. In the case of Bowley, we see an old-school reporter working under new pressure—though he also had the liberty to work on off-deadline stories; in the case of Martin, we see a traditional reporter working on off-deadline stories, but with a new perspective; and in the case of Bilton, we see a different type of journalist covering a story demanding a variety of new tools and platforms. From a close look at a day in the life of Bowley, Martin, and Bilton, a picture emerges of how journalists were adapting (or not) to the values of immediacy, interactivity, and participation—and just how these values were, indeed, contested ones.

Graham Bowley, Financial News Reporter—
January 21, 2010

Graham Bowley is a sandy-haired, middle-aged Brit. He had spent years on the foreign desk after working for the *International Herald Tribune* and the *Financial Times* in Europe. In his spare time, he was writing a book about the Himalayan mountain K2. On the Sunday before I spent time with him, he had a big story in the travel section, as well as a large profile in the Sunday Business section about Morgan Stanley's new chief executive. Bowley said I should spend the day with him while he covered the Goldman Sachs earnings report release, because it would be fast paced and Web-centric, and because I would be able to watch a story evolve from its start on the Web to its final version for the print paper—which also stands as the lasting version online.

In 2010, journalists at *The Times* speculated that many Americans were frustrated with Goldman Sachs, the bank that seemed to be the big winner in the financial crisis. To many observers, Goldman, with its massive role on Wall Street, was now the symbolic representative of Wall Street versus Main Street in American political discourse. Goldman, along with JPMorgan, Wells Fargo, and the other surviving banks after the financial collapse, had been guilty of mistakes that may have led to the financial collapse, as diligent work from journalists, government commissions, filmmakers, and nonprofits had revealed. To many politicians and many in the public,[4] Goldman represented the banks that had created the complicated derivatives and collateralized debt obligations that inflated and then popped the housing bubble, leading the American markets off the cliff and, with them, leading the economy to its worst recession since the Great Depression.[5]

Any story about Goldman in these times, Bowley told me, typically went on the most emailed list, got "boatloads" of comments, and had a good shot at making the front page—though Bowley was going to have to do more than just say how much money Goldman had made for the story to have enough substance to be worthy of Page One: he'd have to make news that all outlets would have distinguishable and unique from the pack, or at least that was the theory. The fourth-quarter earnings, typically released in a period between December and February, were of the most interest in the newsroom and, theoretically, to readers, because they reflected the previous year's total gains and losses and employee compensation. More precisely, they revealed what Goldman employees' average bonuses would be.

Though the story was big news, Bowley had told me the day before that I might be bored watching him, as the process of writing the story itself would be rather routine. Bowley came into the newsroom in time for the 8 a.m. release of the precise numbers, but he had already had a story ready to go for the Web (minus the actual numbers) the night before. At *The Times*, this sort of prestory is called "B matter." It is the canned, ready-to-use material that is prewritten, sometimes weeks before, sometimes days before. The reason: the Web. The goal for such a story is that it will be ready to go up the second the anticipated information is released, whether it is about corporate earnings, unemployment numbers, or election results, for instance.

A prewritten story was usually copy that read almost like a dry press release, and sometimes, it even included quotes that had been compiled *before* the actual event. The journalist would often hedge; some quotes gathered would be positive, others negative. The thinking was that *The Times* could get a complete, potentially more thoughtful story up on the Web, rather than just a quick headline flash like AP or Reuters, hopefully creating some "value-added" content for the reader—something beyond the wire content's quick burst of news. "Value-added" (or "added-value") content was a term journalists at *The Times* used to distinguish their work from that of other news outlets.

The day, Bowley explained, would be divided up by the various releases of information, with the earnings announcement at 8 a.m., a conference call with the Goldman CFO to journalists at 9 a.m., an 11 a.m. investors and analysts call, and at some point during the morning a one-on-one call with the Goldman CFO; then, after many updates, Bowley would wrap up a final story for the print paper. By 8 a.m., all Bowley had to do was wait for the numbers to be released online from Goldman and then put them into a story that looked like the one below, copy that had already been edited by business Web editor Mark Getzfred. The B matter (or prewritten story) looked like this:

Goldman Sachs said Thursday it earned $TK [to come] profit in the fourth quarter, rounding out a year for the Wall Street bank in 2009.

The bank said its profit for the whole of 2009 was $TK billion, and in a move that is likely to incense its critics, disclosed that it had set aside a record $TK billion for bonuses for its employees.

The results show how much Goldman has rebounded from the financial crisis and its single quarterly loss in the final three months of 2008. Its disclosure on bonuses underlines the extent to which compensation will again eat up much of Wall Street's revenue this year.

The bonus numbers are likely to provoke more outcry over the level of executive pay on Wall Street, a year after the government rescued the financial system with billions of taxpayers' dollars.

Many banks are bracing for more scrutiny of pay from Washington, as well as from officials like Andrew M. Cuomo, the attorney general of New York, who last year demanded that banks disclose details about their bonus payments. Some bankers worry that the United States, like Britain, might create an extra tax on bank bonuses.

But these concerns aside, few banks are taking immediate steps to cut their bonuses substantially. Because of the potential criticism, some big banks are changing their pay practices, paring or even eliminating some cash bonuses in favor of stock awards and reducing the portion of their revenue earmarked for pay.

In December, Goldman announced that its top 30 executives would be paid only in stock, with no cash component. Now, nearly everyone on Wall Street is waiting to see how much stock will be awarded to Lloyd C. Blankfein, Goldman's chairman and chief executive, who has become a focus for criticism over executive pay. In 2007, Mr. Blankfein was paid $68 million, a Wall Street record. He did not receive a bonus in 2008.

Promptly at 8 a.m., Bowley checked the wires for results. He saw that *The Journal* had posted the earnings before *The Times*. "It's on *The Journal!*" he shouted, and yelled out the number to Getzfred. Bowley confirmed the numbers independently. After looking at the earnings again, Bowley shouted, "*The Journal* got it wrong." He said this in a rushed, almost competitive tone.

The two then conferred about whether they were going to make net revenue or net earnings the main focus of the story;[6] at this point, Bowley had an income statement printed out with the quarterly earnings. Dan Niemi, the assigning editor, said they should go with the net earnings number of $4.95 billion. "It's more applicable to common shareholders. And say it's above Wall Street expectations," he reasoned.[7] Getzfred and Bowley looked at the hot-button bonus compensation number, and Getzfred said, "This is the lowest [compensation number] ever as a public company."

Bowley stood over Getzfred's shoulder as they fed the earnings number into Bowley's B matter and uploaded the first version of the story to the content management system and onto the Web. Bowley went back to his desk and refreshed the home page. It took a few minutes for the Goldman story to come up on the business page and then emerge on the lead spot on the home page, though the story was already live on the *Financial Times*, Reuters, and *The Journal*.

Bowley worked with Getzfred to tweak the wording in the lead as the two went back and forth with small changes, but the story was up for the public to read. Notably, the story had only been edited by Getzfred: there was no copy editor on this kind of breaking story until after the story had gone up on the Web site. However, for a story to make it into the print edition, it might be copy edited anywhere from two to sometimes seven times before public consumption.[8]

Bowley's posted story was only the first version of the piece, and he would continue to work on it throughout the day. After posting the basic earnings, Bowley began reading up on the bonus pool from years prior, trying to determine what the per-person bonus would turn out to be for this year, compared to the others. All of this was happening at a steady pace, with Bowley checking carefully, so as not to make mistakes that could result in a painful correction online or in the paper or in flaming comments underneath the story from the audience.

He stopped tinkering with the early version of the story (with each change reflected in updates to the Web posted by Getzfred). Bowley arranged for me to take part with him in the journalists' conference call with Lucas van Praag, Goldman's chief public relations officer, and the Goldman CFO, David A. Viniar. The CFO began by introducing all of the highlights from Goldman's earnings. Then, the conversation turned to questions from both the British and American press on issues ranging from the bank tax Obama advocated, to the compensation issue, to whether Goldman was "too big to fail."

Bowley observed that he was starting to get reader email about Goldman, and then he sent a note to Getzfred, saying that he wanted to have comments turned on for the story. Since *The Times* moderated comments before they were posted, the newspaper could have only a few stories with comments live on the site each day. Comments on the story meant that the story would remain high on the home page, in part because of the effort it took to moderate them.

Bowley knew he couldn't answer each reader email as it came in, but on that day, he was well prepared for the regular stream of email that would likely appear as a result of the story: "As soon as you mention Goldman, they just start coming in." Bowley could tell the reader mail apart from something that might be coming in from a source by using a simple trick: if a reader were to click to email a reporter at *The Times* by putting his mouse on the byline, the message that would result would have a big subject line prefix denoting it as [READER-MAIL]. Functionally, this feature flags the email as something the reporter is free to ignore (as I saw with fair regularity).

Bowley was trying to do many things at once—to make sure that he was constantly updating the Web and continuing to report the story. The room he had to maneuver and have the story take on a particular and unique angle was more difficult at this point: he was trying to feed the Web with each bit of new information, and the latest round had just been a pool of press quotes. At this point, nothing really made *The Times'* story particularly unique.

Nevertheless, he was able to get some input from colleagues as he prepared for each step of the major Web updates, and there were some pauses in the online process to think of new angles. For example, as Bowley waited for his individual call from the CFO—one of his first breaks from the Web pressure and his first chance to differentiate his work—he got some suggestions from the Sunday business editor about possible questions to ask. These included probing Goldman on its current outlook toward credit default swaps, as loose regulations on those financial instruments had been blamed in part for the financial crisis.

Bowley responded to the suggestions, noting that he was interested in asking about the Volcker rule, a reform suggested by former Federal Reserve chair Paul Volcker, which would split banks' extremely profitable proprietary trading desks (where banks trade their own funds instead of their clients') from investment efforts on behalf of clients. The reform would also prohibit banks from owning or investing in a hedge fund or private equity fund. At the core of this question was whether investment banks could also be commercial bank holding companies. But he wasn't able, at this point, to use all of these suggestions in crafting the Web story.

Bowley got the call from the CFO and questioned the nature of the bonuses and the Volcker rule implications. Bowley's main editor, David Gillen, head of the financial team, instructed him to consider how Obama's proposed financial regulations might affect Goldman's role. Gillen planned other accompanying stories, aiming to have one reporter look at the legal implications of the Volcker rule for Goldman and another look at the policy implications.

The larger story started to take form beyond just the minutiae of updates from the daily story. After this individual call, Bowley knew this was a chance for him to differentiate *The Times'* story with the angle he was starting to convey. He began slipping some quotes from the CFO into the current Web version.

Gillen gave an order about crafting the story: "Let's frame it [this way] . . . did Goldman blink [in the financial crisis]? It's still up 50 percent?"

Bowley responded: "Is there pain and suffering?" he asked, referring to the way people felt inside Goldman about not getting big bonuses. Bowley also said he would try to get the pulse of what was happening inside the bank. Plans were made to get reactions from the trading floor.

Editor Liz Alderman and Gillen asked Bowley, "What's the A1 [thought]?" Bowley paused for a second and replied, "Washington and Wall Street."

Gillen instructed, "The lead will be the analytical on the bank."

In other words, Bowley was instructed to do a deep dive, looking at how the bank was going to navigate the tricky question of bonuses at a time when bankers were being vilified by Washington—to the point where President Obama was proposing a populist tax on this particular form of bonus compensation.

The A1 thought, the Page One thought, or the A1 story, refers to the story that would be presented to the Page One meeting for consideration for the front page of the print paper. The "analytical" idea of the lead referred to the step-back approach *The Times* would take after the journalist was done updating the story for the Web and began to ready it for the print paper.

After the discussion about the larger trajectory of the story, Bowley had some time to read an analysis from Credit Suisse about the earnings. He asked one of the *DealBook* reporters (whose role it is to get breaking news about Wall Street up on this specific *Times* blog quickly) about the implications of the bonus cut inside Goldman. The reporter noted, "It all depends on what Lloyd [Blankfein] gets."

At 11 a.m., as planned, Bowley sat in on the call between Goldman and financial analysts following the company. The call was mainly conducted in complicated financial jargon terms, with analysts asking for clarification on particular points on the income statements and other questions to help them make predictions about the company going forward. I didn't understand much of the call, which was heavy on financial language. Afterward, Bowley said to me, "Let's turn gobbledygook into English."

Bowley's job, then, was one of translation, taking financial terms and making them understandable for what he saw as the typical *Times* reader: someone who wouldn't understand the jargon. As he and others told me, *The Times* reader was often imagined by *Times* reporters to be an educated, interested reader who may just not know much about business. Most journalists, however, also saw their work reaching major decision makers.

After the analyst call, Bowley made a few additional changes to the story for the Web, again reflecting information that was not particularly unique to *The Times*—though Bowley's translation skills offered the chance to weed out the best news from this call. When satisfied, he noted, "I think we're done updating for the Web, but there will be more later." At this point, I left him alone to write the story for the print paper. He put on his headphones for a bit, then took them off to make calls, including a few to people on Capitol Hill. But mainly, at this point, his focus was on writing, not updating.

At about 2 p.m., Jane Bornemeier, head of *New York Times* radio and a key mover in *The Times'* video efforts, came by with a camera crew. They explained to Bowley that they wanted him and another editor, Winnie O'Kelley, to talk about the Goldman earnings for the camera. Bowley took a second and removed a blazer from the back of his chair and asked, "Can I put this on?" The video was designed to be "ninety seconds to two minutes . . . it's not a . . . recap, it's about your line of reporting," Bornemeier explained. Her colleague said to Bowley, "Give us a sneak peak, but not the golden egg," referring to the fact that she didn't want Bowley to give away the story. This was the first time Bowley had ever been asked to do one of these videos.

At this point, the video shoot was just a pilot for *TimesCast*, which was then planned as a noon Web show to give *Times* readers online an inside look at what the big stories would be in *The Times* by the end of the day. With big breaking news stories likely to make Page One, it was increasingly common for the writing process to be interrupted by multimedia demands.

Bowley and O'Kelley prepared for the camera, slightly bemused. "This is funny," O'Kelley noted. "We don't even work together." Bornemeier prompted them some more: "It's as if we were doing inside eavesdropping on a conversation you were already having."

Bowley's editor mocked him for being British. "He has a great voice," Gillen said, noting that his reporter could sound especially suave with the accent.

O'Kelley asked Bowley a few questions about the Volcker rule and the idea to separate commercial banks. She asked whether there were deeper questions than just those regarding bonus pay. The whole taping lasted about twenty minutes. Bowley returned to writing with his headphones on, and by 4:30 he passed his draft for the print version of the paper to Gillen. "He's a heavy edit," Bowley noted, anticipating significant changes to his style.

He then fielded a call from a Goldman employee's wife. "Goldman Housewife," he scribbled on a pad, looking excited. She had read the Web version of the story and called to complain that her husband wasn't getting the half-million-dollar bonus that Bowley had published. Bowley promised not to quote her but got her number to call her back in case he had a story for which she might be relevant. A few minutes later, a source called with a possible story on delays of bonuses by JPMorgan. "That would be a great story," he told the source. He turned to me and noted, "I love what I do," quite seriously and sincerely, with a big grin on his face.

By the end of the day, the story looked quite different from the B matter. He had written five versions of it, and according to a printout Getzfred gave me detailing the story's history back-and-forth from the Web page, it had been tinkered with in some small form no fewer than twenty-six times. The story had shifted down into the headlines of the home page and never gotten comments turned on; instead, a policy story about President Obama and banks took the second most prominent place on the home page after news about campaign spending. Bowley's story, instead of running on A1 as Bowley had hoped and editors had indicated, ran on the front page of the business section. The headline, changed from the numbers of the earnings, ended up as "Strong Year for Goldman after It Trims Its Bonus Pool," [9] and the lead read like this:

> No one was crowing about their big paychecks at Goldman Sachs headquarters in New York on Thursday. Despite a record 2009, the bank announced that it had set aside only $16.2 billion to reward its employees.

> Only?

If you have never worked on Wall Street, it is hard to grasp how 11 figures could be anything less than an enormous payday. But for Goldman, the financial and political calculations used to tally that number also added up to an uncharacteristic show of restraint.

In a surprising concession to the public outcry over big Wall Street bonuses, Goldman broke with the longtime industry practice of earmarking roughly half of its annual revenue for compensation.

From Bowley's day, we can start to unravel bits and pieces of core themes that appear throughout this book. In this case, the Web values of immediacy, interactivity, and participation are at work to varying degrees. Immediacy was perhaps the clearest value to intersect with his daily newswork: he spent his whole morning rushing to get the story out. There was no given reason from his editors or from Bowley himself, really, as to why he should be doing all these updates throughout the day, rushing to file the next addition to his work with every new source that called. At the same time, there is a felt pressure in the newsroom—something unsettled and often unspoken—that the Web demands more, that people are going to be checking back and demanding additional information. To be competitive, *The Times* feels that it needs to keep bringing new information to people.

Yet we should pause and ask: Is anyone really reading this constantly updated Goldman story twenty-six times (or even five)? What end does all this updating serve? But like *The Journal*, the AP, *The Washington Post*, and every other news outlet covering the story as breaking news, the news will be filed at *The Times* in incremental pieces as each new bit of information seeps out. To break from the practice might leave *The Times* looking bare, which wouldn't square with its aim to be the best newspaper in the United States, if not the English-speaking world, and *the* authoritative news source. Notably, *Times* editors did not have at their disposal data about readers on the Web (known as Web metrics)—while someone in the newsroom was collecting this information, it had not yet made its way into daily newswork. So editors couldn't really make an informed decision about whether people (or the same people) were reading these updates, but they nonetheless felt the pressure to keep the story going.

At the same time, we saw how immediacy is also a contested value. Though newsrooms struggle to be first, they also prioritize being right—and we saw how *The Journal*, for instance, got the earnings figures up wrong, even though it was the first outlet to publish the story. So just how fast should a newsroom go? The story was mainly facts and quick quotes for the morning and wasn't even in the hands of Bowley's main editors until later in the day. During this whole process, Bowley's main editors, Gillen and Alderman, were far more concerned with the big story—the print story, the A1 story. They wanted something that would stand up as one of the top five stories for the entire newspaper at the end of the day. Their involvement was to push Bowley, who was at the same time working on constant Web updates, to be thinking about the bigger picture.

One of the big goals at *The Times* was to take the busy day's Web updates and wrap them into a more thoughtful, analytical piece. This was called a "second-day story," a term people at *The Times* used to describe the kind of story they thought would distinguish their work and analysis from that of every other news outlet. The concept of a second-day story is old—it used to come out the second day after an event happened; but now, in the digital age, the "second-day story" is the same-day story intended for the print edition. In the newsroom, editors and reporters view this as the most important story because it is the summary—and more important still, it goes in the print paper. Yet as we will see, this second-day story has just a tiny lifespan on the Web, which is where most people turn to get their news from *The Times.*

Some of the smaller subthemes that popped up through Bowley's day were the ways in which interactivity and participation intersected with his workflow. When the video crew came marching down, it was clear that there was a mandate from above the ranks to get Bowley on a Web video—and he willingly complied, though he did at first seem confused. This multimedia opportunity was just another way to tell the story—but it wasn't *the story*—it was a deliberate ploy from the newsroom to get readers to pay even more attention to the story itself ("give a sneak peak, but not the golden egg"). What's also interesting about this unexpected moment of multimedia production was that it was completely manufactured, staged, and created by the video team. The other journalists taking part were not used to the routines, practices, or ways of working with these instant quick videos. Clearly, someone was valuing interactive content for readers, but traditional journalists working ASAP were not part of that plan. In other words, creating interactive content was still a messy process, not quite routine in newswork.

Finally, we saw small nods to the importance (or lack thereof) of participation in the newsroom. Bowley got his reader email, and he was excited by the influx, but I never saw him actually read it. Nonetheless, he was well aware that his readers were active and ready respondents to what he said—which is significant and does mark a change from the time when reader responses were not so visible. Bowley knew that people *wanted* to talk about the Goldman story and that *The Times* could be the place for them to air their views. But part of his reason for requesting that comments be turned on had more to do with knowing that the story would then stay up longer on the home page. It didn't seem to me as though Bowley had much interest in what the comments might say (though they weren't turned on, so I couldn't actually be sure), just so long as they were there. Thus, Bowley seemed to understand the idea of the active reader, but to him, participation didn't include actually talking back. Participation was messy, too: Should he answer all those emails? When should comments be turned on? What was *his* role in all of this?

Andrew Martin, Financial News Reporter— February 11, 2010

To give me a sense of a reporter working on a nondeadline day, Andrew Martin allowed me to spend time with him as he pursued a variety of projects. Over the course of Martin's day, I would see him work on three major stories, vet two potential stories, dig up new information, and have a planning meeting with a video editor to talk about multimedia for upcoming stories. Each portion of the day holds important lessons for understanding the news values at work in the digital age—the different rhythm of working on a nondeadline story, the experimentation with immediacy, and the lack of appearance of much interest in the participatory audience.

Martin's beat was consumer finance: he saw his role as translating what the policies of banks and financial firms meant for his audience—the middle- to upper-middle-class, educated people imagined as reading *The Times*. ("It's not likely that I'd write about payday lenders," Martin told me, "though maybe I would, if it was a big enough story.") Interestingly, Martin's own sense of who his audience was put boundaries on what he would write about. He reasoned that *Times* readers weren't likely to be asking for advance loans from sketchy dealers to make rent. But at the same time, if there seemed to be widespread corruption and a real humdinger of a story beyond just the fact that these payday lenders are generally shady, Martin would go all in. I heard the same sentiment echoed by people covering personal finance.

His recent work on debit card charges and credit card machinations, on the other hand, addressed things that literally were in the pockets of most people reading *The Times*. And Martin hoped that his coverage of what he was discovering to be personal finance corruption, coming from big banks to small ones, would indeed reach decision makers in Washington, D.C., and corporate boardrooms and from there catch on with audiences beyond *The Times*.

On the particular day I watched him, Martin was working on three long-term stories: one on credit card fraud with San Francisco–based reporter John Markoff, one on why overdraft legislation had stalled, and a third with news columnist Gretchen Morgenson on the Office of the Comptroller of Currency (OCC). Martin told me that his hypothesis on the OCC story was that this arm of the government might be "where consumer complaints about banks go to die." He explained to me that the head of the OCC, a man named John Dugan, was an opponent of financial regulation. *The Times* wanted to publish Dugan's profile before the vote on financial regulation. Martin was interested in doing the story, especially if the financial regulation legislation meant that the OCC might regulate some part of consumer protection. According to Martin, during the lead-up to the crisis, Dugan had a reputation for being friendly to banks. Martin also was going to spend the day vetting two potential stories and thinking about multimedia potential for another set of stories that he had on his enterprise list.

This day in Martin's life indicates that a nondeadline day can be filled with busily pursuing multiple stories, tracking down sources, and purposefully thinking about new ways to bring information to readers. In fact, Martin's day was frenetic and hard to follow; he switched rapidly from one project to the next. Similarly, as I watched him work, I saw some dynamics about news decision making (considering whether a story was, in his mind, worthy of *Times* coverage) that went beyond just determining whether or not a story fit into a schedule—or whether it was needed to fill the Web site.

Martin began his morning by working on his story about credit card fraud. He was interested in learning why the European Union might be switching to chip-and-PIN credit cards (credit cards that have a microchip embedded in their plastic). He was concerned about potential implications for the United States, especially for travelers abroad. Without a microchip in one's credit card, he noted, doing something as simple as buying a subway ticket in Paris would be nearly impossible.

The United States had not embraced these changes to credit cards, even though chip-and-PIN technology was more secure. Martin was working on this story because a council in Europe was going to make the suggestion that all EU countries switch to chip-and-PIN cards. He made a call on background to get more information, and then he sent his press contact an email asking for more on-the-record information. Martin was trying to figure out just how big a story this would be for the US consumer and how much authority this council had before moving forward.

As he made these calls, Martin explained to me that he was probably one of the very few people left at *The Times* with an actual, physical, metal Rolodex (most people seemed to keep their sources in Microsoft Outlook or saved on Gmail). He then moved on to working on his next story, which meant trying to figure out when the proposed consumer finance protection agency would come up for a vote. He talked to a source who said he'd know more once he heard from Senator Chris

Dodd, one of the sponsors of the financial regulation bill. Martin then called the Senate Banking Committee, hoping to get better information. He didn't want to be behind on the story if the bill was going to have important provisions related to consumer protection, and he also wanted to be ready with a story that could respond to all of the proposals when the bill was ready.

After he made this call to the Senate Banking Committee (with no success), he moved on to another story about overdraft fees. He started Googling the names of banks he had on a spreadsheet. This Excel sheet gave him some sense of which banks earned the most money on their overdraft fees. Some of them appeared to be small regional banks—meaning that people in less populous parts of the country might actually be paying more than people in big cities. Overdraft fees were a heated issue in the fall of 2009, he explained, and community banks had lobbied against major changes. His goal was to find small banks willing to talk about overdraft fees and respond to these seemingly high charges.

Martin began calling some of these small banks, looking for people who were willing to talk to him. When he called and asked to speak to bank presidents, Martin didn't reveal that he was from *The New York Times*. Instead, he waited to reveal his identity until he was speaking to the person he was actually trying to reach.

Eventually, after talking to people at a number of banks, he realized that his data, provided by a consultant, was actually flawed. Martin learned from these conversations and from crunching his own numbers that the ways the figures had been compiled didn't accurately show banks' take-home on overdraft fees, but instead indicated a different amount that banks made from consumers. That project got pushed to the side for the moment with a sigh.

Martin's day shifted as he went from story to story and source to source, cobbling together new bits of information for each story, depending on the person to whom he spoke. He didn't have a regular pattern for when and to whom he made calls; to some degree, he was at the mercy of the vagaries of the schedules of the people he was talking to. At the same time, he often gleaned new information from these calls, including tidbits about new stories, and he made connections that would allow him to gain access to the OCC across the course of the day.

For instance, when he called Representative Carolyn Maloney's office about overdraft legislation, he didn't get enough information for his story, but he did find one juicy tidbit: some history on one of Maloney's challengers for office, a woman whose background included working at JPMorgan and who would most likely oppose the financial regulation Maloney had helped propose. In a subsequent conversation that day, he received more news from Representative Maloney's office: JPMorgan had held a fundraising event for her competitor. Martin figured that this could be a good story and informed his editor, Liz Alderman, "I don't think it's going to be a blockbuster [i.e., Page One], but it'd be a good section front."

Martin also spent a good portion of his day vetting potential stories. The first was a story about Bling Nation, a small startup. Martin let me sit in on this call, which he put on speakerphone, identifying me. Martin listened as the company's representative tried to convince him to write a story about mobile phones with a secured chip attached that could be read by credit card machines. The mechanics were complicated, but Martin was interested because merchants taking advantage of this technology wouldn't have to pay an interchange fee.[10] However, Martin was skeptical because Bling Nation had only been able to convince small towns such as Saratoga Springs, New York, to try the concept, and he decided not to pursue the story.

He paused for a bit and let more developments for his stories trickle in—after calling the OCC again, he requested access to their office in Houston, the home of the OCC's complaint center, and the OCC gave him permission to visit. Martin got excited and started to look at fare prices, but then he admitted, "I should probably tell someone before I book a flight." His comment is notable only if you think about the dire state of most newsrooms, where travel for a story would be highly regulated because of its expense. In this case, Martin didn't even pause to ask for permission; he just planned to inform his editors that he was going ahead with the story. This is a distinctly big, national paper luxury—knowing that he had the budget to travel at a time when most newspapers had cut back on these kinds of expenditures for anything but the biggest stories.

Martin then vetted yet another story, this time on a company that was trying to do something new with accounts receivable. He again allowed me to sit in on his phone call. The company's service was apparently a new exchange for financing—a "receivable exchange"—and Martin didn't exactly buy the concept. "You have to be very careful when you take a story from a small company. Sometimes they are great, but if we give our stamp to them, then it really means that they are getting our endorsement, and then they can use it."

Martin had some down time after being busy all morning and began to prepare for his meeting with his contact on the video team, Brent McDonald, a senior video journalist. Martin noted that McDonald didn't just do business videos; in fact, he had just come back from the Congo. Martin said that I absolutely had to check out McDonald's videos, because they varied from beautiful to painful, and they showed places most people had never seen. The business videos would not match this more exciting fare. Nonetheless, Martin had worked with McDonald for a big series on credit cards that had required a lot of multimedia, and he explained to me that he actually thought some of the videos were better than the stories he had written.

So before he got started on some new projects, Martin wanted to run some stories past McDonald. The interactive element would add to Martin's work, and it would also change his work process: "It's good to know if you are using video, because it changes your reporting a little bit. If it's just me, I can wing it. But if you interview people, you have to ask if you can use a camera." Martin said that, in the past, he had known he always had to be thinking about photos, but it was different now to think about videos: videos were a change in the routine, whereas getting photos for a story had been a constant part of print production for decades. Martin noted that he was more likely to try to get in-person interviews than to use the phone if there was multimedia potential: "It's a little harder with banks with guys in suits. You have to be a little more creative because you get business centers and boardrooms, and they do not make exciting videos and photos."

Martin went over his list of thirteen potential stories, many of which were not on the list maintained by enterprise editor Marcus Mabry. (This is a key detail, because if a story is missing from the list, it is more difficult for Web producers to plan for multimedia.) This was just his own list, which he kept to himself, determining on his own when to share stories with his editors, once they had been further developed through additional reporting. He tried to flesh them out a bit more, to add context, so he could give the list to McDonald when they met later in the afternoon.

Around 4 p.m., Martin met McDonald in the fourteenth-floor cafeteria, where we all got a cup of coffee from the *Times* coffee bar (an actual espresso bar serving things like mocha lattes). Like most *Times* employees, Martin and McDonald used their ID cards to directly debit from their paychecks to pay for the caffeine break.

Martin gave McDonald the list of his thirteen stories and explained his early thoughts that the OCC could be an exciting story because the Houston facility was home to dead bank complaints. McDonald vetted the story from the perspective of a video producer, looking for potential visual representations for the story: "What would [the OCC] show us?"

Martin reconsidered: "I guess it would not be that interesting. There'd be someone with a phone, a guy telling us what they would do. But we could get Elizabeth Warren and, like, two-thirds of the state attorneys general to rip the shit out of them, because the OCC has said that the states have no authority over national bank branches."

McDonald said that the energy from the attorneys general sounded like good video, especially if they could get one or two attorneys general who had been thwarted in their efforts to protect consumers. McDonald noted that real victims with real complaints would truly make the video come alive.

Martin was concerned about this suggestion, because a fair amount had been written about the conflict between state attorneys general and the OCC. But McDonald reminded him that video needs strong characters, and without them, there couldn't be a good video for this particular piece. In other words, the characters could be anyone, but people pushing files around in Houston would make less compelling images than angry state attorneys general. As such, the priorities for video were different from Martin's goals for his print story. And the video story *would* be different from all the print stories written about the same subject.

Martin suggested two other stories, but McDonald rejected them as being too close to the video stories he had just completed for the credit card series. McDonald's rationale was that the video group, a small unit inside *The Times*, needed to be selective about the stories they pursued, so they could be sure that their new videos would present significant value about a subject *The Times* hadn't already covered.

Then, Martin pitched another story that he had tentatively slugged (given a shorthand name) "PREDICT," about how FICO was using credit scores to "drum up business" to determine the kinds of risks people were taking "elsewhere in life." Best Buy was one of the first companies to bite with this new FICO analysis, using it to determine whether to give people credit to buy items like TVs. Best Buy said it would let *The Times* have access in Marin County, California. McDonald said that this could make a good video and that he likely would have to be out in the Bay Area for other stories for the business desk.

The meeting closed with McDonald and Martin going over the full list of possible stories. McDonald was looking for characters and people. Much of the meeting was dedicated to Martin helping McDonald recognize who the key characters would be and giving McDonald enough information so he could determine how the scene would be set to tell the story visually.

On the way down to the business desk on the second floor, Martin explained to me that he didn't always tell his editor if he was pursuing something that would include multimedia. He said he tended to first work it out with McDonald, and if it sounded good, he'd fill his editors in. As we will see, interactives often emerged from this bottom-up process, as well as from top-down mandates like the *TimesCast* crew's visit to Bowley.

I left Martin for the day around 5 p.m., but he was still making calls, looking at old articles on LexisNexis to research Dugan of the OCC, and reading the details of the consumer finance protection bill. Martin worked on three stories for the day, went through a list of thirteen potential stories for multimedia with a video producer, vetted two stories with potential sources, and pitched another possible story for the front page of the business section. The day had certainly lacked a steady rhythm, with Martin jumping from story to story.

Notably, none of the stories Martin planned to write would be on-deadline stories, apart from a possible shorter piece on the financial regulation bill. Even then, Martin would have already done much of the legwork in teasing out the myriad implications of the bill for consumers once it came up for a vote—and was thus immediately newsworthy. So he wasn't writing for the Web, per se, though his stories would of course be Web stories.

Martin's day also highlighted some of the ways that these larger Web values were—and were not—influencing newswork. Here, we see an entirely different view of pace in the newsroom; immediacy was not the concern. Notably, Martin expressed the value of a particular story based on where it would appear in the paper, with the stable print product the marker for value. The longer stories that Martin was working on generally involved spreadsheets, travel, and extensive interviews—none of which was possible on the schedule Bowley was following.

Martin's day highlights best his sense of the importance of interactivity in online news. Martin was fully sold on the value of multimedia to tell stories to readers, so much so that he was thinking of multimedia from the very beginning of each story. This positive outlook and this collaborative, traditional journalist-directed initiative were extremely rare. Martin's past experiences had shown him the promise of multimedia, and he had found a way to integrate this new way of telling stories into his workflow. Other journalists, as we will see, had not. Notably, the steps Martin took to make these multimedia videos a reality were ones that might create difficulty for others in the newsroom. Martin never told his editors or any of the Web producers that he was pursuing these multimedia projects: this was a rare bottom-up process of multimedia creation, and he had simply made it a part of how he did his newswork. In this sense, he had embraced the new faces in the newsroom—video journalists—and included them in his work.

Martin's day helps illustrate that there was no established routine that all journalists followed when seeking to create interactive content. But the lack of regular routine and planning offered an important trade-off: a lot of freedom for Martin. He was able to cultivate a strong, personal relationship with a video editor interested in his work, and he was able to hold this meeting on his own time, of his own volition. No editor was coming to him, forcing him to do multimedia. There were no big plans made, no huge meetings, no hoops to jump through. All it took was for one reporter to feel duly certain that multimedia would be an essential part of telling his in-depth feature stories.

In this way, we can see how the value of interactivity had made its way into the working mindset of a reporter. Significantly, though, Martin didn't quite understand exactly how to have his stories take on a multimedia element. He needed McDonald's help to figure out what would make good video, since the criteria for quality video were very different from those a reporter would use to evaluate or craft a print story. While Martin could interview suit after suit in boring offices, McDonald needed visuals and characters that would provide good sound bites and raw emotion. We can start to see this kind of collaboration as complimentary, with McDonald pushing Martin out of his comfort zone, which could in turn impact Martin's ultimate choice of sources and the tenor of his story.

Nick Bilton, Lead Technology Blogger
for the *Bits* Blog—January 27, 2010

Nick Bilton was the chief tech blogger for *The Times' Bits* blog. *Bits*, which stands for "business, innovation, technology, society," was described on the *Times* site:

> Bits offers a steady stream of news and analysis on the technology industry throughout the day from *New York Times* writers and freelancers. We cover start-ups, tech leaders like Google and Apple, enterprise technology, government policies and the way the Internet is changing how we live and work.[11]

Bilton's duties included posting breaking news, covering news not quite big enough to warrant a full story, noting quirky news, and writing about anything that might attract the attention of a true tech geek. *Bits* was not intended to compete with the "candy" blogs, as some in the tech world call them, such as *Gizmodo* or *Engadget*. Instead, *Bits* was intended to provide original news content and offer analysis about tech issues. Other tech writers on the business staff were also charged with writing two to three blog entries per week.

Bilton's background was different from most in the newsroom. He had gotten his start at *The Times* as a designer and art director and then moved to *The Times'* research and development lab, an actual R&D lab where programmers and designers create and test products that may be the future of *The Times*. These projects include everything from a touch-pad news "kitchen" table, to having guest statisticians pore over data to understand social news, to the seemingly bizarre, like a haptic news mirror, to other "secret" *Times* developments.[12] As a result, he had design and programming skills that enabled him to manipulate images, text, and graphics—and connections with the R&D lab that helped him add to his content.

Bilton was also interested in the changes in media consumption at large, and when I met him, he was in the process of hawking his new book on news as a social experience and the multitasking nature of media consumption. The book, entitled *I Live in the Future and Here's How It Works*, describes someone like himself, a media consumer who is "totally ADD and can do a million things at once. I have to."[13]

The technology pod in the New York office had its own set of cubicles, though there was just a small walkway between it and the area where most of the financial reporters and editors sat. Toward the back windows sat Vindu Goel and David Gallagher, deputy technology editors. In the pod of cubicles sat the New York tech writers—Jenna Wortham, Steve Lohr, and Bilton—as well as (oddly enough) the agriculture beat writer, Willie Neuman. Across from this technology pod was the place where the technology Web producers sat. Toward the back of the window sat Sam Grobart, the personal technology editor.[14] The technology section of the business desk had its own Web producer, because technology and personal technology were among the most clicked-upon "verticals" on the business desk,[15] so these technology sections have their own permanent and stand-alone Web pages. In addition, technology Web producers were often devoted to supporting special projects specifically for the tech writers.

Beyond this collection of staff in New York, the head technology reporter and six other reporters were based in San Francisco. At the time, everyone communicated via AOL Instant Messenger, despite all working in Gmail. Stories and blog posts got vetted, reporters worked out who might write what blog post, and ideas and coordination were exchanged—all over the AIM chat client. This coordination was also coupled with a weekly meeting of the New York and San Francisco staffs that took place via conference call. This meeting was held in conjunction with the media desk to plan coverage for the Monday paper, which had the theme of tech and media news. Proximity, created electronically as well as physically, helped this desk to coordinate its work, as a particularly busy day in Bilton's blogging life at *The Times* will indicate.

I shadowed Bilton on the day that Apple released the first iPad. This was a seminal occasion that had been referred to by technology editor Damon Darlin a week earlier as "the day that will change the world." *The Times* was planning to go all out to cover the device that many in the media industry had said might be a salve for the news industry's woes.[16] The technology pod of the business desk had assigned five people in San Francisco to cover the unveiling of the new device, the name of which was unknown at the time. *The Times* planned a liveblog with a Twitter feed[17] (Bilton would be a voice on the Twitter feed), multiple articles, a column from the tech columnist David Pogue, a video interview between someone in New York and someone at the unveiling, and a steady stream of photos to be fed into the liveblog. This day provides good insight into a number of different challenges facing journalists at *The Times*, from understanding how to deal with social media, to reporting in entirely new online conditions, to dealing with immediacy.

Bilton started his day in earnest around 10:15 a.m., looking for a way to write a *Bits* piece on "What's Not Apple" to get some news out about something other than the new Apple device. He began by looking at other blogs in the tech world for ideas. He had two monitors on his desk, plus a laptop. One of the monitors was set up just as his Twitter feed. He was also IMing (instant messaging) constantly with people in San Francisco and other people in the tech pod, even though he was sitting next to the latter group and could talk to them. He began pitching in to the group effort to find some Apple photos for the liveblog and noted, "I'm one of the only bloggers that posts their own images." He put an Apple icon into the live-blogging software for the Apple event.

Around 11:30 a.m., Bilton took me and his fellow tech writer Jenna Wortham up to the R&D lab, where he used to work. It was on the twenty-eighth floor, and everyone looked under thirty-five. At the R&D lab, staff had undertaken (on their own initiative) to build a software program to monitor Twitter word counts for the Apple announcement. They consulted with Bilton on which words they should track and decided to monitor everything, from iPod to Apple, iSlate (the rumored name), iPhone, iTunes, and Apple tablet. R&D was seeing about six hundred tweets a minute from these searches. Notably, no one knew, at all, what the new device would be called—and they wouldn't until the big Apple product launch.

Back downstairs in the tech pod, Bilton got ready for the 1 p.m. launch. The tech team had pita chips and fruit laid out on the broad wood cubicle dividers as though they were preparing for an endurance run. Bilton's role was to scour the Web for everything he could find about the soon-to-be-announced iPad. The tech team's plan, like that of nearly every other news organization in the country, was to rely on a liveblog to convey the breaking news to readers. This liveblog would have a step-by-step replay of whatever Steve Jobs said at the iPad product launch. For whatever reason, Jobs refused to put his announcements on a Webcast, and as a result, only a select few journalists got to see the launches up close, leaving a very hungry public curious about a product that would not be released for a few months.

Other journalists at *The Times* were going to be manning the liveblog. But just prior to 1 p.m., Bilton began pulling up competing blog sites—*Engadget, Gizmodo, GigaOM, TechCrunch,* and a few others—to see what they were saying about the feeling in the San Francisco Convention Center, where Jobs was doing the launch, to help *The Times* liveblog. These competing sites were tweeting information and pictures. *The New York Times* had decided against using Twitter to capture pictures, with the photo editor making the final declaration that the wireless in the convention center would be fast enough to send high-resolution pictures from the wireless cards in digital cameras.

Live blogs were not new to *The Times.* These liveblogs were far from live, per se. A reporter would write a short bit of copy, it would be edited by an editor, and then it would be posted, often minutes after the event had actually occurred. Other live blogs, like those of tech competitors, did not depend on a formal layer of editing. *The Times* wanted a more formal liveblog with "analysis," rather than tweets like *Engadget's*—but it struck a compromise with what it saw as audience demand for instant information: editors would have a Twitter feed on the liveblog page that, for one of the first times, would include true outsiders presented under *The Times* brand that *The Times* could not edit—a big experiment. Those chosen included top tech people from competing blogs and even the rival personal tech columnist at *The Wall Street Journal*, Walt Mossberg. But this was dicey for the newspaper, as *The Times*, editor Vindu Goel explained to me, liked to know what its content was going to look like before readers did.

Amusingly, the wireless at the convention center in San Francisco went dark for a few moments. Bilton found a pirate audio stream for the tech team, but the sound could barely be heard.

Bilton was shouting out information to his editors, but it wasn't clear how this was getting incorporated back into the liveblog. "The wireless just went out in the room," he said. Then a few minutes later, when it was back on, he went back into monitoring mode. He shouted, "It's starting," as the tech staff in New York wasn't getting much of anything from their staff. Slowly, the tightly edited bits of information began to appear on *The Times* liveblog.

Bilton saw the name on a competing blog—"iPad, they just said it!"—and immediately tweeted it. *The Times'* home page editor was ready for the announcement right away with a red alert right underneath the "*The New York Times*" banner: "Jobs announces new tablet will be called the iPad." But *The Times'* liveblog took two minutes to get the name up. *The Times'* home page then put up a link to the liveblog after some wrangling. (At first, *The Times* was sending people to a rival news site—most likely the AP.)

Bilton commented that the iPad looked like a big iPhone, and the team noted that one of the first things Apple was showing was *The New York Times*. Jobs said, "I can browse *The New York Times* site so easily."

The next big moment was when Jobs began showing off email.

"Email's beautiful," Bilton yelled. He was looking at *Gizmodo,* a rival blog, for pictures, rather than *The Times'* liveblog. Editors didn't pay attention, but Bilton continued to tweet his musings. "The screen is gorgeous," he said, after a rival tech blog posted the screen resolution and information. He went to Wikipedia to look it up. "Amazing," he said, "It's already been updated to include the iPad."

He took a hard look at the size and tweeted, "I can't wait to get mugged with this on the subway #ipad."

He also began IMing the R&D Lab to add "iPad" to the tweet-monitoring list, since now they actually had the name for the new device. There were literally thousands of tweets a second, Bilton observed. There was no set precedent for this little innovation, but it was giving Bilton a great sense of what the rest of the world was talking about on Twitter. But all of this information was internal: no one other than Bilton and the R&D lab were seeing what could have been an interactive experience for *Times* users.

As the event continued, Bilton kept yelling out useful tidbits, posting all of what he was saying on Twitter. When Jobs cursed on stage, Bilton noted from his Twitter that he had just dropped the "F-bomb." But all of his information was coming from rival blogs. This was spot reporting, in an entirely new way, relying on competitors, from three thousand miles away.

The New York Times' blog didn't have any pictures, because the photographer couldn't get enough bandwidth to send his photos wirelessly, as Bilton had predicted in a meeting. Bilton sighed. Immediacy was clearly a problem for *The Times'* liveblog: with its delays for editing and lack of photos, it simply didn't have the pizzazz of the competing tech blogs.

Bilton continued scrolling through other blogs, and he informed the tech pod that the senior vice president of digital operations at *The New York Times,* Martin Nisenholtz, was on stage at the convention center to demo *The New York Times* app. He talked about the "essence of reading a newspaper" and how it would be preserved online. Bilton noted that an Adobe Flash graphic didn't look that great—an issue that Apple and Adobe would battle about as the iPad rose in prominence. Bilton also commented that the Tweet tracker was getting sixteen to seventeen hundred tweets per minute.

Bilton tweeted again: "Wow Apple is launching iBook store to compete with Kindle."

Then he learned that the iPad would only be on AT&T. "Groan," said Bilton. (AT&T was overcapacity at that point, with its network completely bogged down by all the iPhone users.) But the liveblog wasn't capturing opinions like his, just offering, as much as possible, real-time information. As per newsroom policy, the liveblog would stick to traditional, objective reporting. Bilton offered again, still via Twitter, "The blogs said the whole room groaned when Jobs said AT&T."

Still, the editors refused to bite on the bit of opinion. Bilton continued to tweet about the AT&T dilemma, noting that the network would get even worse. Notably, Bilton was tweeting to his followers and only responding to people he knew from the tech world.

The final moment of the product launch was the price point. Bilton was betting and asking everyone on his Twitter feed, "Will it be more than the Kindle?" The prices went live (it *would* be more than a Kindle), and the home page modified the alert. The liveblog, again, took longer to update, though the prices were already out over Twitter. Jobs talked about the "magical" device and closed the product announcement. At 2:37, after the announcement was over, Apple put up a press release about the iPad.

The tech team then had a quick meeting to talk about the day's coverage. Bilton would write a "what's missing" post and a "what people were expecting" post. Larry Ingrassia, the business editor, wanted outtakes for the paper with some of the comments from Twitter—notably, this social media–driven story was the only one I heard over the course of five months initiated by top editors. Ingrassia particularly liked one tweet from the San Francisco–based tech/science writer John Markoff: "You ain't going to strap this to your running shorts." The main story for Page One for the day was quickly hatched: why people might want this and whether it could be successful.

Bilton told Goel that he wanted to do a roundup on what Twitter was saying, noting, "There's a lot going on in Twitter." Goel suggested instead, "Why don't you do a blogosphere post?" This may signal that, at the time, the blogosphere conversation was more important in the eyes of some editors than the Twitter conversation.

Bilton noticed again that there were people chatting on Twitter about the word *iPad* and the perceived association with a women's sanitary product. Goel also started to see a lot of similar references on Twitter but didn't think the conversation was ripe for a post. Bilton suggested writing a blog post on this, but the idea was ignored, for the moment.

Finally, around 5 p.m., the tech editors were convinced that the iPad name jokes were significant enough to merit a blog post—in part because *The Wall Street Journal* had just written a story about them—and they asked Bilton to do it. Bilton replied that that a woman should do it, and Goel tracked down Claire Cain Miller, a female tech writer. Even though Bilton didn't write the post, he still tweeted that the iPad was not winning over women.

Bilton and Brad Stone, a *Times* reporter in San Francisco, began chatting on IM about whether Apple would or would not kill the Kindle—a charged topic without the feminist concerns. They decided to turn their discussion into a series of dueling posts for the *Bits* blog. Stone's was titled "Three Reasons Why the iPad WON'T Kill Amazon's Kindle." The first post had the following subheadings:

The Kindle is for book lovers, and the iPad is not.
Amazon will continue to improve on the Kindle.
The Kindle store will continue to thrive.[18]

Bilton began his counter to Stone's post by noting, "Kindle needs a reboot." When he sent it to Goel, however, the editor noted that Bilton's post felt a little "review-y," saying to me that the "opinion police will come down on them." Bilton turned to me and said, "Reporters are not supposed to have an opinion, even on blogs." The question of just how much voice a reporter should have, especially on social media and on blogs, was still in a state of transition at *The Times*, as we will see later.

Bilton's response to Stone—"Three Reasons Why the iPad WILL kill Amazon's Kindle"—was ultimately edited to include the following subheadings:

Content is changing, but the Kindle is not.

The Kindle's technology isn't evolving fast enough.

The Kindle is too expensive for a single-purpose device.[19]

Despite Goel's warning about the "opinion police," Bilton's blog post still included this kind of language at the end:

> Kindle's store and its reading application for the iPhone are both excellent, simple experiences for purchasing and consuming books. Amazon understands this market better than anyone and could easily sell more books on the iPad than Apple could through its new iTunes bookstore. Amazon also offers an excellent recommendation system, and I can envision some users opting for the Kindle application on their fancy new iPads.

Bilton then turned to finish his post with the live R&D counts of tweets tracked including "iPad" and related terms for the day. He used the image software on his computer, making a graphic from Excel and Adobe Illustrator.

By the end of the day, around 8:30 p.m., when the final blog posts were finished and the Page One stories were edited, the tech team went out for drinks to celebrate the busy day. At this point, Bilton had tweeted thirteen times on his own account. He had written five posts: "Get Your Non-Apple News" (10:29 a.m.); "The Blogosphere Reacts to Apple's iPad" (4:07 p.m.); "Three Reasons Why the iPad WILL Kill Amazon's Kindle" (7:05 p.m.); "Google Adds More Social to Search" (7:41 p.m.); and "Monitoring Twitter's iPad Commentary" (using the R&D lab information) (7:56 p.m.).[20]

Bilton had also actively tracked the dialogue on Twitter to alert the tech pod of new developments, though some of his observations were ignored, while others were turned into stories. The iPad-as-women's-product, for instance, got more attention once *The Journal* flipped out a quick story on the name. But Bilton had noticed the trend long beforehand on Twitter.

Bilton multitasked constantly and was involved in many kinds of conversations. He was, at any one point, tweeting on his own Twitter stream, tweeting on *The Times'* liveblog, IMing with people as far away as San Francisco or as close as the desk behind him, and talking to other staffers. He was also simultaneously tracking Twitter, checking the blogosphere for competing tech blogs, and thinking about new blog posts to write. With these blogs, he wasn't just posting text but actively using Photoshop, Adobe Illustrator, Excel, and a number of other programs to enhance the visual aspects of his blogging. Bilton joked about being ADD—but he was exactly the multitasking information seeker and user of social news that he had written about in his book.

Bilton's day shows a number of nytimes.com experiments in immediacy, reporting, and content production. While the liveblog had been used at other times, especially for breaking news, there were many fits and starts in figuring out how to make it work for such a high-profile event and a noticeable time lag. It was not fast enough to give even people at *The Times* a sense of what was going on at the convention center, even though it was providing nice capsules with analysis. In fact, the way *The Times* learned that the device was called the iPad was essentially secondhand: when Bilton spotted it on a rival blog.

The liveblog brings to a head the tension between *The Times'* desire to remain relevant and timely and its aspiration to have its imprimatur. The liveblog, which involved a multistep process of writing from reporter to editor, and then posting via clunky content-management software, simply didn't get this information out fast enough for even *The Times'* home page to directly link to the newspaper's own coverage right away. Editors argued that a slower response time allowing for more descriptive and thoughtful analysis would appeal to *Times* readers. Nonetheless, the competing news environment—one I could see from Bilton's desk—featured a "fastest finger" approach to getting out an almost live transcript of events.

Similarly, editors had been insistent on high-quality photos from the event. But the wireless speed in the conference hall was too slow to support the high-resolution photos from *Times* staff photographers, leaving the liveblog without any unique *Times* images during most of the event. Hastily, *Times* staffers scrambled for wire photos coming in, but the process of getting photos from the event up onto a liveblog had yet to be fully ironed out, although the problem could have been fixed if the reporters had simply been allowed to tweet what were perceived as lower-quality photos.

What's also novel about Bilton's day was the way he was reporting under these conditions of immediacy. He was relying on secondhand reports from other blogs and those tweeting on the ground of the convention center. This was his version of reporting. This news was coming to *The Times* more quickly than the news from *The Times'* own reporters. Bilton's entire job during the event was to monitor what was happening in the convention center as a reporter of secondary social media feeds. Whether this should be counted as original reporting is quite an interesting question; for example, the name iPad was first found on a rival blog and then immediately posted on *The Times* home page. And blogging in a newsroom was still somewhat novel: Exactly what could or couldn't Bilton say on the *Bits* blog? Though blogging had been a standard part of *The Times'* site since the mid-2000s, format and tone were still questionable: Was it editorial, or was it not?

Participation figured into this day in a variety of ways. In an experiment with social media, *The Times'* tech editors had invited in outside tweeters to join the liveblog (in a sidebar). This meant a loss of control over what would be said, yet it would be hosted by *The Times*. During the announcement, one Twitter user used foul language (against *Times* policies) and had to be kicked out of the Twitter list.

This was not *participation* in the user-to-producer way, but an extension of *The Times* into a more robust conversation with other newsmakers. Similarly, Bilton was using social media and actively engaged in a conversation with other journalists and tech influencers—just not with his audience. These conversations were now transparent for the public and much easier for Bilton and other journalists to conduct in real time. But as far as being a conversational platform for one-to-many, Bilton's use of social media was not fulfilling this role. Thus, participation on these platforms *was* important, but what participation meant to Bilton and the other journalists did not match the more utopian vision of participation in news.

On the other hand, we also saw editors discount the importance of conversation on social media platforms. While Bilton was only following some of the most elite tech types, he was still getting a variety of comments from Twitter. Yet his editors were reluctant to allow him to do a roundup of what was being said there. Nevertheless, social media did have an influence, after the iPad name started becoming a dirty joke—and after *The Journal* had picked up on it. Again, though, this was a conversation of elites. Nonetheless, Bilton's day does show, on a macrolevel, the influence of participation in the newsroom.

While Bilton's day doesn't offer much detail about interactivity, it does suggest that interactivity needs to be *planned*. Bowley's experience, for example, was orchestrated by another department of the newsroom, but in the process of the immediate news cycle, such as Bilton's iPad day, the place for making this kind of multimedia content is not quite clear. Thus, interactive content may be one signal that there are different kinds of pacing for online news, ranging from the immediate to the planned. Nonetheless, Bilton's day offers significant insight into experimentation in an immediate news environment, as well as some additional understanding of how participation was understood at *The Times*.

Three Days in the Lives of *New York Times* Journalists: Reviewed

Across the stories of Bowley, Martin, and Bilton, it should become clear that life inside the business desk of *The Times* was variable. No two journalists shared the exact same role, nor did any single journalist encounter the same tasks each day. The challenge before me is to detail, on a broader scale, how the news values of immediacy, interactivity, and participation shown in each of these portraits impacted newsmaking on a much broader scale at *The Times*—and to draw out more specifically the points of tension and the affordances and opportunities presented to journalists as they embarked on newswork during this time.

Looking back across each of these days, it should be clear that old pressures still constrain and order news values and news routines; it is not as if the digital age of 24/7 Internet news began and everything changed. For example, consider how source pressure continued to impact the kind of news that Bowley and Martin were able to generate. They relied on sources for news, and Bowley was dependent on having key voices from Goldman in order to write an authoritative story. Audience pressure, though often viewed through the lens of the imagined audience as seen by the journalist, has also not changed. Bowley, Martin, Bilton, and the editors we see here were thinking about *The Times'* audience—what *Times* readers might like to see. And while they did not have the kind of Web metrics dangling above their heads showing instant clicks and likes that other newsrooms of the time often used, *The Times'* staff did go by their feel about *The Times* being a general-interest newspaper for the educated and for elite decision makers.

The unrelenting demands for content remain ever present. Before the 24/7 era, this was the pressure to fill a newscast or a newspaper. Now that pressure is felt during bursts of time (like with the iPad release) or throughout the day (as with the Goldman earnings). This content demand, though, does not entirely explain immediacy, as immediacy is encompassed by a much larger notion of self-perception and professionalism, audience pressure, external competitive pressure, and news policy, among other aspects.

The twin pressures of socialization into newsroom norms and professional authority also continue to influence newswork. Bilton's stories were subject to a test for editorializing versus opinion, and his roundup of the blogosphere versus the Twittersphere suggests that the newsroom had not yet adapted to valuing this kind of content. Bowley and Martin, with their different experiences of interactivity, nonetheless demonstrate the impact of newsroom policy on creating an environment that emphasizes this new online value. The unspoken importance of immediacy suggests a conformity around newsroom policy surrounding breaking news. At the same time, we get glimpses of the conflicting nature of professional authority, as journalists note that the important stories are in the print paper.

External pressures are also present in this newsroom—pressures that we will see have been transformed somewhat in the digital arena. Journalists are still extremely competitive with rival newspapers, worrying about not having a story that would make *The Times* look like it was missing out. They are pleased when a competitor gets something wrong. Competition also helps frame the desire for differentiation for *Times* stories. Later we will see that economic pressures do not seem to influence news decisions, but they do make a difference to management. Thus, some of the emphasis on interactivity and participation in the newsroom is tied to an economic result.

These pressures are present and continue to shape news, but my goal here is to explore some of the values of online journalism that are particularly emergent at this time: immediacy, interactivity, and participation. A few major themes emerge from these "day in the life" portraits—themes that are particularly relevant to future discussion. First, we can see the tension in the newsroom between off-deadline production and the needs of immediate online output. We also see the value that was placed on the print product and how *The Times'* sense of its own authoritativeness ran, at times, counter to immediacy. Martin's day demonstrated that off-deadline reporting was still valued and considered important in the digital age, though perhaps other newsrooms do not have the luxury, time, or resources to allow staff to work on these longer stories. Then we saw how interactivity was valued by some and not all and how it has had different points of origin and emphasis in the newsroom. Its place in the daily news cycle was also unclear. Finally, we have seen the different ways that social media, commenting, reader mail, and audience perception influenced the ideas surrounding participation in the newsroom (or not).

The next chapters show how these vignettes offer a starting point for investigating the emergent significance of immediacy, interactivity, and participation in online journalism. Each chapter devotes careful attention to the integration of each Web value into journalistic production, looking at the complicated experience of being a journalist in this era of digital transformation. The next chapter looks more closely at how immediacy emerges as a contested value—one that pits ASAP news against the vaunted daily print product.

Chapter 3

The Irony of Immediacy

The Daily Show, perhaps the site of the greatest media criticism of its day, sent "reporter" Jason Jones into *The New York Times* newsroom. His mockumentary piece about the sure death of newspapers seemed to epitomize the situation in which *The New York Times* found itself in 2010—supporting and producing a legacy print product with more than 160 years of tradition but needing to remain relevant in a world of instant information. As the introduction to the segment put it, "Back in the days before the Internet, the only way you could find out what was going on in the world was called a newspaper."[1]

Jones walked through the newsroom, quipping that it felt like "Colonial Williamsburg," and laughed at the newspaper's landline phones. His two interviews, one with executive editor Bill Keller and the other with associate managing editor Rick Berke, formed the backbone of his investigation into "why the last of a dying breed prefers aged news to real news."

Before interviewing Berke in his office, Jones offered this voice-over: "Even today, there's some who still think there's merit in publishing news 24 hours after it happened."

He asked Berke: "Why is aged news better than real news?"

"I've never heard the term aged news," Berke replied.

"Well, it's yesterday's news," said Jones, pointing at the newspaper on Berke's desk. "Give me one thing in there that happened today."

Berke stumbled. "Nothing happened [in] here today . . . [pause]."

Berke didn't have much of a rejoinder to defend his print paper.

Jones was posing as the ambassador of a generation who found the print paper to be a historic relic of a bygone era, something someone's grandmother might read (as he informed viewers). And for Jones and *The Daily Show's* fans, the only news that mattered was the "real news"—the news that was happening now.

The Daily Show's satire underscores a crucial point: *The Times* was still engaged in producing news for the next-day print newspaper cycle, a fact that seemed antiquated to a comedy show writing for the under-thirty, digitally savvy crowd.[2] The segment, of course, fails to mention the 24/7 nytimes.com site that was continually being updated. Also left out was the fact that many journalists were writing "real news" ASAP, today.

"Aged news" versus "real news," though, is one way to explain the competing understandings of immediacy at *The Times*. Immediacy has always been a news value, from Renaissance Europe to the present: getting the news out as fast as possible, as quickly as the technology of the day would allow. In the case of the contemporary print newspaper—the newspaper of the 2000s—immediate meant today's news *tomorrow,* in print form. The end of the era of multiple editions and the dominance of one-paper news markets generally meant one, single final product capping off a twenty-four-hour news cycle. Breaking news in print form was old compared to CNN's constant streaming feed, of course. For the print paper, breaking news had, ideally, more context, time, and space to be brought to a story. Immediacy was the next day.

But in a digital arena, whether the news outlet was broadcast television, cable news, legacy print, radio, or an online-only outlet—none of this mattered. Everyone now shared the same capacity to distribute content at the same time. The Internet meant these news organizations were equalized: whether they liked it or not, they were always on, with audiences always present. The new immediacy of online journalism was ASAP journalism: journalism for now, not journalism for tomorrow.

What *The Times* faced, then, was a culture clash. Producing the print paper required a mentality that virtually ignored the reality of online journalism. Those primarily concerned with print journalism were thinking about news that would appear in the print paper the next day, in a form that would last "forever." The print news cycle took twenty-four hours to complete. But in the online context, immediacy meant a new journalistic biorhythm, a quest for "nowness," for true *immediacy*, which marked the boundary between the newsroom of the austere, print Gray Lady and a newsroom with ADD. Little wonder, then, that the online journalism value of immediacy, as it was understood and interpreted inside the newsroom, was a *contested* value.

This chapter juxtaposes the two fundamentally different routines of print and online news. The focus is less on the impact of print and online on journalists; instead, it is more on the overarching process of producing the newspaper for both print and online. The underlying argument is that the 24/7 cycle and the NOW cycle ordered newswork in almost completely different ways, resulting in a conflicting institutional understanding of immediacy in the digital age. Print still won hearts and minds, but the future of *The Times* was online, and journalists working with the Web internalized this as living in a world of constant pressure to produce content.

Here, you will see a detailed outline of the print production cycle at nytimes.com. The emphasis on print begins with reporters and editors, who see the print product, and the print diurnal cycles, as the defining aspect of what it means to be at *The Times*. The Page One meeting was even billed by *The Times* as the moment when editors get to decide what news is most important to the world. A number of sections offer detailed conversations about story development and story placement. On a more global scale, these conversations give a sense of how people at *The Times* talk about journalism and develop stories. More directly related to this chapter, though, is the fact that these conversations, the focus on story development, the series of meeting after meeting, the collaborative decision making—all of this allows stories to develop and debate and exchange to occur, and it requires *time*. The Page One and business page meetings give a sense of these exchanges, and an anecdote helps establish how immediacy for the print paper is *tomorrow*.

On the other hand, a look at the Web cycle of news production is sharply different. Here, we'll see the online production cycles of the home page, during the day and at night, and the business Web page. Unlike the print production cycle, there are (virtually) no meetings for the Web. One person, or sometimes two, decides when, where, and what stories go on the home page and, in the case here, the business page. One person writes and edits the final Web headlines and summaries, though there may be some suggestions from various Web editors. The most significant task is making sure that there are enough new stories up on the Web page so that the page appears "fresh"—so that the imagined audience demanding this content will keep coming back for more. This way, nytimes.com looks like it constantly has something new. But even in this constant crush for more, now, at times Web journalists still look to the print paper for guidance, and they rely on its production cycle for most of the Web site's content.

Aged news and real news coexist in one newsroom. Yet they are sharply different, with their own practices and routines. Immediacy is a journalism value that orders news routines and professional role perceptions and that takes its cues from internal and external pressures on news production, but it has different meanings for print and online journalism. This chapter, then, offers an overview of the distinctions between print and online, while the next chapter, a slightly different look at immediacy, focuses more on the experiences of traditional journalists as they go through the metamorphosis of suddenly being in a 24/7 online world. The irony of immediacy is that *The Times* in 2010 was still a newsroom obsessed with yesterday's news while it was simultaneously focused on the NOW!

The Fetishization of the Print Product

From the outside, it looked as though the newsroom structured print and Web in unison. Journalists wrote unquestioningly for the Web (at least insofar as almost all stories would eventually appear online). Traditional journalists had ready access to their section's Web producers, who sat right by the desks of main editors. The 24/7 Web newsroom was well in place by 2010. But to many journalists, the print paper still represented their best work. The print paper also signified the completion of the daily news cycle and comfortable, predictable routines and rhythms, and it offered a clear way to assign value to stories. As Larry

Ingrassia, business desk editor, told me, "The print product is the final product."[3] This final product reflected the news judgment and layers of editing that required the work of dozens of journalists throughout the newsroom.

Symbolically and professionally, most editors and reporters didn't judge home page "play," or prominence, to be an enduring victory. That was ephemeral, a fact they seemed to recognize. *Real* success was getting into that elusive spot on Page One. Page One was corporeal; it simply mattered more, both to journalists personally and to the larger institution. Reporter Brian Stelter told me, "I know that my promotion and my time here depends on getting Page One or A1 stories. That's what matters most."[4] Another reporter expressed to me, "A1 is the prime real estate; yeah, editors are paying attention to the top ten [most emailed], but what really matters is the A1. That's what they are judging you on." One reporter expressed frustration that online-only articles (like blogs) were basically ignored, even if they made the most-emailed list. The reporter said, "I can be on the most-emailed list with my blogs, but if it isn't a Page One story, it doesn't seem to matter." As at least a few journalists told me, employee reviews with editors monitoring their progress didn't even take into account home page placement, blog traffic or posting, most-emailed stories, or other measures of online success. Instead, editors were concerned with the number of Page One stories, total bylines, story length, and story placement—traditional print measures of success.

On occasion, a reporter might be particularly insistent about the home page, but I saw it rarely. One weekend, Steven Greenhouse had a story about unpaid internships that had failed to make the front page. On the Saturday that it appeared in the newspaper,[5] Web producers and the business desk weekend editor David Joachim noted that Greenhouse was waging an email campaign to get it on the home page. With little else happening on that Saturday, Greenhouse secured a key spot for a few hours, and his article rocketed up to the top of the most-emailed list, though it had been buried in the business section. The incident shows the influence of the Web (particularly during the weekend, when churn is slower because there are fewer new stories).

So while some reporters and editors worked actively to promote their stories online, the emphasis and value still lay in the Page One story. Editors fought to get stories on Page One—in fact, they devoted a considerable amount of time in meetings arguing to get what they saw as the best stories of their respective desks on Page One. They thought about long-term projects in terms of whether they had the potential to make Page One. For instance, reporters Peter Goodman and Catherine Rampell's series on the Great Recession, which had no definitive time peg, was explicitly engineered to get A1 play. The stories were two thousand to thirty-five hundred words, and editors were willing to wait until the right moment and right news balance—hopefully on a Sunday, when the most readers would have the physical paper—to reward their reporters for their hard work and, presumably, show the prominence of this work.

In fact, *The New York Times'* response to *The Daily Show* illustrates the seriousness with which they took the Page One ritual itself. Though couched in language designed to suggest the equality of print and online, *The Times* ran an article that responded to the Stewart piece, called "A Snapshot of the World at 4 p.m." It featured a dramatic account of the afternoon Page One meeting. Accompanying this article was an interactive feature called "Deciding the News" (perhaps an unwitting reference to Gans's book) that offered a panoramic view of the vaunted Page One meeting table. *The New York Times* took a direct shot at *The Daily Show,* noting, "The comic got the laugh but missed the larger point (not to mention the Web site)."

The article begins with this dramatic tone, relaying events as they appeared on Tuesday, June 30, at roughly 4 p.m.:

In Baghdad, vast parades for the withdrawal of American troops. In Minnesota, Al Franken wins a disputed senatorial election. In Honduras, crowds denounce the recently ousted president. And in Albany, the business of the government continues to be a joke.

Meanwhile, at the offices of The New York Times, a meeting was taking place. Eighteen editors had gathered at a table to discuss tomorrow's news. The table was formidable: oval and elegant, with curves of gleaming wood. **The editors no less so: 11 men and 7 women with the power to decide what was important in the world** [emphasis added].

The power to decide what was important in the world. Yes, this was the Page One meeting. The meeting that would, in the eyes of *Times* journalists, order the *world's* conversation about current events. And it would be done via the front print page of the newspaper, designed to become yesterday's news. The article continued to defend Page One practices:

> Every afternoon at 4 o'clock, the top dogs at the nation's paper of record descend upon a third-floor conference room to decide what news is truly fit to print. It is a 30-minute meeting at which energetic argument is hardly unfamiliar; but at a moment when the front page (and the rest of the physical paper) may be headed for the shredder, it is also an anachronistic throwback, a ritual with the whiff of obsolescence in the air.

> Or so the paper's critics tend to think.

The story then ends on this note:

> "This meeting will always determine what we feel are the most significant stories of the day," [associate managing editor] Mr. [Charles] Strum said. "At least until later in the evening, when everything tends to change."

This is a reminder that 4 p.m. is not the end of the news day, of course; the front page will have to be remade if something major happens, as it did when there was an earthquake in Haiti in 2010 that struck around 5 p.m., after the Page One meeting.[6]

Though the Web page was displayed on a huge screen in every Page One meeting, editors rarely commented about what was on the page. When I asked Jim Roberts, assistant managing editor, why no one had anything to say about the Web during Page One meetings, he responded this way:

> Print is still the medium of choice. Still, the vast majority of people [the audience] take their cues from print. What we do in print is more symbolic and more permanent than your home page, which can be erased and altered in a handful of keystrokes. . . . It's not like they are not paying attention. It's just that I take it as a compliment that the executive editor rarely tells me that I have overplayed or underplayed a story.
>
> It has happened, but it doesn't happen that often. We go into that meeting and in the version of the meeting held the Web site is displayed in larger-than-life fashion. If someone had an issue, I'm pretty sure I would hear about it. I think some of it is just a matter of just their own interest, and some of it is a matter that they seem to think that we are doing okay.[7]

This comment was worth highlighting because Roberts, who was charged with leading Web efforts, acknowledged the dominant cultural role of print. Even though he was *in charge* of the Web, he still thought that top editors were still more interested in print. Roberts' response also suggested a theme we'll see throughout this chapter: the Web site was simply left alone to a set of people in the newsroom who were charged with taking care of it—and in the end, the rhythms of print and Web could not be truly integrated. It was okay not to focus on the Web, because everyone charged with its production was doing a good enough job that it didn't *need* the attention of Page One; the Web was running smoothly on its own terms in the background. The focus on Page One by top editors emphasizes a focus on tomorrow's news, not today's news—what immediacy for newspapers used to mean before online journalism.

Publisher Arthur Ochs Sulzberger, Jr. has been fairly quick to say in public that *The New York Times* could be imagined as a digital-only publication. "We will stop printing *The New York Times*, sometime in the future, date TBD," he told a London audience.[8] However, many at

The Times found it hard to envision a time without the print paper. The truth was that, despite both the tremendous infrastructure costs required to print the physical newspaper and its massive circulation declines, *The Times* made most of its money from its print product. As executive editor Bill Keller told me, "It's not going away any time soon."[9] This focus on print seemed to belie the much larger focus on immediate information flow in the information age. And given the trends elsewhere in the news industry, this focus on print, with the careful selection of tomorrow's stories, seems almost quaint. Journalists seemed to be relatively unfocused on the economics of print versus online; to most journalists, print was iconic, and online was ephemeral, and this was what mattered.

Unlocking the Mystery of the Print Newspaper

The print cycle kept some journalists' attention insulated from the immediate, publish-now deadline. Instead, immediacy meant the same thing that it had for decades: getting the stories out by the end of the day. This process, especially when viewed in contrast to the online news production process, underscores how the print production cycle allowed enough time for editors and reporters to focus on story development, planning, and analysis. In this section, I offer some context for understanding the Page One meeting, and then I detail the kinds of conversations journalists had during Page One meetings. The goal is to underscore how journalists discussed and refined with each other the stories throughout the day, aiming to be on Page One. The conversation also shows how these set times offered a clear pause in the day for this conversation to take place. Notably, there was no mention of the Web, as Roberts noted.

Every weekday, editors met at 10:30 a.m. in the Page One conference room on the third floor. On any given day between 20 and 40 people could be in the room, including Web, video, multimedia, and photo. Editors from each major desk pitched their top stories for the day to the managing editors and executive editor, but the meeting was also an opportunity for others in the room to provide feedback about these stories, something that would help them think about how their stories would develop over the course of the day.

The meetings followed a predictable pattern: the foreign desk reported first, followed by the national desk, D.C., business, metro, sports, and then other sections of the paper, like media or environment, that do not have stand-alone sections in the newspaper, or if they do, these sections only appear once a week. Later in the day, an afternoon meeting was held to refine the stories and finalize what would go on Page One, though this, of course, could change if there were developments after 4 p.m.

Editors were most likely to pitch top breaking news, investigative stories, or exclusive features that had a loose "time peg": stories that were not tied to a major news event but happened to be deemed particularly interesting. For example, one breaking news story pitched to Page One was a story about the Financial Crisis Inquiry Commission. This news featured high-profile Wall Street bankers testifying to Congress about their views on the financial collapse[10]—but what they would actually say was unknown at the time of the meeting. One example of an investigative story pitched during my time at *The Times* was about how New York governor David Patterson's top aide faced domestic abuse charges.[11] A particularly memorable feature story pitched by the business desk was about the Chinese real estate bubble, in part the result of pictures of housing developments with homes styled in over-the-top, tacky nouveau riche decor. As managing editor Jill Abramson noted, looking at the ostentatious homes, "These are just terrible. We need to have photos of these."[12] There was no clear timeline for the story, but it was considered important news that no other news outlet was likely to have.[13]

Editors came back from the Page One morning meetings trying to interpret the reactions from the managing editors and executive editor, hoping that, if they changed a particular aspect of a story, reframed a lead, or answered a question the editors had, they might be able to earn their story a coveted place on the front page. On the business desk, for instance, editors might come back from the meetings saying something like, "Well, Jill [Abramson] seemed interested in this. She had a couple of questions." Or there might be a joke, often referencing the predilections of the Page One editors. As one editor put it one day, "They are really interested in the Prius recalls, because half the people in the Page One meeting drive a Prius."[14] Editors knew they had to develop a story further if they were going to ensure their pitch a spot on the front.

A look at the conversations throughout the day across a variety of meetings illustrates the way that stories evolve over the course of the day. The stories change—in part, because editors get new information about each story. But the meetings also serve to guide editors (and subsequently reporters); the questions they face from their colleagues point to holes in evolving stories. And the check-ins are ways for the editors in charge of each story to stop, think about what they know, and try to summarize a story's importance for this group of eleven men and seven women who will decide the most significant stories of the day. Thus, the following descriptions of Page One exchanges help explain the way stories develop—and the questions editors have.

The morning after the attempted Times Square bombing on May 4, 2010, when a terrorist loaded a car full of explosives and drove it into the heart of the city, the metro desk offered the following stories:

> We are trying to get information about him [Faisal Shahzad] and his life in Pakistan . . . and see if people appear in court . . . and find out what happened in the 48 hours he got from Times Square to the [airport] gate at JFK.[15]

By the afternoon, this introductory statement had turned into a plan for the following stories, as outlined by metro editor Joe Sexton:

> Let's talk about the bomb package. [Faisal] Shahzad was arraigned this afternoon . . . They charged him with terrorism and weapons of mass destruction, and it seems like he got terror training in Pakistan. They are making arrests in Pakistan.
>
> The second story will be a tick-tock—how the [authorities] put it together. The car was left running. The house keys were in it. They got the [vehicle identification number] from the engine block. A 19-year-old girl was able to describe him to a sketch artist. There was a photo array. We have cell phone records

[that show that the calls] were prepaid. The [police] contacted the seller of the car. He had been receiving calls from Pakistan. He had no interest in the engine or the car except the cargo-hold. . . . We are looking to see how he was able to board the plane even though he was on the no-fly list and paid in cash for a ticket to Dubai.

Then we're doing the best to say what we can in a profile.[16]

Other editors also contributed to the conversation. For instance, business editor Larry Ingrassia asked, "What percentage of people buy tickets in cash?" And Keller added, "Was this supposed to be a suicide bomb?"[17] Representatives from the metro desk responded that they would look into both issues further.

Over the course of the same day, the conversations about coverage of the massive BP oil spill in the Gulf of Mexico also shifted between morning and afternoon meetings. The spill had only just started, and editors were trying to assess its scale. In the morning, the conversation followed this outline: Jim Roberts, the associate managing editor, started off by asking, "What's the latest on spill?", referring to the story by its slug. National editor Rick Berke responded: "BP executives are testifying privately in D.C. The peg is that BP safety records may have many safety lapses in the past. This may be one big story." Keller asked, "When they testify, is it a closed session?" Someone from the D.C. bureau chimed in on the phone via a conference call, noting, "It's not formal . . . and they are not expected to make comments public."[18]

Berke then commented on another developing story:

We have a valve story. Bill Nelson [a US senator from Florida] had something in 2000 about oil rigs shutting off remotely through acoustics. This is required in other countries, but when Cheney came to the White House, it was different. With the oil industry, it's not a requirement in the US.

Jim Roberts instructed, "If the weather is clear, it would be good to go after that." Managing editor Jill Abramson asked, "What's the damage?" It was still unclear how bad the spill was. Berke noted that a photographer would capture the damage that was clear to the naked eye.

The morning meeting helps editors refine their reporting throughout the day. By the afternoon, the stories have gone through further development, and they are ready for another presentation to the Page One meeting, this time as more clearly formed narratives. The discussion continues, however, as reporters still have ample time to work on the stories before deadline, as the afternoon discussion about BP demonstrates.

By the afternoon, the BP story had taken on a different focus. Berke gave a completely different update:

> With BP in Congress, there's a story about fishermen developing. [Ken] Salazar [US secretary of the interior] is blaming BP right now, the [attorneys general] of Gulf States are demanding reimbursements for damages, new details are appearing in the settlements . . . There's a cool new detail on the inside of BP. They were going to apologize with an ad campaign and are now doing something aimed at individuals and social media to say BP is a great company.

Abramson asked, "Have they hired a consultant?" Berke answered, "They've hired a crisis expert from Alaska. They are trotting out the president of BP everywhere. BP has had these years of 'beyond petroleum.' They had this clean image." Keller asked whether the PR story was going to get lost in the larger stories planned for the day. Berke considered the question, answering that it would be prominent in the story or maybe constitute a separate news item focusing exclusively on the PR campaign. Keller thought that this PR angle might be the more interesting part of the entire saga so far.

This conversation reveals how a small story about a closed hearing morphed over the day. Furthermore, the conversation details that, while Berke knew that a BP story would most certainly be on Page One, the reporting and story shaping were not complete. He did, however, have new details to bring to the conversation. The meeting was a back-and-forth opportunity to consider how to develop the story, even as the print deadline approached.[19]

In the end, three stories about the Times Square bombing made the front page, with editors assuming that the metro desk would answer the questions raised. The BP public relations story also made the front. The next question regarded which story would be the fifth Page One item: a story about European market struggles, news about the merger between United and Continental Airlines, a story about Italian opera stars losing weight, or a story about Alzheimer's patients who go missing.

The room seemed to nod in consensus in the afternoon that the clear winner for the fifth slot was the Alzheimer's story, in part because, as the editor of the story noted, "more people that go missing are elderly than children, and people just don't know that."[20] The front page was planned to reflect a mix of stories on most days, some with a breaking-news feel and others with more of a feature feel—such as the story about Alzheimer's patients. This was a particularly busy news day, with much breaking news, so Page One was dominated by these stories. But notice that space was left on the same page as the Times Square bomber for a story that could have easily been about Italian opera stars going on diets.

Roberts offered a small update on the Web in this afternoon meeting:

We were able to get the latest version [of the would-be Times Square bomber] about the suspect being a citizen. We want to thank Culture for doing a great job with the Tonys. There is a great video with the search story [the story about Alzheimer's patients getting lost]. There's a print and interactive timeline [of] the forty-eight hours it was until we caught [the would-be Times Square bomber].

Notably, no one at this meeting offered any input into what should be leading the Web page, where stories might go on the Web page, or where multimedia might be included. And there was no praise for Web efforts, either, despite the quick turnaround required to build the extensive interactive timeline about the would-be Times Square bomber. The multimedia and video editors didn't give updates to the room, either. Note that the majority of the editors were focused on the *story* of the forty-eight hours before the Times Square bomber's failed attempt, not the interactive timeline that would visually detail, for the *Times'* Web readers, where the bomber might have been.

Every once in a while, editors might look up to check on a breaking news story while in the Page One meeting. On the day that the business desk broke a story about the Securities and Exchange Commission (SEC) indicting Goldman Sachs for misleading investors,[21] Ingrassia commented to business editors later in the day that he was in the Page One meeting when he noticed the story: "I was just watching the Web page, and I saw it go up, and it was great. It was just up there, and it was *boom*. Fantastic."[22] But as we saw Roberts comment, the home page was rarely a point of discussion.

Understanding Immediacy for Page One

The lack of focus on the Web didn't mean that these journalists weren't concerned with immediacy. Breaking news simply meant something different: breaking news was for *tomorrow's* paper. The Times Square bomber story was a breaking news story, but the main editors were not thinking about Web updates, just how to frame the most complete update for the main stories in the newspaper. Immediacy was aged news; it was yesterday's news; it was not online journalism. "Stale" meant waiting an extra day (e.g., the day after tomorrow) to publish. Journalists nonetheless felt pressure to produce content to meet the requirements of expected news output (the print paper), but the focus was on filling the print page—a stable page with clear deadlines—rather than the felt content demands of the ASAP Web.

One incident from the business desk illustrates how a breaking news story evolved into a front-page story and also demonstrates the front-page need for immediate news with a tomorrow deadline. The Page One editors valued hard news with a time peg, but they were not focused on making sure that this news was available as it was happening. As they prepared the page for the next day, they still wanted to have this breaking (but aged) news, and without it, editors grew concerned.

On February 10, 2010, the San Francisco tech team alerted the business desk to a breaking story about Google. The news was brought up for discussion during the daily 2:30 business news meeting. The editors thought they might have a good chance for Page One with the story, because it was breaking news that was appealing (it was about a big company, Google) and had a definitive time peg—but for *tomorrow's* paper, rather than immediately, for the Web—on a day that didn't have much breaking news for the next day.

That afternoon, Google had announced that it would be trying to put a form of broadband into communities that it claimed would be faster than anything else on the market. Google was promising to do this for free. During the meeting, editors Adam Bryant and Marcus Mabry tried to finesse the story into a Page One pitch. This was a day when there was particularly bad weather on the East Coast, and Page One was low on breaking news. He knew that top editors were hoping for something to fill that void.

Mabry commented on the story: "Is this the future of the Internet?" David Gallagher, the technology editor, responded, "It's Google's attempt to push Internet companies." Gallagher was careful to note that it was not a business venture, but an innovation by Google to explore new fiber lines. Bryant asked, "If this had to be risen as a bigger deal, could it be done without lying to [the] reader?" By using the word "risen," he was referring to the idea that stories "rise to" Page One if they meet certain standards of quality, such as having a particular, unique angle, or if they are important breaking news.

Gallagher pushed his story, but he warned Bryant not to make too much of it: "It seems unlikely that this is a move that Google will somehow become an ISP [Internet service provider], but this is still really interesting, and they will end up making a lot of money." The editors discussed how this was potentially "massive," but no one really knew what to do with the broadband that Google was unveiling, because it was "so high-speed."

Bryant had a follow-up question: "Has Google transcended the species barrier like a fish that is not in water, or is this not a big deal?" This meant, essentially, had Google gone from being an online tool and operating system to providing infrastructure? Gallagher answered, slightly equivocating, "This is one of their more interesting moves." Mabry noted, "They are news-free at Page One." Bryant pointed out that it could be worth a "refer," or a mention on the front page that refers to something inside the newspaper. The technology editors were instructed by Bryant to "pump it as much as you can before it bursts." Gallagher responded that such reporting was possible: "No one else is doing it." Bryant added jokingly, "Use the word 'hegemony.' That's a Page One word."

"News-free" didn't mean that the newspaper didn't have news, but that the newspaper didn't have any news with a direct time peg for the next day. In the print world, the news peg was still *tomorrow,* rather than breaking news now. This anxiety about filling the front page recalls the fear of not having enough content to fill the paper captured by 1960s and 1970s ethnographies. These content questions for the print paper are different from those for the Web page, as instead of the immediate need for more news, the concern is with filling the page with news for the next day. Thus, there is pressure, but the demand for more, now, ASAP, is experienced differently in the newsroom by those closest to the print cycle. However, for *The Times,* it wasn't a question of whether there was enough content, but whether there was enough *good* content to fit aspirations for a great front page that included breaking news.

The exchange also revealed some of the demands of the Page One stories, even if they did have a tomorrow time peg—that there needed to be some broader impact and "game-changing" news, rather than just a quick development. This idea was reflected in Bryant's comment about whether Google was becoming a new species of tech company. And, perhaps notably, the conversation also reflected the fact that stories could be manipulated to a certain degree to become Page One stories—and would go through this angle reformulation thanks to set times for conversation like the business news meeting. In this case, the story would be framed as a particularly interesting innovation in Google's broader effort to have its hands in all sectors of the technology world—hence Bryant's comment about "hegemony."

But when thinking about print and online content creation, perhaps the biggest and most obvious difference between working on something for print and for the Web site is that the print paper actually has a deadline. To meet these deadlines, reporters and editors worked in what was generally a predictable fashion, with reporters' work punctuated by Web needs. The deadline of the first national edition, which was published in more distant markets, was 9 p.m.; the deadline for the first city edition, distributed to places like the far reaches of the Connecticut suburbs, was 10:15 p.m.; the second national and city editions, which were intended for the rest of the East Coast and New York City, respectively, closed at 11:30 p.m.;[23] and there was a final edition at 12:30 a.m. The newspaper could stop the presses after 12:30 a.m. "in the event of the Second Coming or news of similar importance or controversy," as night editor Keith Leighty put it.[24] Deadlines for each page on the business desk were staggered to the 9 p.m. deadline, in order to help with the flow of content to the copy desk.

Business News and the Print Life Cycle

The business desk's daily cycle further illuminates the print newsroom's distinct set of rhythms, practices, and routines, which were quite different from those of the Web. In fact, the business desk editors' schedules and the three major meetings of the day were totally oriented around developing stories for the print paper. The conversations around these stories had almost nothing to do with the Web. But the advantage of not being caught up in the NOW of the Web site meant that journalists had the chance to debate, discuss, and, as we just saw, perhaps oversell their stories for the next day's newspaper.

The first and most comprehensive meeting was between 11:00 and 11:30 a.m., typically lasting about half an hour. This meeting gave editors a chance to ask each other questions about story angles and to consider aspects and questions reporters might want to pursue. Later in the day, when they had a better sense of what Page One might look like, editors had a 2:15 (or 2:30) p.m. meeting held with everyone standing up around a cluster of editors' desks. The point was to see which stories might have developed enough to be pitched again for Page One and to check on the status of stories for the front of the business page. Finally, there was a 5:00 p.m. meeting where editors discussed the placement of each story on the front of the business page. The decisions about story placement were intended to signal to readers the importance of each story. Other meetings later in the day involved fewer editors and helped plan the next day's coverage.

Conversations about business stories typically revolved around these two separate but related decisions—story development and placement on the page. For instance, during one 11:00 a.m. news meeting, *Times* editors began talking about a way to frame a story about the massive agribusiness Monsanto battling with the Justice Department.[25]

Editor Justin Gillis explained that Monsanto was worried about its patented seeds becoming generic. Gillis noted, "Monsanto has a giant monopoly over innovation and patents. There's a suspicion that they do stuff [the Department of Justice] doesn't like around the edges." Editor Tim O'Brien noted, "There are so many restrictions Monsanto poses against farmers." Editor Winnie O'Kelley added, "If [farmers] somehow use a Monsanto seed without permission or use it in the wrong way, or one gets into their crop, they can't sell it on the market." Gillis explained, "The basic allegation is that Monsanto is screwing over small companies." Editor Adam Bryant asked, "Is this a story about an evil capitalist conspiracy or patents?" Gillis replied, "It's Monsanto. People have been complaining about it for years. They buy it because they like the seeds, but they hate the company." O'Brien noted, "You don't have a choice." These conversations detailed how a reporter might go about developing a story. In this case, it meant directing a reporter to take an aggressive stance reporting Monsanto's often nasty treatment of farmers.

Another example shows how a question from editors can prompt further reconsideration for a story's angle. Deputy technology editor David Gallagher presented a story on the evolution of Google Translate into an accurate translation service during an 11:00 a.m. meeting.[26] He explained: "We have translated [the slug]. There is this algorithm of electronic documents from the UN and the EU, and your computer can basically learn to TRANSLATE it. Google is using the entire Web and has huge amounts of data to work with to [learn to] translate words [into other languages]." Ingrassia followed up by asking whether there were outside linguistic experts in the story and whether this was something that would cost people jobs. Gallagher pointed out, "We have experts. . . . No one says that this is as good as a human, but it's really pretty good. It could make it unnecessary for small businesses to have translators." Later, as the story was pitched for Page One, this new angle was added to the story's reporting, following up on Ingrassia's concern that there might be human translators now put out of business.

Thus, built into these meetings were the space, time, and presence of other editors to help consider the merits of particular stories within the context of the larger news landscape. These regular pauses in the day were necessary to give editors a chance not only to think about story angles but, on rarer occasions, to rethink the ways they were framing stories. But as we will see with online story production and Web content, the same kinds of conversations do not take place about content for the Web, due to the speed that journalists feel is necessary to remain up-to-date online.

The Devotion to Placement

Perhaps nothing seems more foreign to the Web cycle than the attention spent thinking about the very deliberate placement of stories in the print paper. The Web changes and refreshes, while the print paper is for good. Editors on the business desk spent some of their time hoping to pitch one or two Page One stories a day, but their main concern was filling the business section, and particularly its front page, with a variety of news. As with those in the Page One meeting, journalists on the business desk are concerned with breaking news for tomorrow but also with having enough feature stories to represent *The Times'* distinct reporting. Editors focus on the front page of the business section as a way to argue about the importance of stories, which is theoretically dictated by their placement on the page.

When editors spoke about the placement of stories in the newspaper, they were speaking in a specialized language, known to *The Times* for decades, despite sounding like babble to an outsider, with codes for editors to assign importance to stories. The codes for story importance featured such terms as "down-page," "top of the page," or "display," each of which connoted different levels of importance. Depending on the day, each code word could mean something different. A "display" story signified a story that had art on the page: a photo or, more common on the business desk, original art. The display on the business desk was an ever-present source of concern to the editors—a constant demand and pressure of print news that needed be filled, albeit with a particular standard of news.

As Winnie O'Kelley noted on February 18, 2010, when the print section had no display by midafternoon: "Did Dan solve the display problem?" The page needed illustrations and photos as much as it needed stories. If there was no big breaking news that warranted the display, and no backup feature stories that could serve as the display, the business desk was in serious trouble in terms of page design, as visuals were seen as likely to draw readers in to the content. In these situations, editors were often dissatisfied with the layout of the page, but they would resign themselves to publishing it anyway, saying something like, "Well, this is the best we've got for today."

Take, for example, the language used in the morning meeting on March 29, 2010. The editors were speaking in "slug" terms to refer to the stories while discussing their placement on the page. Editor Justin Gillis said, "Housing has to run, maybe it should be a display? Or oil could be a display later in the week." Ingrassia commented, "Is that a display, or could it just be a down-page story?" (Here, he was signaling that this oil story might be less important.) Gillis relented: "Oil could be a down-page story." Ingrassia then noted, "Well, we could have housing as a display, maybe oil at the top of the page."

At 5 p.m., the editors would gather around again, and this time, Ingrassia would make the final call. Often, stories that have been slated all day as dress page stories, or stories to go on the front of the print section, are switched out in favor of a late-breaking story (for tomorrow) that seems to "add to the mix."

One meeting I observed helps elucidate how the editors discuss the final placement of stories and how a new development can change their careful planning. Often, Ingrassia, just standing and looking at the page layout (with the page printed in real size), would change his assessment of how to place a story. The stories originally slated for the

March 5, 2010, paper were about the Greek debt crisis; the International Monetary Fund; solar power; and the latest sign of recovery, that shopping retail sales at all the major department sales had shown a big uptick despite bad weather in February 2010. Ingrassia asked, "Will our readers have a hard time reading this IMF story? Will they see this as a hard news story? IMF is more analysis, but the Greece story is the news lead." The editors decided on a different design, which they thought would help readers: Larry said, "Let's do a two-story package with headlines with a subhead," which effectively placed the IMF and Greek debt as two stories together for the reader, set in two columns side by side.

However, at the moment when the page was about to be finalized, *Dealbook* blogger and financial reporter Michael de la Merced alerted editor David Gillen that the SEC had charged a psychic with running a Ponzi scheme. The journalists joked about how the psychic was predicting profits. "Why would they charge a psychic? This is just ridiculous," editor Tim Race said. Gillen argued, "We have to have a fun story. This is just great." But another determination entered into the equation: just how much money the psychic was being charged with stealing. The alleged figure was $6 million, and one of the editors noted, "That's a lot from a psychic." Ingrassia shrugged a bit: "This has to be really well written." Gillen promised he would edit it.

The editors decided to move the economic indicators story about retail sales inside the print paper. Though retail sales are one of the few economic indicators that may make the dress page because they predict the state of the economy, the psychic was just more "fun." Another one of the editors commented, "[The retail story is] strong, but it can go inside." Just as the Page One story had taken a feature story for the front, this lighter fare about the SEC psychic would add to the mix.

A senior editor could spend his or her entire day absorbed in news meetings discussing the angles and placement of stories: 10:30 a.m., Page One; 11:00 a.m., business page; 2:15 or 2:30 p.m., business page; 4 p.m., Page One; 5 p.m., business meeting. Expressed through the careful selection and arrangement of stories, their choices reflected considered editorial judgment. The finality of print, with its regular and specific deadlines, brought a sense of order to newswork. But this routine of putting the paper to bed each day seemed largely to ignore the reality of a world with fast-paced information flows and the capacity for near-instant transmission of information in a way that had never before been possible. That development has largely been left to people who spent most of their time thinking about the Web. However, reporters often found themselves caught between this old world and the new world of immediacy, as we will see in the next chapter. But first, it's important to juxtapose these print routines with online routines—and in so doing to see how online editors dealt with immediacy as part of their workflow.

Life Behind the Home Page: Online Rhythms

Online newswork departed from the regularly scheduled process of decision making, planning, and editing a story that dominates print production. In fact, it operated according to an entirely different rhythm. Production for the Web was a frenetic activity, often with little clear strategy about how, when, and why stories should be posted. Online news production was largely a response to the perceived pressure of immediacy, defined as ASAP, constant updates for online journalism—and in parallel, immediacy emerged as a value that structured and ordered newswork and gave journalists a particular vision of their role as professionals.

Yet journalists did not speak directly about "immediacy." Editors could not explain to me why they thought stories should be updated as quickly as new information was available, and Web producers could not explain to me why they believed there was a need to keep the pages constantly updated, or looking "fresh." "Fresh" was a quality that Web producers and others charged with online journalism associated with their presumed sense of what the audience wanted: something new, something different. But just like "feel" or "news sense," "fresh" depended on a journalist's (most often a Web editor or Web producer's) individual judgment, honed from the time they'd spent thinking about Web production. Determining what is "fresh" is one way to explain how journalists tried to make sense of the constant presence of a never-ending deadline in the digital age.

"Fresh" was also one way for journalists to deal with the fact that they had no control over when audiences might be clicking on Web content. However, they did know that, at least at *The Times*, there were always thousands of people looking at the Web page at any given time. The goal was to keep them coming back. The understanding from journalists working on the Web was that fresh content was better. Updated content brought in new readers or kept readers coming back, so the home page could not be static, or at least not for very long. The morning newspaper delivered to your home (if you got one) should look nothing like the home page you opened at work in the morning.

What the home page editor did during the day, when most people were getting their news online, was relatively unstructured. While the home page editor had some sense of when he would add new stories to the page, there were no conversations between him and the managing editors or executive editors, for example, about which stories should remain in place during the day. Instead, it was up to the day's home page editor and the continuous news editor, Pat Lyons, to make these decisions.

I asked associate managing editor Jim Roberts why there were no formal Web meetings like the print meetings to decide coverage and story placement. He told me, "You've seen how fast the Web moves. You can't sit around and plan for that. It's too quick for people to stand around and debate."[27] This comment was a clear recognition that the print process couldn't work for the Web. There were some meetings that lasted no more than ten or fifteen minutes, and they didn't offer much guidance about which stories should lead the home page and when. The morning Web meeting was an opportunity for journalists to tell other staff what stories might be coming down the pipeline, but the home page editor I followed over the course of one morning, Mick Sussman, said he rarely paid attention to this meeting. In fact, he admitted that he couldn't hear it from his desk. Decisions as to what column of the Web page to put a story in, or how to order the stories, or how long to keep a story in place, were the kinds of things left up to the home page editor and his or her supervisor, not decisions made by committee—particularly during the day, when most people in the United States come to the site.

And in the evening, there were two "handoff" meetings to make

Web producers from around the newsroom aware of content from across other sections and to inform the night home page editor. But there was no debate over home page play, no extended discussion over what stories merited the most attention, and very little conversation about the stories themselves—just reading down a list of what stories were available. In this sense, consider that an editor for print could spend his or her day in meetings talking about story placement, while on the Web, there were virtually *no* meetings that offered the same kind of opportunities.

Instead, in looking at the online rhythms of Web production on nytimes.com, the picture that emerges is not one that involves many actors, but instead focuses on the activities of a single individual. Thus, in looking at the home page editors and the online business editor, we get a sense of the rhythm of each page, a rhythm that is articulated through the vantage point of one person. This is distinct from what we saw in the print rhythms, where the portrait of newswork is an extensive detailing of collaborative discussions. The close-ups of individual Web editors/producers, though, underscore the imperative of immediacy that faced the online newsroom.

Rhythms on the Home Page: Daytime

On April 2, 2010, I spent the day with Mick Sussman, one of the morning home page producers for the US edition.[28] His shift was from 7 a.m. to 3 p.m. He explained to me that his goal was to have something new up on the home page about every ten minutes (keeping the page looking "fresh"). The big changes that he made were in the "A" column, or the leftmost column going down the home page; the photo spot, which he tried to change every thirty minutes; and the "B" column, or the column underneath the photo spot, which was a prime spot for a news story other than the top of the "A" column. Sussman was also constantly rotating out blogs in the "on the blogs" section, but he admitted, for instance, that he didn't have much knowledge about style or sports, so he often relied upon other people to alert him when something was important.

Sussman had to write headlines for nearly all the stories he put up on the home page, though Pat Lyons, the continuing news editor who, in theory, supervised him, would offer suggestions, as would other editors and Web producers via IM. Sussman also often had to write the Web summaries for the stories (the short blurbs under the headlines), though he relied on what came from copy editors or the Web editors. But the nuances of the Web page itself often demanded that he do the last-minute editing of these summaries before they went in front of millions of nytimes.com readers, often going up without any kind of editorial oversight other than his own news judgment and copy-editing skills. Lyons would provide feedback if something needed to be tweaked, but this was a publish-first mentality. As I watched Sussman work, I noticed how much hand coding and manipulation of the Web site he had to do: his job involved not only journalistic judgment but also considerable Web skills.

When a new story popped up in his queue, usually over IM, Sussman would send a headline to Lyons, also over IM. If Lyons didn't respond, Sussman would just put up a headline. When I was observing Sussman, he asked Lyons about putting up a story on a conspiracy movie. When Lyons didn't respond, Sussman put the story up. His justification was, "I think this is pretty interesting," and he noted that he always liked conspiracy stories. For about half an hour, this story was in the section right underneath the main photo on the home page—a prominent spot. This is an indication of the latitude that Sussman had over the page, shaping it to his own interests. A few minutes later, the foreign desk alerted him to a story on Saudi Arabia, and Sussman decided to put this story on the home page. While these stories often went through layers of debate and discussion at each individual desk, their quality depended on this editorial judgment. A breaking story, for example, might be headed to Sussman without quality checks, as we will see in the next chapter. To some degree, Sussman depended on the quality of work provided to him. However, Sussman was ultimately in control of who saw what story, and for how long, on the Web.

Sussman explained that his goal was to balance the home page content so it was distributed evenly among all of the different sections of the newspaper (a goal echoed by other home page editors). His other, perhaps most important duty was to keep the news constantly updated in order to make sure that nytimes.com had both the latest content and new content, so people would have reason to keep coming back to the page. "In six hours, there should be a complete turnover of the page," he noted. "There is an imperative to keep the page looking fresh for readers, so I am constantly tinkering with it, looking at blogs, reading subpages, and seeing if there is other content to pull up for the page."

When I watched him, he spent most of his morning preparing for the jobs-numbers story (a story we will see from the reporter's perspective in the next chapter). First, he had to prepare an alert, and then he had to deal with constant changes to the headline for this particular month's story (the April 2010 numbers). Sussman also checked to make sure that *The Times* hadn't missed anything by watching the wires when he had a chance.

Noon EST was a big time for updates to the home page, as many people would check the Web during their lunch break. Sussman put entirely fresh content on the home page, such as a story about attacks in Israel and a *Times* feature story on Senator Kirsten Gillibrand.[29]

On his own, Sussman learned that President Obama was speaking at noon, and decided to make sure he had a video link on the home page so the president could be featured. Sussman made three other major updates to the B column while I watched him.

Each major update consisted of changing the big picture on the home page. The course of the afternoon went as follows: At 1 p.m. Sussman's first update was to put in *TimesCast,* the five-minute *Times* video that included (at the time) some highlights of the Page One meeting and interviews with reporters about breaking news. At 2 p.m., he put a photo of President Obama speaking in the main picture space. He then inserted international news into the second slot, underneath the jobs report. Then, by 3 p.m., he had made another major switch, moving news about New Jersey governor Chris Christie into the column beneath the main photo. All of these changes seemed a bit superficial— but they each made the home page look completely different.

None of the other editors was consulted when Sussman made these changes. To be even more clear: one person was writing the Web headlines, as well as the copy that went underneath these headlines. *One person* for millions of potential readers. And there was no copy editor for these Web headlines.

While other people in the newsroom IMed Sussman with suggestions for Web summaries and headlines, only he knew exactly what would fit together on the home page. And ironically, most of the time, he was only giving a very quick read to any of these stories, if he read them at all. His attention was focused on the lead of the story, the headline given by the desk, and the guidance of other Web producers. As far as I could tell, he wasn't making any errors, but the entire process seemed like it could leave the home page vulnerable to mistakes. Yet the system did seem to work. Only rarely did anyone in the newsroom complain that a Web summary did not represent a news story—and of course, that could quickly be changed.

Sussman had figured out a routine to keep *The Times'* home page constantly looking different. Roughly, the rules went something like this: He would put up a new blog post every ten minutes, which he culled from his RSS feed. Some repositioning of stories took place every twenty to thirty minutes. New stories were added as they came up, if they seemed to meet Sussman's internal criteria of newsworthiness. A major, visible change to the home page was made every hour. Sussman checked the competition three times on the day I shadowed him (CNN, BBC, *The Washington Post, The Wall Street Journal*) but only once mentioned a competitor's story to Lyons. Rather, he was preoccupied with updating the home page with *Times* content and wasn't paying much attention to anything else.

He barely had time to run up to the cafeteria during the day, and he made sure to do so at about 11:20 in order to be ready for the big noon push. Sussman had tried to make the continual rotation of stories more predictable and routine, but it depended on everyone else in the newsroom feeding him a continuous supply. At a place like *The New York Times*, with over one thousand people in one building, as well as the *International Herald Tribune* staff in Hong Kong and Paris, keeping updated original content on the home page was quite possible, during the New York news day at least. Nighttime presented different challenges, as we will see next. But for the day home page editor, immediacy, with some undefined sense of "freshness," ultimately influenced almost everything, from when Sussman ate to his near-continuous workday spent changing and updating content on nytimes.com.

Where Print and Online Converge in Online Production

Ironically, while the immediacy of trying to keep the page updated seems to reign during the day, night production of the home page online relies on cues from the print paper. In this odd way, the two newsrooms converge. The night home page editor was still concerned with keeping the Web page "fresh," but she had also been instructed to use the guidance of the front page and section editors when selecting news stories for the home page. And the locus of production of most of the news, the New York bureau, shuts down for paper deadlines in the evening, so the amount of brand-new news that can be placed on the Web site slows to a trickle.

The night I observed Lillie Dremeaux, April 5, 2010, was also the night of the worst mine disaster in American history.[30] Thus, I got to witness Dremeaux in an on-demand, breaking-news environment, where her Web summaries would be *the* latest anyone coming to nytimes.com would know about the disaster if they happened to just want a quick headline. Each subsequent Web summary that night changed as more details of the story became clear. Thus, Dremeaux's job took on added importance. She was not just refreshing the home page to keep things looking interesting; she was also refreshing the home page with the breaking news coming out of the disaster.

At first glance, her routine was much the same as Sussman's. She was in constant communication with night editor Gerry Mullany about when new copy would be available from the copy desk, as by this time of the night, most breaking stories were now in their final form, and feature stories set for the print paper were being prepared for the print deadline. Like Sussman, she was continually bombarded by IMs from other Web producers with requests to get their desks' content on the home page. She also seemed to be making constant changes to the page, and she kept only a minor eye on the competition—with this research never affecting what stories she chose to put where—though she did make a note in an email of which competitors she checked.

Dremeaux paid attention to one of the two night Web meetings, the 7 p.m. meeting, where Web producers informed each other and Mullany of what content was available. This meeting was to help Dremeaux know what the big stories for the day had been, and each Web producer from each desk had the chance to pitch his or her big stories for home page play. In addition, as the night home page producer, Dremeaux was also guided by the decisions made by print editors. But it would be up to Dremeaux to decide when, where, and for how long material would appear on the home page. Her goal was to give each section's strongest dress page story (or printed section story) play on the front page for at least some period of time.

Over the course of the night, the home page became increasingly static and began to look more and more like the print paper. Around 9 p.m., Dremeaux printed out a mockup used to guide the print Page One designers that showed where each story on Page One would go. This mockup guided where she placed each story. Using the visual cues about the most important story in the paper (the lead story in the right-hand column) and the off-lead (in the left-hand column), she would place these pieces in the most prominent places on the Web site (the A column or under the B column). She would also be sure to have the other stories that made Page One in prominent places. As Dremeaux put it:

> The front page tells me what are the five or six most important stories of the day. I follow that because there are some really important editors—the most important editors at *The Times*—saying that this is what we think is important. And the home page should reflect that. [31]

Strangely enough, the home page late in the evening was most like the paper people would see in the morning. In fact, the individual section pages were remotely copy edited—by a university professor. Web producers could not go home until they had gotten their "Cowling note," a brief email that alerted them to capitalization issues, spelling problems, and so on. As Web producer Cate Doty noted, "The Web site is most edited when no one is looking at it." [32]

Dremeaux had an added constraint that Sussman did not—she had to make sure that there was enough new content to keep the home page looking "fresh" in the morning. Since the home page had already run through many stories throughout the day, Dremeaux had to be careful to save some of the major stories of the evening (which would be in the print paper the next day) for the morning.

This way, the following morning, when no new news of major significance to US readers had yet occurred, and very few US reporters were on duty, there would still be new content for the page. Thus, the need to keep things "fresh" by keeping the Web site looking new can be seen as a recent constraint on newswork in the sense that it might shelve news for a little while. In such a case, keeping things fresh may actually make them, like day-old bread, a little bit stale. Immediacy imposes a driven focus for new content on journalists and the Web page, but when there isn't any (or enough) new content, the Web site tried to balance the desire to keep the home page looking ASAP with the reality that journalism is not, in the end, ASAP at *The Times*, at least most of the time.

Still, by the time most people woke up, the home page would look completely different from Dremeaux's carefully matched headlines and the carefully edited section pages, with the news that had come in from the foreign desk and the business desk heading the site, and the home page producer cycling in the remainder of the material that hadn't made the home page the night before. As Doty put it:

> The interesting thing is that when I wake up at 10:30 the whole Web site is different. So the Web site is totally edited when no one is watching. The page will look completely different from now (12 a.m.) to the morning so that's kind of a fascinating thing to note.

Thus, the life of the home page producer revealed some particularly important online imperatives and values at *The Times*. There was considerable importance placed on keeping the Web page looking as fresh as possible, particularly throughout the workday. The home page producer employed the breadth of content available throughout *The Times* to make this possible. What Sussman and Dremeaux did each day didn't vary much, and both had their own routines. However, what stories to place where, in the end, was up to them, with perhaps limited supervision from their editors. Writing the Web summaries and the headlines fell down to one or two pairs of eyes, at most, versus the multiple rounds of copy edits for a news article. The home page producers had considerably more latitude and less oversight than anyone working on the print side of the newspaper, and for the most part, they were making decisions about which stories were most important based on what news happened to be available at each particular moment.

Online Rhythms on the Business Desk

Most days when I was doing my research, I would get into the newsroom in the morning and prop myself up comfortably in a chair next to Mark Getzfred, the online editor for the business section, before heading off to do any other research. Some highlights from his work days, which began when he took the train at 6 a.m. from his home in Connecticut and read on his Blackberry and Kindle until he arrived in New York by 7:30 a.m. or so, then ran to at least 5:30 or 6 p.m., show how the business desk attempted to fill the need for online content. Like Sussman, Getzfred took to his job with intensity, underscoring the obsession with the new and what was now online.

Getzfred began his day trying to find fresh stories for the business Web page and the business global page (the main business pages) that had not been in the business section the night before. He started by searching through *International Herald Tribune* content that had come in from the night before; the business desk relied on the content from the partnership with this paper owned by The New York Times Co. to help fill the morning edition.

So, for instance, on January 12, 2010, he spent his morning (as he did most mornings) reframing a story from the Asia bureau of the *International Herald Tribune* (*IHT*) on Japan Airlines' struggles with bankruptcy, just to get something new on the page. He followed this up with a story on Airbus, the European airline manufacturer, another story that had come from the *IHT*. Both stories went up (though in different places) on each of the business pages.

He would constantly scan the wires, and he would begin rewriting a markets story even before the US markets opened. An Asia-based writer would have left off this story in the very early hours of the US morning, it would have been picked up by the European markets writer in the Paris bureau of the *IHT* by early morning US time, and then Getzfred would begin filling in the details about premarket trading in the United States, gleaning content from the wires. He noted that this was one of the most popular stories on the site—"people like reading about markets and we give it a little context" (again emphasizing how *The Times* hoped it was providing value-added content). Around 9:45 a.m., he stopped for a brief fifteen-minute meeting to discuss what was going to be available on the Web site with the other Web editors. This was the meeting that Sussman said he couldn't hear—despite the fact that this was one of the few moments when Web editors got together to talk about stories. Notably, this meeting only described what was available and the importance of these stories at a particular moment.

He would then rush back downstairs and continue to rearrange the business pages. He explained to me on March 1, 2010, his sense of the pressure that he felt on the Web: "There is some pressure, but it's not like we are twenty-four-hour news with always something to fill, but there is some pressure." And then he began filling the business pages with a series of stories that would generally be trivial by the end of the day, either inside the print paper or not even present at all, such as any story about economic indicators, hearings, or reports. A typical story from that day was one he took from the wires about the fact that personal spending was up at the expense of the personal savings rate. Another was still more about the ongoing Toyota brake failures. He explained: "Akio Toyoda apologized again. . . . [It] probably won't go in the paper."[33]

Getzfred told me later that these stories were nonetheless likely to make the home page, as "the home page, particularly in the morning, is always looking for news. They want something fresh they can put up there."[34] While Getzfred declined to say he was working at an immediate pace, he rarely took breaks, even for lunch. His focus was, indeed, on keeping the Web page looking new, in part because *Times* readers, as he put it, "wanted to see something else," and "we have to respond to what is changing throughout the day."[35]

On that March morning, he IMed Lyons, the editor who worked closely with Sussman, to alert him that a Federal Reserve Board member would be retiring. His IM said something to the effect of "Donald Kohn is retiring," to which Lyons replied, "Who is that?" Getzfred explained, and Lyons IMed back to note that they didn't have much, so it would go on the home page—*even though Lyons didn't have any idea who Kohn was.* The home page in the morning and the business page in the morning were both hungry for news, even news that wasn't of much substance, as long as it could be cycled into the spots for readers with news from the day, rather than news from yesterday.

Getzfred continued most of his day filling content as he could with wire stories and updates from reporters (like Bowley's continuously updated Goldman story; see Chapter 2) and keeping the markets story up to date. He would shuffle around stories and put in new *Times* content when he had it, but most of the time, new substantive stories from the business desk, the kind talked about in the news meetings, weren't ready during the day. So as a result, the business page during the day was a mix of blog posts being pushed out by the six or so major blogs and small chunks of news—unless there was something major brewing.

Getzfred spent his day hunched over the computer, constantly scanning stories, rewriting AP content, making sure that his markets reporter was staying on task, and keeping the business Web page filled with new content as soon as he had some. Notably, this was not even always "good" content, content that would even be talked about in *Times* news meetings; it was just new. Stories about corn subsidies, for example, might be leading the page for a good part of the morning—until 10 or 11, when some better content might be flowing in from more substantial *Times* news. In most cases, there was likely only one story, like Bowley's Goldman story, that could really feed the business page with original, print-discussion-worthy content until later in the afternoon or evening.

Getzfred was also the first line of defense for making sure that breaking news got on the Web site as fast as possible. On January 12, 2010, that meant making sure *The Times* had two fairly important updates. The first came around 5 p.m., when *The Times*' media writer Bill

Carter got a scoop that Conan O'Brien would refuse to be *The Tonight Show* host if Jay Leno was moved back to his old 11:35 p.m. slot. At the time, this was big news: *The Times* was the first news organization to have news about O'Brien's decision.

The second was a bigger story, and it underscores the rush to get out big news. Though January 12, 2010, was the day that the Haiti earthquake struck around 5 p.m., EST, no mention of this was made around the business desk. Instead, the news that had Getzfred and the rest of the business desk in breaking-news mode was Google's announcement that it was—for now—pulling out of China because of security breaches.

The news was broken on the tech blog, *Bits*. Getzfred then alerted the home page to the news. The home page didn't like the wording and, after briefly posting the *Bits* blog, took it down and put up an AP story. Getzfred quickly wrote a roughly three-paragraph story on the statement to give a "staff presence on the page" and also to give the main reporters for the story a running start.[36] *Bits* then reposted a new version, which Getzfred passed to the home page, which the home page liked. The full article then followed, updating Getzfred's headline version, which stayed on the home page until something more substantial was ready. Getzfred was motivated by speed and by his sense of pride in having a *Times* stamp on the story.

"Update, update, update" was the unwritten mantra for Getzfred, and as such, he kept a steady stream of stories flowing on to the business page Web site. When the business page went through an update in April 2010 to focus on even more immediate material, with the goal of highlighting new stories throughout the day, the emphasis on newness and constant updates only increased.[37]

After reading a draft version of this book, Getzfred thought this made him appear like he was waiting for news to happen, when in fact, he felt that he was actively preparing for scheduled events he knew would generate news, working with reporters to generate prepared matter to respond to these news events, and making sure that stories were available as soon as possible on the Web. Notably, though, this focus on the now, this ASAP need for content, underscores the importance of immediacy in online Web rhythms. Though the print and

Web business pages started to converge in the evening, in part due to the slower trickle of content, the felt imperative during the day was for more new content, now. The business Web page, and the home page too, both paused online as *The New York Times* in New York went to bed, but in the morning, what was there would be gone, and the cycle would begin once again.

Print and Online Routines

Thus, two dynamics were at play, print and online, and ultimately, print was the most important factor, not least because it occupied the value system that was most dear to traditional journalists. Immediacy meant two different things in a newsroom that had two processes of news-work ongoing at the same time. There was both the old world of immediacy, where breaking news meant tomorrow, and the new world of immediacy in online journalism, where immediacy meant "fresh" constant updates and where the home page would not look the same in any way after six hours.

The print news cycle ultimately fed the home page and the business Web page with content—but generally, it took until the end of the day for the authority of print news to begin to inform how Web stories would look online and what prominence they would have. By that point, most people would not be paying attention to nytimes.com. By 9 p.m., when the major print stories for the day had been fully fleshed out, copy edited, and prepared, the home page finally began to stop its immediate churn. The home page editor, though, didn't need any raw numbers or traffic data to have the sense that most people had long ago signed off of nytimes.com, at least among readers in the United States, and that the busy focus on keeping readers on the page had long subsided. In fact, these numbers were not readily available to the Web editors.

Yet by morning, the important stories from the print paper—the value-added content, the front-page stories—would be quickly washed away by stories with relatively small bits of significance. Sussman would be left with the previous night's leftovers, some foreign stories coming in during the day, and filler stories from desks like business that were of such little significance that they might not even make the print paper.

On the other hand, we might see the Web site as doing quite well according to *Times* standards, despite moving so quickly. Even without the layers of editorial judgment, those charged with constantly updating the Web site do it well; they are trusted for their facile judgment and their competency as headline writers and copy editors, all their work done rapidly. These Web editors have their own sense of traditional news norms; they do weigh the importance of each story, given the significance to readers—though in practice, this may not always work in the quest for "fresh" content, as we see with Getzfred and the early-morning business Web page.

The compulsion to continually keep providing more content had become woven into the fabric of nytimes.com; immediacy has created a system of worth, order, practice, and routine for online journalism. In this way, what journalists spoke of as "fresh," and I conceptualize as immediacy, takes its shape as an emergent value of online journalism at *The Times*. Immediacy ordered how the majority of *Times* readers would see the newspaper's content. What is missing from this conversation is the "why" for the focus on online updating. This had become incorporated into how Web journalists understood their mission—and their sense of what was important—but other than the simple explanation that readers wanted to see what was new, there was little reflection on what made immediacy important. This further suggests that this value was emerging, as journalists had yet to define and truly reflect on its importance, beyond daily routine.

Culturally, nytimes.com was not the print newspaper: there were no long meetings; multiple editors did not labor over what stories were placed where; and online moved quickly, all thanks to the imperative that more readers should see new content. Decisions were left to two people, generally, rather than a group of people debating what would be the agenda for the day. Perhaps at the end of the night, print created a pause, but during the day, a visitor to nytimes.com would have no clear insight into what the "11 men and 7 women with the power to decide what was important in the world" considered the most important stories.

The great irony for this newspaper was that immediacy was a compulsion, but print remained, at least for the time, more important in setting the tone and significance for news stories in the daily rhythms of top editors and traditional journalists' senses of order. The seemingly clear rules of print production did not always (and often did not) meet the needs of online news production. Thus, news making based on these two value systems suggested competing work routines. In this chapter, what we see is the process for shaping and creating public-facing content for readers, both print and online. My goal is to offer a larger sense of process, rather than the experience of particular journalists, though the individual nature of the Web production job requires a close look at the daily practice of these journalists.

The tension between print and online immediacy is particularly poignant for traditional reporters, who must serve two masters. Though print matters more, the daily process of the Web often captures their attention—creating competing pressures. For journalists, this uncertainty is often unwelcome and makes their lives quite difficult. In the next chapter, we will turn to how journalists who work with text experience the ups and downs of online news production in an era when immediacy means NOW.

Chapter 4

Immediacy

TO WHAT END?

In some ways, business health reporter Barry Meier was pretty lucky. He wasn't working on a big breaking story that was sensitive to immediate time deadlines. Instead, he had been given the time and space to plug away at an evolving story on failing medical devices. So far, he had found that thousands of all-metal artificial hips were faulty. He wasn't writing for a daily deadline; instead, he and his editors were biding their time for a big Page One story.[1] After all, it wasn't like artificial hips had to be linked to a particular day's news agenda, though editors surmised this would eventually be an important story.

So Meier had the time to report, report, and report, gathering more and more data and tweaking his story. He waited, with his editors, until there was the right mix of news stories on Page One for the head honchos to decide that his hip story would be one of the most important of the day. Eventually, Meier's first front-page splash propelled enough interest for a high-profile series of articles on medical device failures. A year later, he could say that the faulty hip replacements could be called the "most widespread medical implant failure in decades."[2]

But he wasn't writing for the Web, unless you count the fact that such stories would ultimately be posted on the home page and the business Web page, at least for a few hours. "I don't write much breaking news on my beat," Meier told me. "I'm the wrong person to talk to if you want to hear about writing for the Web."[3]

On the other hand, Steve Lohr, an old hand on the technology beat and the author of a book on the history of computing, had a different perspective about immediacy in the new news environment. Lohr wrote both big stories and incremental, daily stories on his beat. So while he might be working on, say, a story about digital data or supercomputing, he was at the same time charged with covering IBM. This meant that he needed to respond to major company press releases, cover vaguely notable IBM tidbits and gossip of the day for the *Bits* blog, and write up anything that had to do with IBM earnings. So on any given day, Lohr could be writing for Page One, the front of the business page, the blog, or the instant demands of the nytimes.com Web site. The seemingly endless demands and conflicting priorities frustrated him. He was particularly bothered by the intense focus on speed.

As he told me when I shadowed him, "It didn't used to be like this. People caring about every little detail of the day. It's not horrible [writing Web updates], but it's not what I want to be doing."[4]

He didn't clarify whether he meant that his audience or his editors cared about these constant updates, but it was certainly clear to me that he preferred stories that weren't just event-driven but instead inspired by his reporting efforts.

Juxtaposing these two experiences is significant: Meier fills a vision of the old world of news, whereas Lohr is subject to the demands of online journalism. Some at *The Times* may escape its pull, but only the most vaunted have the opportunity to be totally immune. Instead, for the ordinary *Times* journalist, the environment of online news demands the kind of rapid production Lohr dreaded—an acceleration of the journalistic workflow for an ever-demanding audience—whether editors expecting new content for the Web or the paper's readership. Covering breaking news for the Web was almost a test of endurance, as journalists stared down the unrelenting demand to be first and fast; the presence of pita chips and donuts on big news days were not just for morale, but for energy.

As we will see in this chapter, Lohr was not alone in feeling harried, if not disheartened, by the pace of online news production. While the last chapter looks at the disconnect between print and online in a more global sense—at the organizational level of *The Times*—this chapter provides a close look at what the conflicting nature of immediacy meant in 2010 for the on-the-ground reporters and editors on the business desk. The people covered in this chapter are traditional journalists charged with the majority of original news gathering in the newsroom. They were caught in a struggle in a newsroom that couldn't quite decide what immediacy meant: Was it today's news for today, now, or today's news for tomorrow?

Inside *The Times*, immediacy constrained, ordered, and influenced newswork in a variety of conflicting and confusing ways. On one hand, editors and journalists worked together to assemble breaking stories as quickly as possible, often not without error. On the other hand, *The Times* encouraged journalists to take a step back from the minutiae to give a big, sweeping update (the "second-day story") and write a story for the print paper that would last. Two different goals—one day, one reporter. The result: general exhaustion.

And to what end were the big second-day stories, the tomorrow stories, in the churn of online journalism? Even those protected from doing tedious online updating were now subjected to the demands of the Web site's churn: journalists saw their hard-won Page One story or even long-term investigation fade from the home page within hours. Sure, a story remained on the Web site somewhere, but often out of easy public view, somewhere even reporters commonly had trouble finding it.

New, discordant rules seemed to apply to the competition. Sometimes, the competition really mattered online—if *The Journal* had it, so must *The Times*. On the other hand, sometimes the competition was ignored entirely. The situation with scoops was similarly unclear. Scoops, once the great shining pride of the newsroom, were now caught in a netherworld between print and online; a scoop posted to the Web site could be eviscerated by the competition in a matter of hours, but a scoop put in the print paper could be rendered meaningless by the crush of Web news overshadowing the morning paper. Scoops were central to the journalism ego, but what they meant in the digital age was quite different—and unclear.

The purpose of this chapter is to bring together this variety of experiences of traditional journalists in the immediate online journalism environment: covering breaking stories, writing second-day stories, sizing up the competition, understanding churn, and assessing scoops. Each dimension explored here underscores how immediacy is, indeed, an emergent and contested value of online journalism. Journalists do not know what it means, but they know that it is increasingly ordering how and what they do and that it is essential to the quality and perception of the work they do. Journalists face a Sisyphean struggle with the ever-present content demands of the Web for more, new, now; yet after they produce something, they are only asked to start afresh and produce more. As this struggle goes on, immediacy in turn reorders news routines, practices, and role perceptions of what it means to be a journalist and to do journalism in the digital age.

A New Catch Line at *The Times?*

Online newsrooms live in the now. *Gawker,* for instance, notes, "There's a new catchline on the media kit: Whatever we think. Whatever we know. That's what we'll publish."[5] And this mentality has similarly caught on at *The Times,* where journalists write what they know as they find it out. We get some sense from Bowley in Chapter 2 about what immediacy feels like for journalists at *The Times,* but I was also able to capture one particular story as it unfolded, headline by headline, lead by lead—for what was, at the time, the all-important "jobs" story.

The jobs (or unemployment) numbers for the previous month are released by the Bureau of Labor Statistics at 8:30 a.m. on the first Friday of each month. During the Great Recession, the "jobs" story usually made the front page and was the subject of much attention. In the newsroom, these numbers were viewed as a bellwether for the economy, and outside the newsroom, politicians and pundits made much noise after their release.

This story is a good example of *New York Times* journalists running about like Web hamsters in action and of the repercussions of creating breaking news content. Along the way, there were missteps and errors in the crush to get the news out fast. As reporter Peter Goodman began to shape the story for the print paper, as he had been instructed, he got word from Page One that his lead wasn't "breaking news" enough—even though, by the time his story would go out in the print newspaper, the story, on the monthly employment report, would be about twenty-four hours old (depending, of course, on when a reader picked up the print paper in the morning), underscoring the old immediacy versus the immediacy of online journalism.

Goodman spent most of his time writing big feature stories about the state of the economy. This is an important side note, because not all journalists face constant immediate pressure at *The Times* all the time, so when they do, it is perhaps all the more jarring to their daily routine. For instance, Goodman was hard at work on the feature series mentioned earlier, called "The New Poor," a Page One-or-bust series. Still, Goodman, despite his vaunted status in the newsroom, was also on call to write a big breaking story for the Web.

The goal for the "jobs" story, at least in its breaking stages, was to be able to post it the moment the new numbers were in. This was a far cry from the richly textured stories that Goodman usually wrote. Nonetheless, the newspaper tried at least to somehow make sure that this humdrum story might have a bit of a different flavor from what competitors would write about the jobs numbers. This was the supposed "value-added" element to separate *The Times* from the "commodity news" that other news outlets would have.

So as we saw with Bowley's Goldman story, the strategy was to create B matter that could be put up as a placeholder to differentiate *Times* content, with a prepared lead ready to insert the latest numbers. Reporter Javier Hernandez, with guidance from Goodman, actually prereported the jobs story with quotes from people about the possible numbers. In fact, as Hernandez joked to me, he had even gotten quotes from a factory that had people "banging down its doors to get jobs," as well as a quote from an unemployed person frustrated with the situation. Hernandez added, "We always try to find at least one unemployed person for this before the story gets written."[6]

In the case of this story, we can see some of the strengths and limits of immediacy. On March 5, 2010, Web editor Mark Getzfred and Hernandez were ready for the unemployment numbers. At 8:30 a.m., these numbers first came up on the Department of Labor Web site, and nearly instantly, CNBC repeated the numbers on the air. Getzfred sent an IM to the home page editor to request that he put up an alert across the top of the home page.

Hernandez put the numbers into his B matter. In February 2010, job losses were down, from 109,000 at the beginning of January to current losses of 36,000. The unemployment rate remained steady. The headlines and leads changed rapidly over the course of the morning, as we can see below.

> **Headline 1, 8:47 a.m.** "36,000 Jobs Lost in February; Rate Steady at 9.7 Percent"
>
> **Lead 1, 8:47 a.m.:** "Friday's losses were less than the estimates by economists, who said that a series of winter storms were likely to affect the employment numbers."

There were a few typographical errors in the rest of the copy of this first story, including a stray comma and an extra space, and a sharp-eyed reader alerted *The Times* to the errors.

> **Lead 2, 9:26 a.m.:** "Just as unemployment in the United States seemed to be abating, the government said Friday that the economy was hit with another round of job losses last month."

Hernandez then added this section to the story, following it with an analyst's comment:

> The job losses reported Friday were less that [*sic*] the consensus estimate of a 68,000 decline for February.
>
> At a time when doubts about the recovery are surfacing, the report did not offer a clear snapshot of the economy's underlying health. Analysts generally expect the jobs market to improve this year, but only at a grudging pace.

Headline 2, 9:31 a.m.: "U.S. Job Losses in February Obscure View of Recovery"

At this point, Getzfred had encouraged Hernandez to start adding his "value-added" content about the unemployed worker and the company with job hunters. But after Goodman arrived at the office, something important happened: the lead and headline completely changed in tone.

Headline 3, 9:41 a.m.: "Jobless Rate Holds Steady, Raising Hopes of Recovery"

Lead 3, 9:41 a.m.: "The economy lost fewer jobs than expected, the government reported Friday, bolstering hopes that a still-sputtering recovery is beginning to gain momentum."

Note that the changes were from "hit with job losses" and "grudging pace" to a "still-sputtering recovery."

This third lead and the dramatic change in tone are noteworthy. The initial *Times* online story had added the wrong emphasis—seasoned editors, in the rush to put up the numbers, had missed the big picture. Goodman had come into the newsroom around 9:40 and, with a quick look at the numbers, alerted the team working on the story that they had gotten it wrong: this was good news for the American economy. Getzfred and assigning editor Dan Niemi had seen years' worth of jobs reports, but they hadn't picked up this detail from the numbers. Instead, it took someone who wasn't working minute by minute to pause and think about the report.

The headline and lead had been wrong all morning. The breaking news was misinterpreted for the first two hours of the day. Immediate is not always right. This is an important lesson, as readers may not read the story again; policy makers may begin to issue statements; and, in the case of business news, financial decisions may be affected.

Then, Goodman's day officially began after Hernandez stepped down from the immediate update duties. Around 10 a.m., Goodman took over the story, working to add more substantial analysis, though he would also be providing more online updates—with the goal being a 1 p.m. deadline for the first "print" deadline, for the *International Herald Tribune*'s Europe edition.

The lead changed again around 11 a.m., and Goodman became the sole author on the byline for the article.

Lead 5, around 11 a.m.:

The American economy lost fewer jobs than expected last month and the unemployment rate remained steady at 9.7 percent, the Labor Department reported Friday, bolstering hopes that a still-tenuous recovery may be starting to gain momentum.

The government's monthly snapshot of the job market found that another 36,000 jobs disappeared in February—hardly cause for a celebration.

Yet compared to the monthly losses of more than 650,000 jobs a year ago, and against a backdrop of recent news that increased the possibility of a slide back into recession, most economists construed the report as a sign of improvement.

"It's strikingly good," said Dean Baker, a director of the Center for Economic and Policy Research in Washington, who has been notably skeptical of signs of recovery in recent months. "It's much better than it had been looking."

The analysis was starting to take shape. Goodman had had a good three hours since getting into the office to analyze the trends in the data and begin taking the story in his own direction. The time gave him the chance to provide more analysis than the prewritten story ever could.

He provided additional analysis as the 1 p.m. *International Herald Tribune* print deadline edged closer:

Even as the report eased worries that the economy might teeter back toward a decline, it did little to dislodge the widespread notion that the recession has given way to a weak and uncertain expansion, one that is unlikely to provide the robust growth in hiring needed to cut significantly into the teeming ranks of the jobless.

Some 15 million Americans remained officially unemployed in February, and more than 4 in 10 of those had been mired there for longer than six months. The so-called underemployment rate—which counts people whose hours have been cut and those working part-time for lack of full-time positions, along with those out of work—reached 16.8 percent of the work force, up from 16.5 percent in January.

This version, 950 words, would be printed in the *International Herald Tribune.* It would also remain the online version for most of the workday.

After the Page One meeting at 4 p.m., editor Winnie O'Kelley came over to talk to Goodman, concerned that his lead was "too featurey." Goodman had been told by O'Kelley to take the story in a more thoughtful direction throughout the day. O'Kelly had likely figured the news would seem stale by the next morning, having been up on the Web site all day, but Page One still wanted the hard news.[7] The story would, indeed, be aged news by the time it hit the next day's newspaper stands and driveways. But this was immediacy for the print paper.

The final story was posted to the Web at 9 p.m. Though Goodman made only one Web update on his own (the *IHT* update), a team of journalists was required to keep this story up to date and ready for the Web with breaking news and added analysis—four people, one story, and five updates before 1 p.m. But when the morning crush subsided, Goodman had a chance to do some "real" reporting; he had time to speak to the secretary of labor and a number of economists, and he also analyzed the economic data. He had left the morning immediacy of the Web behind.[8] Having access to the secretary of labor (Hilda Solis) and the nation's top economists was a *Times* luxury that few other papers could replicate. In Goodman's case, this meant a huge advantage for *Times* coverage, with "value-added" content from top sources.

Online journalism demands the quick story, the instant interpreta-tion. But the print story Goodman began preparing for the next day's paper demanded the attention of a journalist uninterrupted by con-stant updates. However, the home page and the business online editors wanted new updates with fresh insight about the jobs report. Good-man provided some, essentially rewriting the morning story by early afternoon. The immediate updates had the newsroom in constant mo-tion, but focusing on them also meant the story was actually wrong for a good part of the morning.

Were these journalists hamsters running around simply to publish what they knew now, as opposed to what they would know with some analysis—publishing for publishing's sake? Or was the goal to produce a seasoned story with deeper quotes and more analysis, albeit "aged news" that would be old by the next day—but immediate according to print standards? This jobs story underscores the tensions facing the newspaper and a team of journalists, as they tried to navigate a thicket of competing imperatives over what immediacy meant online, what their obligations were to this goal, and what they ultimately were sup-posed to be producing for the print newspaper.

The "Second-Day Story"

In the world of immediacy, instant news updates are privileged by those manning Web operations until other, print-focused editors determine that it is time to focus on the print story. These more print-focused edi-tors also want a big take-away piece the *same* day for the print paper. In the newsroom, this is called the "second-day story," a name adopted from the old model of a follow-up piece released the next day that was used to explain the news story as it had evolved over the course of the day.

Wire news organizations have been updating stories throughout the day over most of the past few decades. And at the end of the day, these wire services will often do a "write-thru" to finalize the lasting edition of a story, or the big "take-out," as many journalists refer to this story. But now, print newsrooms are doing the same thing. However, the second-day story in the digital age is different for newspapers, and perhaps also for broadcast and cable news channels planning their evening coverage, as the story needs to offer more than just a summary of what has been on the Web all day. Unlike the wire story, which every outlet can use, the second-day story now aims to be unique and specific to a particular news organization.

The second-day story routines reflect how people have adapted to using technology to advance the news. First, because the story is intended for the print edition, the second-day story has to be built to last. In the past, there hadn't been competing Internet coverage that was up all day for readers to consume on multiple outlets. But the built-to-last idea suggests that, even with content that is constantly updated on the Web, the print version of the story should not "feel" old, because it will bring readers a more complete version of the story. Thus, in the Web age, though the second-day story form uses old technology (print) for its distribution, it is a new type of story because it requires journalists to take a step back and find something new that represents what *The Times*' final word will be on the matter after a long series of updates. It is now a "magazine" story for the daily news cycle, as one editor explained to me.

The result was crushing to some of the journalists I met, who hadn't expected their life goal or their tenure at *The Times* to fulfill these competing imperatives. The pressure to do both the immediate story and the second-day story was difficult for many reporters, as they felt compelled to serve two masters. For some reporters, including those who had come from wire services, being at *The Times* was supposed to mean more time for considered reporting. They weren't supposed to have to keep up with constant rewrites, and while they didn't mind writing for the Web in principle, they didn't want to have to chronicle every small development of a story. These reporters felt breathless at times, as they tried to figure out how to feed both online demands and print demands.

Reporter Ed Wyatt explained how the process of updating a story online made him feel like the wire reporter he was when he began his career. Wyatt had recently moved from working as a business reporter in the Los Angeles bureau to covering regulatory affairs out of Washington, D.C., for the business desk. Unlike other reporters I spoke to,

Wyatt seemed to have an explanation for the obsession with immediacy: keeping up with the competition:

> When I got out of business school, I was working for a wire service, Dow Jones, and the emphasis there is speed and getting a story up as fast as possible, reporting a story with enough info to write a headline and two or three paragraphs and send that out. . . . Now without a doubt, I will write something for the Web immediately, [and] it's almost exactly like reporting for a wire service. . . . I didn't think that I would be at *The Times* as a wire service reporter, and it is a trend back toward that, and it is discomforting. You have to react to what's out there from AP and other newspapers but also react to what every blog has posted out there.[9]

Wyatt also felt that he had to match everything other organizations were covering on any breaking story, including blogs *The Times* now found reputable. He saw this as a consistent complaint:

> It's a common complaint about the arena that we are in that as reporters you have to respond to everything . . . everything. Every blog report. Editors see it and they want to know why don't we have [it]. And sometimes we don't have it because it's not true. Sometimes other people have different sources. Sometimes we can learn something and we can confirm it, but it leaves less time for original thought when you are chasing everyone else's reporting.

Notably, few reporters mentioned to me that they felt they were chasing other people's reporting. But this fear is worth noting and perhaps subconsciously drives some of the frenzy.

So, with this note about competition and added value in mind, how well do second-day stories work? I asked Wyatt how he felt about second-day stories more generally. He noted:

> It's good in theory. . . . Yeah, it make senses that we want to do that . . . and we want to have added value and we should in the

story for the newspaper, but if you have to spend time writing the updates and story for the Web, it cuts into time [you need] to ruminate for bigger thoughts. It's good theory, but in practice doesn't always work.

To Wyatt, overlaying the second-day-story approach with a need to write Web inserts was something that cut into his ability to craft the larger narrative for the paper, even though there was considerable pressure to come up with something new. Wyatt, at least, had been unable to see how to make a new routine work where he could cover a breaking news story online and still write a differentiated second-day story. The promise of a new routine was there, combining both online and print, but he couldn't do it yet.

Other reporters also found the pace of reporting and writing the second-day story difficult to maintain. As one reporter said to me:

The pace is simply unsustainable. Maybe you can ask someone to come in here early in the morning and start doing that, but they are going to burn out. You can't have someone doing that regularly. Maybe the young people can handle it, but it is not a way to do this. And then you turn around and write a longer story for the paper. That's like two entirely different stories in one day.

This reporter had adjusted to the idea of writing for the Web, but not the demands of the new routine—and she or he wondered whether doing so was even possible.

Other reporters had a mixed view. I spoke with Jad Mouawad, who was responsible for less breaking news. When he was responsible for a breaking story, he said, he also saw it as similar to the wire service where he had started. Mouawad also had not expected to be doing constant updates at *The Times*. Instead, he wanted to spend his time thinking about the big story, rather than putting out inserts as they came. He told me:

I came from a newswire [Bloomberg], so the whole immediate reaction, immediacy reactivity, bang a story and get it out, bang six stories [and] get them out each day, that's something I am used to, but it's not something I thought I would be coming over here and finding. That's a big surprise to me and one of the biggest changes I've seen in the six years I've been at *The Times*.

The immediate needs of all the news all the time on the Web has taken over. We are now asked to do a lot of things, get news out very fast, feed the Web site, the *International Herald Tribune*, and do eight or nine versions, do something for the Paris deadline, and flip the story around and write a second-day analytical piece that seems fresh. This is not what you would have done ten years ago.

There are more demands on time. Some reporters in the newsroom [as they work to promote themselves] send out tweets, some will proactively use their own social networks to reach more people, but I'm just working on that.[10]

Journalists were not unprepared to work at this intense pace, but they were still trying to figure out how to perform the balancing act *The Times* had asked for, between producing online content and producing the second-day story. A very senior reporter told me that online writing meant thinking about things she hadn't expected to:

I spend more time than I ever thought I would thinking about online. Of course I would always have to think about photos, but now I am thinking about online as well. . . . At this stage in my career, I should be spending my time having long lunches and cultivating sources. But that's not the reality. Things are moving much quicker.[11]

The reporters acknowledged that they were more than capable of producing a second-day story for the print paper, but the breakneck pace of doing so made it hard to sustain this effort on a daily basis. In fact, to them, it was antithetical to the very idea of being at *The Times*. Many saw what they were being asked to do as cutting off potential venues for more in-depth reporting opportunities. The need for speed was harming the ability of journalists to dig deeper and to spend more time looking for stories; after all, it's hard to cultivate stories if you can't get out of the newsroom for lunch. This complaint, voiced by a few journalists, did not seem to have changed the overall quality of what the Page One editors believed *The Times* could provide, but some journalists certainly felt they didn't always have a chance to do their best work.

Ironically, despite the seemingly endless demand for online content ASAP, *The Times* print newsroom wanted that second-day story. So this really meant journalists had to be writing—and reporting—two entirely different types of stories at the same time: a breaking news story for the Web and a longer, more thoughtful, "value-added" story. It was this "second-day" story that seemed to matter at the end of the twenty-four-hour news cycle, while the in-the-moment updates mattered during the news day.

Here, we see the way in which immediacy emerges as a contested value for journalists as they go about trying to do their work in the online newsroom. On one hand, in breaking news situations, they are given the imperative to work swiftly and produce regular updates to feed the demands of the Web. Immediacy is ASAP; immediacy is valued as the essence of nytimes.com online journalism. But on the other hand, immediacy creates a strain on the lived experiences of what reporters are actually able to do: it is exhausting and hard to sustain and certainly not what they thought the illustrious *New York Times* was supposed to care about. On the other hand, they're told to scale back their pace on the very same day and write something lasting— something for tomorrow but written today, a story that will make the aged news seem, well, less aged and more a symbol of *The Times* setting the agenda. So reporters are caught in the middle of a newspaper that has not figured out what it wants to be—and the strain is telling.

Churn

To many other journalists, the result of immediacy was not just physical exhaustion. There was also, at times, a defeatist attitude when journalists realized that their work—even their best work—would not be on the home page for very long. They understood that the Web site was focused on getting out new and fresh content, but to the journalists with whom I spoke, this also meant that readers didn't have the chance to absorb the stories that these journalists had spent so much time on. What was the point of writing a second-day story if it would only be on the Web site for a short time? It would reach the print readers, but not the Web readers who, having seen the story developing over the course of the day, might never see the final story unless they checked back in the evening or early in the morning. Even big projects could fade into the netherworld of the Web site; though there might be subpages showing a big series' content, chances are that the home page would stop linking to this content after a day or two.

During my stay at *The Times*, business editor Liz Alderman was rotated up to the home page to get a better sense of *The Times*' digital experience (she was on a year-long visit from the *International Herald Tribune's* Paris bureau). She had the perspective of both the home page and of editing on the business desk and commented on the churn:

> We here at the home page think we should be changing it every five minutes—but there's a real question of how often to update—is it for the news junkies or every few hours? . . . I don't know why they update the Web when they do. It's different . . . if you are cranking something out versus [putting out] a polished narrative.[12]

Alderman questioned the discrepancy between what she understood to be her goal on the business desk—pushing her reporters to create "value-added content"—and how long this content would actually last online.

Other journalists were similarly frustrated by the constant motion that seemed to make their stories disappear. As reporter Diana B. Henriques complained one day:

> I'll have a Page One story one day, and then my sources will call me and tell me they can't find it online. It's because it's disappeared by morning into the headlines. That's life, I guess. It's

good for the paper, but I don't know what to tell my sources. Sometimes it's as if my story didn't exist.[13]

By morning, Page One stories were gone from the home page—and largely gone from view, as well, unless a journalist, source, or reader happened to be Googling a particular story. So that important story Henriques wanted to send to her sources wasn't featured anywhere prominent anymore (though late at night, it would have been).

To those closest to the Web, this churn of stories was just fine. As editor Kevin McKenna explained to the business staff one day:

> You're not going to find stories up there all day, you're just not. These stories have to move and change as we have new content. This is not the [print] newspaper. It has to be more dynamic. You're not going to find your story from this morning's paper still featured on the [business] Web page by 4 p.m. That's the nature of the Web.[14]

But to many journalists writing these stories, immediacy was not a particularly fulfilling newsroom value. From the perspective of workflow, it meant pushing out content as fast as possible, only to then rewrite the same content for the next day's print paper. To what end, though? All that work went into stories that would quickly be replaced and then forgotten in the six-hour turnover Sussman had mentioned. For *Times* journalists, ASAP online rhythms meant that a day's—or a month's—hard work could be displaced with a few clicks and a few hours on the home page.

Competition in the Digital Age

The Times' attitude toward competition online further underscored the ambiguity surrounding immediacy in the newsroom. Depending on my vantage point, one day I would see journalists vexed by the appearance of a story (or the speed of news) on a competing news site, while on other days, journalists paid no attention to the competition online.

Watching journalists discuss what appeared online suggested that *The Times* hadn't quite made up its mind about whether to try to keep up with the competition or to be aloof and follow its own path.

A snapshot back to Mick Sussman, the day home page editor, illustrates the unpredictability of whether online competition matters. He was monitoring the competition—*The Washington Post*, the BBC, *The Wall Street Journal*, and CNN—but I only saw him actually check them three times. Here he was, the home page editor, only just barely paying attention to the competition. From my observation, these quick checks did not impact what stories he placed where or which stories he thought were most important. In fact, only once did he point out that *The Post* had a story *The Times* did not. Sussman learned that it was a *Washington Post* story about governors quitting and how that could be dangerous. But Pat Lyons, his editor, pointed out that the "could cause danger" perspective really didn't make it news, so that story was nothing for *The Times* to be concerned about.

Nonetheless, on the same day, those concerned with the home page were stressing about not having the same photo that other news outlets were using on their home page. Sussman and the global home page editor were debating whether to use a picture of a Muslim teenage widow who had set off a suicide bomb in Moscow. Other news outlets had splashed the arresting photo on their morning sites, but *The Times* did not want to use the photograph unless *it* could independently verify the picture. Eventually, the home page photo editor was able to identify the photo's origins, and the group decided to give the picture "a good run."

So did these top online editors *care* about having what other news sites had, or did they not? Sussman illustrated that he didn't want *The Times* to miss major stories, but he didn't let the home pages of other sites dictate his own news judgment. At the same time, not having a key photo that others did have absorbed newsroom conversation for at least thirty minutes, a seeming eternity in Web time. Standards for competition were hard to understand in this constantly updating Web world.

In other instances, the simple presence of a story could prompt business editors to react and encourage a response story. In chapter 2, we saw how, when *The Journal* posted a story about the iPad's name being potentially offensive to women, an account that the tech desk had initially dismissed suddenly got written about in a blog post. Other cases elucidate how a minor story popping up on *The Journal* home page could set off a chase to get something for *The Times*.

On April 13, 2010, assigning editor Dan Niemi noticed that *The Journal* had splashed a story about Lexus being downgraded in *Consumer Reports,* just the latest after a long series of struggles from Toyota: "Sometimes people will see this stuff and think it's a big deal, but I argue against it. There's not much credence to *Consumer Reports.*" He added, "Sometimes people will see something on *The Journal* but their Web page just splashes stuff, it's not always important." Nonetheless, the auto team had a blog post on the subject, and the home page was pushing it for the front. As more details became available, the story emerged as a significant detail in the Toyota saga of 2010, in part because Toyota was pulling this Lexus model off the market. But was the early story—the *Consumer Reports* story—worth chasing simply because *The Journal* had it?

Some journalists argue that it isn't important to keep up with the latest developments. As one editor explained to me, the goal was *not* to beat Bloomberg, *The Wall Street Journal*, Marketwatch, Reuters, or the *Financial Times* every time they published something. As one editor explained, "You don't go head to head, you're zigging when they zag, you're competitive on the big story." In other words, the big story matters, not the small wins.

Is immediacy about chasing down the small story? Is it about being the first to get out the story—or is it not about beating Bloomberg? *The Times* hadn't quite figured out whether it wanted to be the comprehensive site that captured everything or to be more selective in its offering. Despite the ambiguity, one thing was clear: Competition meant something new for online journalism, where an immediate response could counter another newsroom's offering. Instead of waiting for the next day to respond to something *The Times* had missed, the newsroom could respond ASAP. The question before these journalists, though, was just how to balance these instant demands, these quick stories, with the more significant stories that would end the day.

A Scoop in a Web-First World

Building on the idea of competition, scoops in a Web-first world further illustrate how immediacy remained a contested value. The fact that *The Journal* had the Lexus post up before *The Times* was not really a scoop. Scoops had to focus on more than just small developments—the scoop valued in the newsroom is the one that shows the clever reporting of a dogged *Times* reporter. But then a question arose: publish the story online first or wait for the print paper? Saving the story for print meant that it would be blatantly clear the next morning that *The Times* had something *The Journal* did not. But online, the win would not be so clear: *The Journal* could pull together a "matching" story to make up for what it had missed the night before.

One certain advantage for *The Times* in the digital age was that *The Journal* had fairly early print deadlines for three editions, between 6 and 7 p.m., between 7 and 8 p.m., and between 8–10 p.m., which generally meant that anything *The Times* put on its Web page at 9 p.m. was unlikely to make it into the print edition of *The Journal*. At least on paper, *The Times* would win the morning, and to people for whom print mattered most, that would mean *The Times* had won. As we have seen, some of those people are at the head of the news organization.

When weighing what to do with a scoop, *The Times* had to decide what mattered more: putting the story up first online or putting the story in the paper. But there was a great fear that these scoops would be ephemeral—that these hard-fought stories that ideally demonstrated distinct *Times* reporting would be eviscerated by an ASAP culture of immediate 24/7 reporting. The value of a scoop inside the newsroom had little to do with what journalists believed the story offered to readers, and much more to do with reporting prestige and beating the competition. Scoops were different from covering breaking, event-driven stories. These were humdingers, special stories, exclusives that no one else, theoretically, had the gumption to find. And it was all the more important that a scoop would be a win.

When journalists talked about scoops during my time in the newsroom, they considered the competition, but they were also considering their own self-worth. The better the journalist, the better the news organization, the more frequent and enduring the scoops. Inside the newsroom, scoops were rewarded. In fact, some newsrooms offered not just internal emails from top editors brimming with praise, but even small financial rewards for big reporting successes. Some of the scoops close to my time in the newsroom came as the product of intense investigations, like the *Times'* scoop that New York governor Eliot Spitzer was taking part in a prostitution ring.[15]

Financial editor David Gillen explained his view of what scoops meant in terms of a story that he thought counted as a scoop, even though it wasn't the first story on the topic up on the Web. He explained that his reporter had written an exclusive story about how a Galleon trader's wife was about to file a "crazy lawsuit for $500 million," which, rather significantly, included allegations of insider trading. *The Times* couldn't run the story until the suit was filed, but a Bloomberg reporter was in the courtroom when it finally was and "snapped the headline." Nonetheless, Gillen counted the story as a win:

> The snap . . . didn't take the suit for what it was, which was outrageous allegations and a crazy tale. . . . *The Times* story hit the Web site in eight minutes, and it was this utterly complete yarn about the story. I said we beat Bloomberg. Every day we lose to them, but nobody had that story, we beat them, and CNBC credited us with the story because we had the most complete version.

He went on to note, "You can win in the morning and lose the story. I'd rather win the story." This idea of "winning the story" seemed to fit into the overarching idea, echoed by many editors at *The Times*, that the longer, more fleshed-out story, the "value-added" story, was the one that would ultimately matter more. And similarly, winning the story also seemed to me a way to enshrine the time journalists needed to do in-depth reporting that might ultimately carve out more important facets of the story. But winning in the morning was what the Web demanded, and the question before *The Times* was whether any readers would still be around to see who had won the story by the end of the evening.

A hard-fought scoop about Goldman Sachs illustrates the conflict editors faced about how to time an exclusive story. In late May, reporters covering Goldman Sachs discovered that Goldman's clients were worried that the firm had "dueling roles"—both gaining profit for itself and making sure its clients were making a profit. These two goals would seem to benefit both parties. However, Goldman was "shorting" the very toxic assets clients wanted them to sell—or betting against their clients. As such, Goldman was putting its own interest ahead of its clients'. The reporters had documents proving that particular clients, such as Washington Mutual, were concerned.[16]

On May 18, 2010, O'Kelley told the editors at the morning business meeting that Page One editors wanted to see the story right away, so it could go up on the Web as soon as possible. "They want CLIENT on the desk now," she said, referring to the story slug. But the story wasn't actually posted on the Web until the evening for a number of reasons.

O'Kelley explained to me that a strategy affected when "CLIENT" would be placed on the Web site. She noted, "If you put the story up at 6 p.m., you give the competition more time." The business desk, at least, didn't want to release the story in a way that could put *The Journal* in a position to match it both online and in the morning's print paper, though other editors at the newspaper were eager to break the story. This indicated to me that the norms about when to push out a scoop were still being informally contested and negotiated inside the newsroom.

But the story was also complicated, and putting it on the Web before it was ready might even have been dangerous for the newspaper. "It's a story you don't want to rush. It was carefully lawyered," O'Kelley told me the next day. The story went up on the Web site at 9 p.m., past the early print deadline of *The Journal*. In this case, this strategy gave *The Journal* a chance to match the story online, but not in print, signaling how, on the business desk, at least, *The Times* still thought the print-edition scoop was what mattered. And even after the story was posted to the Web, the reporter who had gathered up the long paper trail of documents supporting the scoop wanted to make them public—but wanted to be sure they would not go up at the same time as the story.[17] If the documents went up too soon, they could give other journalists at rival news organizations a chance to write their own credible, document-based stories. As a result, these documents were posted at midnight. *The Times* alone had the scoop. O'Kelley tried to explain how the strategy worked:

> It depends on a story. When it's a matchable story and there's direct competition, we still hold things back, but it doesn't happen that often. This was one of these cases where we had to weigh the competitive point for how easy it was for *The Journal* to match it.

A number of conflicting online priorities are revealed through this Goldman example. First, there was pressure for the story to be put online immediately—this time from top editors. But the business desk pushed back, concerned about competition. So here emerged a question that flowed through many of these scoops: Was *The Times* going to put its stories out before the print deadline for its paper, or was it going to wait and publish these scoops after someone else could get them? This uncertainty surrounding how to deal with a scoop illustrates the tension surrounding immediacy: some in the newsroom wanted the ASAP win; others wanted a compromise; still others seemed to think that the Web stood in the way of *The Times'* authority, originality, and competitive edge, because print was more important. Whether readers would actually notice a scoop (and where) was entirely absent from the conversation.

Immediacy, Online, and Print in a Digital-First World

Immediacy emerges as a contested value as it is negotiated through a wide variety of work routines and experiences of journalists at *The Times*. The tension between print and online underscores how traditional values clash with online journalism values; the two production cycles and their aspirations are distinct from each other. Print privileges long debate, communal conversation, and lasting stories, while the Web emphasizes quick turnover and rapid decision making in the hands of just one or two gatekeepers. The print world values story development and the belief that *The Times* ought to provide a distinct, authoritative, and lasting voice about a story or issue. Online, the churn of stories makes it nearly impossible to achieve this permanence (though, of course, the stories never vanish entirely from *The Times'* sight, just from the readers' likely ability to find the story).

Journalists don't talk about immediacy as a "value." In fact, to some degree, immediacy seems imposed by technological forces of digital production seemingly outside journalists' control, such as the speed of the networked information environment, for instance. But ultimately journalists are the ones deciding that immediacy matters—and this value is articulated by the emphasis on a variety of actions and strategies to create content. Journalists manning the Web site have decided it is important to keep the site looking new, "fresh," and continually updated. Why? Because immediacy has become a way that *The Times* has begun to define what counts as good journalism in the digital age. Journalists charged with providing rapid updates to the Web on breaking news stories do so to feed the demands of editors pushing for this content and to meet the expectations of the hungry Web site. But the Web site itself isn't even capable of being hungry; it's the journalists and editors at *The Times* who have decided that immediacy is going to be critical to establishing *The Times'* authority in the case of breaking news. Immediacy has become a defining principle that guides routines and motivates actions in *The Times* newsroom.

But clearly, immediacy is far more complicated: the realities of producing online journalism to meet this new standard run afoul not only of established understandings of worth in the newsroom but also of the actual capacities of journalists to do their jobs. Immediacy is a contested and emergent value that has not been fully accepted by the newsroom, as print still retains its era of mystique and importance. Journalists don't want to have their stories be part of the churn of online; they want something lasting, and their editors think about and plan for the elusive Page One spot. From the perspective of developing the value-added content that *Times* journalists talk about, there seems to be no probable way of supplementing the process of developing news stories through critique and conversation without regular daily meetings that follow the print news rhythm. Just how to value a scoop in the online world—whether it is online first or print first that matters—underscores the ambiguity of immediacy in the digital age.

Traditional journalists find themselves at the crossroads, trying to understand what immediacy means while still trying to work in the service of "aged news." At times, they are the hamsters described by Dean Starkman, updating content for the sake of updating content. They are asked to write multiple versions of the same story, only to write an entirely new story up to *Times* standards for the print paper—leaving them exhausted and disheartened. They see their top stories vanish from the home page in six hours and then further reduced to headlines in subpages within a day on a site that, according to editors, receives 50 to 60 percent of its traffic from the home page.

And yet often, as we will see in the next chapter, journalists are asked to do more than just write stories—they are also asked to make their stories go beyond just text and include interactive elements. Interactivity does offer a pause to the churn, at least temporarily, as journalists work to think about new ways to tell stories to keep people on the page longer. Interactivity offers journalists the chance, at least most of the time, to think off-deadline about the potential for their work. But as the next chapter makes clear, interactivity, too, is a contested value in online journalism. The impetus for interactive work comes from both the top and the bottom of the newsroom hierarchy, but that does not mean that journalists have figured out how to incorporate it into existing routines or that they even welcome it as a new addition to their work. The next chapter, then, goes beyond immediacy to tackle interactivity and its influence on the practices, norms, and expectations at *The Times*.

Indeed, there were new values orienting journalism practice in an online journalism world: immediacy, interactivity and participation. News routines were being restructured and renegotiated in this uncertain environment. What these values meant, and what consequences they might have for journalism, was emerging through both practice and normative assumptions about what journalism ought to look like in the online journalism world. Interactivity—often called multimedia by journalists in the newsroom—brought a new lens to storytelling and presented the audience as more active agents of news consumption. Interactivity challenged how traditional journalists understood their work and, in fact, reoriented the very structure of the newsroom.

Chapter 5

Interactivity

WHAT IS IT? WHO ARE THESE PEOPLE? AND WHY?

When newly anointed Pulitzer Prize–winning journalist Matt Richtel gave his thank you speech in front of *The New York Times'* staff, he made specific mention of *Times* staff members that no other journalist had ever given a nod to at this kind of gathering: the people who make video games in the newsroom. He proclaimed, as if it were still a surprise to him, "And, we have video game making skills. Old-world journalism is the essence of new-world journalism. The series was long form [journalism] with video, audio, and, yes, video games."[1]

The "video games" had made an impact on the newsroom. Not only had the games themselves generated massive Web traffic, but they had taken Richtel's series about "Driven to Distraction"—driving with cell phones—to a whole new level. Safely, from the comfort of your computer, you could try a simulation of texting and driving. One of the games tested your ability to navigate highway toll booths while responding to text messages about your favorite dessert from a mock cell phone.[2] The subtext of Richtel's statement to the newsroom was quite powerful: traditional journalism was only one element of telling stories now. Interactivity enabled journalists to create a whole new experience for readers.

At the same Pulitzer festivities, Michael Moss, who had won a prize for explanatory reporting about tainted beef, lauded his videographer for being able to really make the story of one survivor particularly vivid. One of Moss's stories detailed victim Stephanie Smith's descent into a health condition that ultimately left her paralyzed. But you didn't really feel the impact of what had happened to Smith until you saw what had become of her. An emotional video told her story: she was twenty-two when she went to her mother's for a home-cooked hamburger. The careful Web video narrative showed us that she was now in a wheelchair, partially brain damaged, with clearly impaired speech as a result of salmonella. This video accomplished something, Moss said, that his stories had not been able to: it put a personality behind the story of tainted beef, one that anyone reading his story could click on and see. This was a new, powerful way to do journalism.[3]

From the bully pulpit of a Pulitzer win in front of *The New York Times'* New York newsroom, these two journalists were proselytizing about how multimedia storytelling had fundamentally changed the journalism they were able to do—and, indeed, had helped them win journalism's highest honor. This was significant: despite the presence of many new, talented journalists who had the expertise to shoot video, create interactive graphics, put sound to audio, and beyond, many traditional journalists had yet to see their new colleagues' value. But these Pulitzer winners were impressing upon the newsroom that working with these new faces was the future; not only had it helped them garner their prizes, but the kind of journalism they had helped create was establishing a new standard for online journalism. In fact, interactivity in online journalism was emerging as a new value orienting the products, processes, routines, and normative professional assessments of journalists inside *The Times* newsroom.

Most journalists in the newsroom used the word *multimedia* to express this new kind of storytelling in journalism. However, I use the term *interactivity* to talk about the large value reorienting online journalism, bringing the on-the-ground conversation of journalists up to the conceptual level. Interactivity is a concept long used in scholarship about user-to-computer interaction, and it helps explain on a broader level the new capacity of users to control the way content is selected or presented to them, whether text, audio, video, multimedia, or something else.[4] Thus, interactivity combines two concepts: online, not only are there new tools for storytelling, but readers are also more directly involved in manipulating their experience of news content.

This chapter underscores the emergence of interactivity as a guiding, albeit contested value of online newswork at *The Times*. Gans and others argue that news values are the result of the clash and combination of external, internal, professional, and normative pressures on journalists. The emergence of interactivity as an online journalism value follows a similar pattern. External economic pressures motivated top newsroom executives to hire new staff and to talk boldly about creating interactive forms of storytelling for both business and editorial reasons. Internally, there was a felt top-down mandate to incorporate interactivity into daily workflow; journalists were compelled to take part in a variety of newsroom initiatives that promoted the centrality of interactivity to their lives. From a professional perspective, journalists negotiated what it meant to do newswork at a time when there were new journalists with new tools and new capacities in the newsroom—some with titles and abilities that many traditional journalists had never even heard of. There was a reassessment of what it meant to *do* journalism in an online environment, as journalists struggled to incorporate interactivity into their workflow. Some journalists readily welcomed the opportunity to try out new forms of storytelling, while others clung steadfastly to old traditions, despite recognizing that the future of online journalism required being able to incorporate interactivity into their work product.

Interactivity was both contested and affirmed inside the newsroom; like immediacy, it was a felt imperative and a new value orienting online journalism. In this chapter, we see how journalists negotiated interactivity as part of their workflow. First, we see top-down/external pressures for encouraging interactivity in the newsroom, illustrated by the comments of top management executives. To management, interactivity was both a strategic way to get clicks for dollars and good editorial planning. The focus on interactivity from the top could be seen in a variety of ways, most explicitly through the presence of multimedia, interactive news, and Web producers brought in to create the fancy Web work that would make a story live beyond its text concept. A brief introduction to these new types of journalists and the way they discussed stories underscores the emergence of interactivity as shaping online journalism in new ways.

Traditional journalists negotiated what interactivity meant for their work in a variety of ways. A common theme emerged: there was no clear routine for incorporating interactivity into online journalism. For some journalists, this meant considerable frustration. As I spoke to many journalists, it became clear that interactivity, at least to almost all traditional journalists, was the "other"—an intrusion on workflow, a mandate from the top, and a task done by *someone else*. For other journalists, however, interactivity was a tremendous opportunity from the bottom up to experiment with new forms of storytelling and embrace the potential of online journalism. In fact, this chapter offers a snapshot of multimedia and traditional journalists coming together to create a project from the bottom up. Overall, the newsroom, for the most part, accepted that interactivity was, indeed, going to be a value orienting online journalism—but what interactivity meant, and how it would be integrated into workflow and professional practice, remained contested.

The Practical Reasons for Embracing Interactivity

To top management, there was a clear reason to embrace interactivity in the newsroom: it was one possible strategy to respond to the felt need to create a more profitable model online. Both top business executives and newsroom managers were well-aware that they needed every eyeball on the Web site to generate as much revenue as possible. One common strategy was the idea of making a Web site "sticky"—the principle of getting people to stay on a site for as long as possible—as opposed to conducive for bouncing from site to site.[5] Time-on-site is a valuable Web metric that could be sold to online advertisers, and more sophisticated Web measurements could actually track just how much a user was manipulating online content. The better the result of each, the more online content providers could be justified in charging for advertising.

Creating a stickier Website did not have to compete with *The Times* editorial mission—in fact, it could complement it. Whenever top brass spoke about the future of interactivity (or "engagement") at *The Times*, they noted both the editorial and the business goals achieved through the process. Developing user-to-computer interaction, as well as participation via social media, were crucial next steps in the future of the news organization. Senior vice president for digital operations Martin Nisenholtz noted in a speech to the University of Pennsylvania Wharton School that *The Times* was focused on understanding how "the roles of engagement [for the user] are so different online." He then gave an example of the traffic accomplishments of a recent audio slide show to illustrate the economics of an interactive environment. Nisenholtz told the audience, "Our investment in video is also paying off with increased engagement. User sessions that include a video view last much longer than those that do not, on average." Human connections, via interactivity, could be bought and sold for newsroom survival.

But business goals also benefited editorial content. Nisenholtz went on to explain the following:

> One of our great accomplishments over the past three years has been to build an intersection between technology and journalism. . . . Certainly we've made great strides in digital storytelling, in data visualization, in video and multimedia, all of which is helping to build a tighter emotional bond, greater engagement.

For him, one of the core questions to answer was this: "What is 'storytelling in an interactive network'?" And his answer was that content must "creat[e] an essential human connection." He implied that text storytelling wasn't enough; there had to be even more, such as a Web video that would speak to the audience in concert with a much larger explanatory reporting piece. *The Times*, he felt, would have to find ways to incorporate new opportunities for interactivity at a time when users had increasing control over their information environment.

Nisenholtz was a top business executive, but his understanding of the benefits of interactivity from a business and an editorial standpoint differed little from the opinions of those in the upper echelons of the newsroom. Managing editor John Geddes spoke to the twin needs of economics and a more sophisticated understanding of the way people engaged with storytelling in the digital age. As he put it:

> The world is changing and consumption of information is different. How people want to consume it is changing. . . . That is going to be the long-term differentiator for *The New York Times*. There are going to be many ways for people to become aware of information. . . . We have to appeal to people [in new ways]. . . . There is huge money [coming] soon from this.

Interactivity would be key for *The Times* to survive in a digital environment; the top brass hoped to develop a focus on creating content *other* than text that people could consume. And if *The Times* could do this well, it could capitalize on ad dollars and make money off the efforts.

On the other hand, Geddes also noted the new mandate ahead for *The Times* and its editorial mission:

> I think the job for us is to write [the story] once and edit and present it in various ways for various audiences. . . . We have to do things across multiple platforms. We have to re-learn how to publish in new ways.
>
> We have to get past the written story bias. . . . There is a logic in not being defined by print and not by thinking about the limitations, but thinking about what is possible on the Web.

At the moment, as Geddes acknowledged, the newsroom was still stuck in a print-first mentality. But interactive content was a way to rethink entirely what it meant to create *Times* stories, and it made sense in a world that was no longer exclusively defined by the paper experience.

Nisenholtz and the business team would provide the budget for hiring the multitude of staff that could create interactive content. Geddes and his cohort of top editors would be charged with setting the newsroom mandate. But the trickle-down of this understanding at the top about the importance of interactivity to the business model did not translate to the rest of the newsroom. To other journalists, interactivity was yet another felt demand of doing journalism in the digital age; it was a new editorial aspiration of online journalism, but not a business strategy. Top-down demands came packaged as editorial missions, and the few bottom-up efforts were envisioned as new ways to involve the audience and gain traction for a story in the newsroom.

What was clear, though, was that interactivity was going to be embedded in *The Times*, whether traditional journalists liked it or not: a massive team of video, multimedia, and "interactive" journalists were now part of the newsroom, along with Web producers whose skills went well beyond content distribution. These were the new faces in the newsroom—meeting new job descriptions that had never even existed at *The Times*. As one traditional journalist put it: "I know who some of those people are, maybe I know their names, but really, if you asked me, I have no idea what they do."

We saw Andrew Martin, in Chapter 2, visit a videographer on his own initiative to discuss new stories, without asking his editors or even giving a second thought as to whether this effort was worth his time. *This was rare in the newsroom.* Martin had realized the merits of video after working on an exhaustive series and now wanted to have it in all of his stories. He was embedding it into his workflow, adapting and changing how he was planning to report his story, and working hand in hand with one of these new faces in the newsroom. This was bottom up, and he was in the minority. But for those who got it, like he did, interactive journalism was, indeed, part of the future of *The New York Times* and less of an obligation.

An Introduction to Interactivity

Before seeing how interactivity made its way through the newsroom as a contested value negotiated in newsmaking, it is important to have a sense of the players in the newsroom charged with creating the interactive experience for the user, most notably video, the interactive news team, multimedia, and Web producers. These journalists were now part of the established process of creating the big-gun stories like Pulitzer packages, sitting in on early meetings when these stories were just in the process of being hatched. From the view of top editors, having these people present was not just icing on the cake; it was also a must for any major series—and both Richtel's and Moss's projects involved these groups from the start.

There is, of course, one important caveat. *This* is about *The New York Times*. Not every newspaper can afford to have incredible documentary video teams led by people who have won Emmys or an entire team devoted to creating interactive graphics. The luxuries at *The Times* in terms of size and potential quality were simply not scalable to other, smaller newspapers. That does not mean, however, that other newspapers at the time were not trying to increase their interactive content. Quick scans of job ads, journalism school offerings, and the like show the demand for journalists who, as a *Milwaukee Journal Sentinel* ad put it, have the ability to "improve design, content, community, user interfaces and information architecture" and can also "develop digital news and information applications." In other words, this value of interactivity in online journalism was percolating everywhere, but it could be seen on a massive scale at a place like *The Times*.[6]

Video at *The Times*

At *The Times*, the video unit occupied a permanent home in a corner of the fourth floor. When you walked into this area, video producers were hunched over software not seen elsewhere in the newsroom. The equipment, from cameras to a small backdrop set, also made this area distinct. The offices that line this corner were filled with people who have Emmys from their days in television poking out of their shelves and desks. And the stories that came out of this unit were not the text stories written by traditional journalists.

Instead, as video head Ann Derry described it, her staff was trained and practiced in the ethos of "documentary filmmakers," doing work that was "not any different than the documentaries but [was] now tied into the news cycle as a four- or five-minute piece."[7] In her view, it was important for the video desk to figure out stories that really merited being told through video:

There are some projects that are great projects but are just not visual. The best projects that lend themselves to video will have good visuals and good audio and good characters, and I think the best video is one that is complementary, not the same story.

The video department made "cherry-picked"[8] selections about which stories it would be involved with, due to a paucity of videographers and a wealth of stories. Similarly, not all stories are well suited to video, especially when the video head runs her shop like a documentary film site, rather than a 24/7 breaking-news desk. So there was unlikely to be an iteration of nytimes.com TV covering live, breaking news events under Derry's reign, though videographers were sent around the country and the world to capture compelling stories that would be folded into the Web.

The home page had a video player that Derry carefully guarded. What was there should be "broadcast quality. . . . What you would see on TV is what we produce and should be able to produce because it's *The New York Times*. We bring the technical craft of the high-quality film- and television-making and the journalism of *The Times*." But video was not alone in, well, producing video. The video desk overlapped with the Web producers, who also shot videos, and with the multimedia desk, which often also included video elements. And reporters might go and shoot their own videos (of varying quality). Derry noted that these overlapping roles at *The Times* meant that "everyone has a stake in this."

Interactive News, the Multimedia Team, and Web Producers

Other forms of interactive content invite the user to become part of their own storytelling process. Web producers, the interactive news group, and multimedia designers all help produce these user-to-computer creations that make the Web site sticky and change the practice of storytelling. Notably, the divisions among the groups I mentioned are quite blurry, because what appears to us as an interactive experience can come out of one of these groups at *The Times* or perhaps even these groups working together to create a single package. These journalists may not come from traditional journalism backgrounds at all, but may instead be specialists who know how to program or who understand the vagaries of Web design. Others may have gone to school for journalism but now specialized in these new ways of telling stories. And the very existence of these teams was still quite new: the interactive news team had only been created in 2009.

The interactive news team in 2010 was charged, generally, with the creation and display of tools allowing users to manipulate data. This group, with its strong programming background, created lighter projects like interactive Oscar ballots allowing users to cast their votes and in-depth graphics letting users go through and figure out the water quality of their homes. Led by Aron Pilhofer, this group actually was both a business and an editorial desk, as its mission was to help develop the Web site, as well as to create editorial content. Pilhofer, a former data reporter, had taught himself programming skills; his desk was the melding of these two aspirations. Though the team worked on news projects, it often worked more like a software team, going into "agile mode" (a form of software production) to create big projects, and it relied on those skilled with user experience, design, and back-end programming.[9]

The multimedia desk (not to be confused with the more general term *multimedia* used by many at *The Times*) was also a crown jewel of the newspaper. It had won an Emmy in 2010 for the series *One in Eight Million,* which profiled fifty-four New Yorkers in weekly episodes. The desk was led by Andrew DeVigal, a former staff artist and graphic journalist and later a Web producer. DeVigal was aware that, to Nisenholtz, "engagement was the new black," but it was also an editorial mission ("part of the consumption of content"). One of the goals of the multimedia desk was to put a layer of visual narrative with photo and video onto a story in a way that could do more than just complement the print story. DeVigal noted that the goal of multimedia was to "create character-driven narratives that are beautiful and visual," and he emphasized the importance of using audio to serve as a backbone for the underlying experience. But there was crossover between his team and Pilhofer's, as DeVigal's staff also created interactive graphics and included people with backgrounds in programming.[10]

The lines between the interactive news desk and the multimedia desk were quite confusing, as Pilhofer explained:

> Generally, I would say we are more about building backends, specialty/event Web sites (Oscars, Olympics, elections). If there is a database involved, we're involved. Multimedia is more about visual/audio storytelling, character-driven multimedia. They also build storytelling tools for producers. That's a radical simplification, and there's a lot of overlap.[11]

The teams often worked together. For instance, the project *Faces of the Dead,*[12] a multipage living memorial to Iraq and Afghanistan War casualties, which combines video, audio, and interactive graphics, was created by members from all of these teams.

Web producers are also key to the interactive content creation at *The Times.* They may shoot video, for instance. And while most are not heavily engaged in programming, they use templates to create audio slide shows, timelines, and other graphics that respond to and complement *Times* content, as Danielle Belopotosky did for Sewell Chan's Chairman of the Federal Reserve Ben Bernanke's interactive timeline (see the introduction). These Web producers may also make audio slide shows. Sometimes, they are tasked with coming up with multimedia ideas for stories or are the center point for coordinating a larger multimedia project for a specific story.

Whatever the role descriptions of these individuals and teams, *The Times* has many people at work creating a multimedia experience for users. The work of these particular groups—multimedia producers, graphics, interactive graphics, and Web producers—is a signal not only that a story will be told in a new way but that the user can choose how much or how little he or she wants to learn about the story and can construct his or her own experience of the narrative.

The felt need to create these teams and hire these people signaled a strong investment in interactivity as part of the growing space of *The*

New York Times on the Web. These new people, who might not have been fully integrated into the daily work routines of newswork and whose job descriptions might still have been uncertain, were creating new venues for storytelling. And one of the most notable differences was the way that these journalists actually talked about creating stories for the Web with interactivity in mind. Their sense of what was significant, removed from a print-first bias, offers some insight into the way multimedia workers at *The Times* thought about their role at the newspaper.

The People Who *Are* Interactivity

The people who grasped interactivity were generally separate from the traditional newsroom. What had once been the print/online divide was now mirrored in the interactivity divide between the print/online newsroom and the multimedia journalists who were working to create content that others in the newsroom liked but didn't quite understand. After all, these journalists' jobs didn't exist ten or even five years ago. From their conversations with each other, it is clear that they had a much different understanding of the potential of storytelling. A typical Web producer meeting and the design of the interactive news desk suggest some of these major differences.

In the newsroom, Web producers were helping advance what *The New York Times* would and could do in terms of multimedia. Each week, all the Web producers who were working during day and early evening hours had a Tuesday-afternoon meeting in the Page One conference room. Only the folks explicitly manning the actual production of content on the home page at that moment were missing. In these meetings, generally led by the news editor for nytimes.com, Amy O'Leary, or by Fiona Spruill, the editor of emerging platforms, the members of the Web team would go through the brightest spots at *The Times* and on competition sites.

One meeting seemed to bring home to me, as an observer, just how in tune these Web producers were with the kind of content that was possible in a more sophisticated Web environment for interactivity.

Shortly after a massive 7.0 earthquake hit Haiti in 2010, Web producers gathered for a show-and-tell of the best Web coverage of the story.

The producers began by comparing general coverage, noting how the CNN page was focused on how to help, while the *Miami Herald* site had actually begun translating things into Creole. News sites other than *The Times* had shown up higher in Google News searches, in part because they had focused on pushing out headlines, instead of writing longer stories.

But the heart of the meeting was a comparison of Web graphics. *The Times* had been able to use satellite photographs to allow readers to zoom in on the damage via an aerial map, giving readers the chance to use their mouse to see the ruins.[13] "I think this really gives people a chance to see for themselves inside what this actually feels like," O'Leary said.

O'Leary also began to go through some of the slide shows that *The Times* had taken, highlighting the work of photographers and Web producers who had brought together text and photography to tell a compelling story that went beyond the photos themselves. The photos, she acknowledged, told their own story as well, but the captions and text gave readers a sense of place. Notably, in these instances, Web producers had worked with photographers closely to get the adequate context and select the best photos.

The Web producers compared *Times* interactive graphics to competitors' sites—even those of international newspapers. Nevertheless, though the interactive news team, along with Web producers, had worked on a twenty-four-hour schedule to put together a graphic series of maps to help readers understand the damage,[14] their efforts were not comparable to *El Mundo*'s work.

El Mundo, the Spanish newspaper, had gone beyond what *The Times* had done. Amy O'Leary explained, "*El Mundo*, which for those of you who don't know, is the main newspaper in Spain. They did this destination site." She went to the site and showed that it had even been configured to show a shaking screen: "*The Times* is not yet configured to do that kind of interactive."[15]

The conversation then began to focus on whether *The Times* should consider purchasing a 360-degree camera like CNN had. The

360-degree camera allowed viewers to "use [their] mouse to click and change the view . . . zoom in, zoom out, and change the angle," all while the camera was moving on top of a CNN van.[16]

Everyone in the room marveled at just how cool the effect was.

"It really feels like you're there," said one Web producer.

"It's amazing," said another.

"So should we get one?" O'Leary asked.

Another Web producer pointed out that it was very expensive, and O'Leary agreed.

One Web producer pointed out: "There's no narrative rationale for context or impact; you're just zooming around."

Adding to the conversation, another producer noted a difference between CNN's coverage and *The Times'* work: "There's no real storytelling. There's a reason that you want a panorama inside with text."

O'Leary agreed: "You want to script, annotate, or map this thing, and it would be difficult with this technology."

The Web producers agreed that, while this might be the right technology for CNN, a news organization focused on the visual, it was not the right type of technology for *The New York Times*.

The conversation at this meeting reveals a number of important views of interactivity among those most open to the idea. O'Leary began the meeting by looking at competitors, signaling that, from the top of the Web producing hierarchy, there is a strong recognition that this part of the newsroom, at least, views interactivity as a central entry point for readers/viewers to major events. And to them, interactivity *was* workflow, something to be expected as part of any breaking story—hence the twenty-four-hour attention by the interactive news team and multimedia producers. And the focus on the competition shows that these Web producers did not want *The Times* to be left behind on the latest advances. To them, a subject like the Haiti earthquake concerned a far-away place that many people had never been to, giving photos, visual storytelling, and interactive graphics the opportunity to tell the story in ways that text simply couldn't.

But for these journalists, interactivity was not just about putting a camera up on a screen and giving readers the chance to scroll around. Interactivity did give users control over how much they saw and when they saw it, but *The Times* had control over the key message of each story. To these journalists, it was important that each interactive element tell a story with a narrative arc, with a clear and defined purpose. This way, the graphics could stand alone and inform the reader; they could be used not just as supplements to text, but as stories in themselves. However, the integration of these new journalists into the existing workflow, as well as the acceptance of interactivity into the daily life of *The Times*, was generally deeply contested. Most felt interactivity was a top-down imperative, and nothing seemed to demonstrate this more clearly then when *Times* head honchos decided to mess with the Page One meeting.

TimesCast

Cameras? In the meeting that *The Times* described as journalists sitting around a table gathered to decide the most important stories in the world? Should these conversations be recorded? The answer, for a brief time in the newsroom, was yes. The push for interactivity from the top meant that *Times* journalists were now going to be engaged in a new experiment called *TimesCast*, a five-minute Web video that would include snippets from the Page One meetings.

The Wall Street Journal had been steadily attracting viewers with *The Hub*, a five-minute newscast about the day's stories. It was rumored among business desk editors that top editors had launched *TimesCast* to compete with *The Hub. The Times'* five-minute program was intended to offer juicy tidbits for the true news aficionado: First, viewers would see bits and pieces of the Page One meeting, with editors giving tidbits of top stories. Then there would be short interviews, much like the one with Graham Bowley described in the second chapter, just to whet people's appetites for the big stories in the next day's paper. The goal was to bring people inside the daily workings of the newsroom without giving them too much information about exclusive news.[17] And the economic rationale for the experiment was made clear to the newsroom by the big ad buys of FedEx, which had purchased (in advance) short commercials to air before *TimesCast*. As one business editor noted, "This thing is going to bring in some money. Did you see how big those FedEx ads were?"

The plans for *TimesCast* had been in the works for months before the launch. When I started my research in January, videographers were wandering through *The Times* newsroom with their cameras, trying to figure out which meeting would give viewers the best visual of a day in the life at *The Times*. Editors in Page One meetings prepared for the spring launch of *TimesCast* for months, and they were literally coached by video editors about how to act in front of the camera. Page One meetings, until the decision to tape them, had been a free-flowing conversation. But the presence of the cameras interrupted this. The editor directing the meetings told the other editors to present a "lightning round" of non-exclusive news for the camera and then instructed them to hold their exclusive news until the video team finished taping. The practice-makes-perfect implementation of this new routine in the meeting took months—and editors kept messing up. In fact, the break between lightning news and exclusive news was imperfect, and editors had a difficult time getting used to the practice. Once the tapings began in earnest, video editor Ann Derry had to keep reminding editors that she could edit their comments if they slipped out of the "breaking news first, then exclusive news" order.

The introduction of *TimesCast* was controversial. I was at a meeting in the newsroom (not in the business section) where editors complained that *TimesCast* was "horrible," that it "looked like acting," and that the conversations seemed "forced." Others were concerned about the competition, noting, "I think the only people watching this are our competition." In the initial days of *TimesCast*, people were bemused by a *Gawker* write-up of *TimesCast* called "Desire under the Big Red Stairs," which turned the broadcast into a mockery drenched in sexual innuendo.[18]

In another vein, *TimesCast* also meant that editors could have their mistakes broadcast over the Web. These mistakes might happen in ordinary conversation, but now anyone could see them. For instance, Bill Keller misspoke on the second day *TimesCast* was live on the site (March 23, 2010). He made a mistake about Britain expelling the head of Israeli intelligence. This mistake was caught by a Reuters reporter, and soon thereafter, the "story" was blasted across the blogosphere. Clark Hoyt, the public editor, wrote about it in a weekend column:

> "Agh," wrote Keller when I sent him [the Reuters reporter's] message. "This is why I went into print rather than TV." Because *TimesCast* is taped and edited, Keller said he should have said, "cut," and given a more careful summary of the story then in progress. Ann Derry, the editor in charge of the paper's video operations, said, "Several pairs of eyes view every segment— and the entire show—before it goes up." She said they all missed Keller's errors and will "'button up' our procedures going forward."[19]

Some on the business desk warmed up grudgingly to the idea of *TimesCast*. David Gillen, the editor principally responsible for financial news, told the morning business meeting a month after *TimesCast* debuted that he was ready for prime time. He announced, "For *Times-Cast*, I'm keeping a tie in the drawer." And then, he commented about who he thought happened to be watching the video:

> I was asking [in the Page One meeting] are people looking at this? But apparently some young people are. Someone tweeted it when it was late and said, "Where's my *TimesCast*?" More people are looking at it than I thought.[20]

Another business editor, however, was a little more hesitant about being constantly on guard. She was worried that she might be asked a question that could be put on video for the public at any time. She was asked about a story for *TimesCast* and was barely able to get something off that "sounded intelligent and like I knew what I was talking about."

But the new reality at this time in the newsroom was the message that everyone should be ready to be on *TimesCast*: people needed to be prepared for the things they said to be distributed on the Web. Interactivity via this new multimedia initiative was a new reality. And it came from the top. Jane Bornemeier, a major developer of *TimesCast*, was pleased to see how far the newsroom had come by allowing people to shoot in meetings: "If you had tried this a few years back, this would be no way. You can tell how far we have come."[21] But perhaps this change wasn't due as much to letting cameras into these meetings as, perhaps, to a begrudging acceptance that including multimedia was the new reality.

Ironically, the *TimesCast* Page One meetings had become less meetings than forms of acting for the audience. The meetings actually took longer, as editors went into free-ranging conversations after the cameras went off. The editors eventually got sick of having the cameras obstruct the natural flow of conversation, so the video crew was kicked out of the Page One meetings. But the Graham Bowley–type interview, where a reporter is asked with little preparation about a breaking story, continued to be featured prominently on *TimesCast* and paved the way for future *TimesCast* iterations.

The mandate to experiment had come from the top, and experimentation meant an adjustment period for journalists. *TimesCast* faced resistance as a top-down imperative. While some journalists were willing to accept *TimesCast*, others were threatened—especially when it compromised the vaunted Page One meeting. Nonetheless, this was a powerful lesson: journalists were going to have to accept the presence of multimedia in some way, whether they liked it or not. Interactivity was imposed as a new online news value from above, at least in this situation, and journalists were not quite sure what it meant for their future.

The Multimedia Virus?

One journalist grimaced at a colleague on a brutal breaking-news day, "multimedia is a virus." This might have been said in a moment of fury: he had just been asked to record a podcast, shoot a video, and then write a breaking news story. And he hadn't even met most of the people ordering him around to do these things. It was as if the drive for interactive content had infected the newsroom—and indeed, it had—and he'd been forced to catch it. Not only that, but the virus was so infectious that, suddenly, all these new people with strange new jobs had multiplied, and there was nothing he could do.

To traditional journalists, interactivity was, of course, something that could add to the value of online journalism. But most wanted as little as possible to do with it. They were frustrated with the imperative of more interactive content: just another new demand in the ever-increasing expansion of their jobs in the digital age. This was yet more work. The integration of multimedia journalists into the newsroom was made more difficult for a variety of reasons: first, most story ideas still came from traditional reporters; second, these multimedia journalists had a variety of overlapping titles and responsibilities; third, they didn't quite fit into the ordinary workflow. Perhaps most frustrating of all to traditional journalists (other than the fact that they felt like they had to do more work) was the failure of interactivity to mesh with their reporting.

Trying to accommodate the demands from the top to help create interactive content was "onerous," according to one journalist. Another's response illustrates the conflict some felt about the message of interactivity—that along with the paper, he was going to have to choose what to focus on, because not everything could be done. It was simply too much work:

> We are trying to do everything. The place has to figure out what it does best and what we are good at. In a time of limited resources, we have video, multimedia, audio, and we can be doing all these endeavors. But we can't be about blogs and multimedia and have a shitty paper—or maybe we can.

Echoing the theme that multimedia meant more work, editor Damon Darlin put it this way:

> It's a lot to ask of reporters if they are reporting to think of video. . . . It's more time out of their day. They have to think about how to fit it into their life and style of reporting. There are dedicated video who are conceptualizing and editing it, but it [workflow] is something that the paper as an institution has to figure out.[22]

Darlin noted the fact that multimedia could feel like an added obligation to the work that reporters already had. Interactivity was the new reality, but it was also added pressure on an already overtasked staff.

Reporters were especially frustrated, because they did not know how this new imperative of interactivity would fit into their work routines. There were now new people that they had to get along with, fit into their reporting schedules, and generally be aware of when they might otherwise just be focused on writing a story. If the reward for writing a big story was freedom from immediate deadlines, the punishment was now being forced to do interactive content.

One reporter working on a long series complained about how he was now being forced to work with interactive staff:

> It hits me that this multimedia stuff is hellishly disorganized and usually ends up being a whole mass of logistical conversations and email miscommunications about what the story is, and in the end they don't do the thing they were going to do. . . . They haven't figured this out at all.

He went on to explain his typical experience: He'd pitch a big story, likely aimed for A1, which would then catch the attention of someone working with interactives. He would almost immediately begin hearing footsteps from multimedia staff members, video team folks, and so on, which underscored the lack of coordination between all of the teams in charge of multimedia content. He continued:

> I just start getting emails from people, and sometimes I've met them and sometimes I haven't and I don't know what they do. . . . I have to have [all these] emails with different people, and they want the story before I have done any preliminary reporting. I don't know the focus of the story yet. And when I am reporting, I don't want to have to spend an hour of my reporting time with a video producer guy because that's time I'm not doing the story.

In echoing the theme of miscommunication, this reporter's words demonstrate just how emergent this culture of interactivity was in the newsroom, with journalists with overlapping goals asking for his time.

Journalists were especially resistant to the differences they saw between traditional and interactive workflows: these journalists were frustrated that they would have to change how they worked in order to fit in with these new people who had different job demands and expectations. Interactivity was an interruption. One reporter similarly noted the clash between interactive and traditional workflows:

> I'm a print reporter, so my interviewing style and management of story style is different. Eliciting information from people who don't want to talk to you is different from persuading them to get on video or taped in some fashion. The timing is different. I have to get the people who I want in multimedia earlier, but I might wait to the end of the story to talk to them.
>
> . . . There's a fair amount of wasted effort on both sides. I can't figure out the arc of the story, and sometimes it means that someone has to be interviewed by me and then by someone else.

Other reporters echoed this refrain of competing work routines:

> The writing part can go very slowly. Sometimes reporting can take three, four, five times to get everything you need [e.g., calling a source]. With filmmaking, they want one direct shot because they don't want to keep flying out to do this.

For journalists, then, interactivity often meant doing more work and coordinating different workflows.

From the perspective of traditional journalists, interactive work processes themselves were actually incompatible with traditional reporting. As with immediacy, there was a felt, urgent demand for interactive content, with an even more confusing idea of how it was supposed to fit into journalists' reporting lives. Writing for the Web they could handle, but directing a multimedia team was not something

they saw as their job. They didn't doubt that interactivity was important—no one said this—but they didn't want to have this become part
of the normative process of their newswork. The perspectives of these
individual journalists could also be seen, though, in larger organizational attempts to incorporate interactive content into the newsroom.

Multimedia Meetings: Trying to Bring
the Process under Control

Because interactive content was not yet part of the everyday work flow,
some editors struggled to bring some order to the process. In these efforts, there was a veiled hope to make the connection between print/
online text production and multimedia production more coherent. This
way, workflow challenges could at least be coordinated. Business desk
editor Kevin McKenna and Web editor Amy O'Leary decided to have
regular meetings to plan multimedia content, but this wasn't a practice
common across all departments. In fact, as far as O'Leary knew (as the
news editor for the Web site), no other desk had these meetings.[23] But
what was also clear was that interactive and more traditional ways of
thinking did not quite meld; multimedia staff thought of different ways
to tell stories and sometimes envisioned their work as stand-alone offerings, whereas traditional journalists thought that this work was a
complement, if not an add-on, to what was already being offered.

Almost every Tuesday, after the morning editors' meeting, McK-
enna invited the business Web producers, the graphics staff assigned
to business, and the enterprise editor to a brainstorming meeting to
think about multimedia potential for upcoming stories. The idea was
to discuss which upcoming exclusive and feature stories might benefit
from multimedia treatment and whether that might be in the form of
an interactive graphic, a slide show, an audio slide show, or a video.
But sometimes, unfortunately, the people who could make the projects
happen were not in the room to provide the necessary information.

The enterprise editor often had an outdated list of stories, or his
list might not include the independent efforts of other journalists (like
Andrew Martin's separately maintained list of stories in Chapter 2,

which he was hoping to plan for multimedia but hadn't shared with his editors). The list was so poorly maintained that stories on it had sometimes already run in the paper; or they were slated to run without enough time to create a multimedia process; or they were otherwise on the list but not useful to multimedia staff, because they were simply ideas and not even coherent story prospects.

At the meeting, it was easy to see how communication breakdowns could result in missed opportunities for multimedia. In one meeting I attended, the photo editor had already taken pictures for a story about Wal-Mart plaintiffs who were suing the company for sex discrimination. O'Leary asked about the potential characters for multimedia. Vindu Goel, the new enterprise editor, noted, "We are working on a new draft. . . . The women's photos have been taken [a few weeks ago]." The photo editor also noted, "We have taken the photos of the principal people."[24] Multimedia was too late; it had been locked out of the planning process. The Web producers all paused for a moment. O'Leary noted, "These could be great audio clips." Goel responded, "Let me see if the story focuses on that."

This exchange reflects two perspectives. The first is that photo and traditional journalists were working on one vision of the story—in their eyes, the leading part of the story—whereas Web editors saw a multimedia story standing apart from a print story, offering a different perspective. Goel suggested that he had to see whether the story would focus around the two women whose lives had been shaken by Wal-Mart. But the story could do more than this—in audio or video form, as Web producers indicated. However, the mentality that many reporters and editors in the more traditional newsroom had was that multimedia was simply an additive, meant to support the text article.

Despite their drawbacks, the multimedia meetings were brainstorming sessions, with everyone boisterously sharing ideas about what might make an interesting multimedia presentation. In this way, the meetings provided an opportunity for people to formally come together to try to figure out patterns and practices that could help streamline the myriad potential approaches for any one multimedia opportunity.

Consider, for example, the meeting on January 19, 2010. The first story discussed was a piece coming out of Detroit on how US cars were getting smaller. The conversation went from people envisioning a slide show of the evolution of the size of cars in the United States (despite the fact that, as the graphics editor pointed out, there were no hard metrics for this) to another story about businesses that watch people shop. The story was premised on the fact that some stores were installing video cameras to observe customers' purchasing behavior—without the customers actually knowing that the stores were doing so. Web producer Tanzina Vega pitched the story with information she had gotten from the reporter:

> It's like a video ethnography. They are in stores. There are these cameras in stores tracking what you buy and how you buy it. The guy behind it is willing to talk and go on record. Whether a retailer will let us do it [go inside the store] will probably not happen—but the guy will analyze everything and give us good access.

Seth Feaster, a graphics editor, added, "It's like anthropology; they [the stores] are looking at us." Amy O'Leary added, "I kind of want to see the ethnographers talking. Even from file photos, there has to be something he uses for his sales calls."

This particular multimedia pitch was one I followed through to its creation, and as such, I was able to watch it evolve from an idea in January to a story in late April. It took months and months for the story to be reported and additional time for it to become a multimedia graphic.[25] The story went all the way to the head multimedia editor at *The Times*, Andrew DeVigal, especially after Vega told him that it was aimed at Page One. In this case, multimedia designed an entire graphic, but it was considered ancillary to the rest of the story by the traditional journalists. And it could not be produced without the reporter's help.

These meetings underscore the kind of tensions at play between multimedia journalists and traditional journalists concerning differences in workflow and attitude. Even when editors bring multimedia and traditional journalists together, unless the story happens to be a major Pulitzer effort, there is considerable confusion over what stories will get multimedia treatment and, if one does, just how that will be incorporated into the workflow. Multimedia was regarded by most traditional journalists, even the journalists at this meeting, as a complement to news stories, not another storytelling vehicle. However, some journalists did understand that interactivity was more than just a burden, and more than just a supplement, that, indeed, it could be almost more powerful than their own efforts.

The Appreciative

While I've painted a bit of a negative portrait, some reporters were in fact quite pleased with the results of multimedia, seeming to understand that multimedia storytelling took advantage of the Web in a way that their text stories did not. Their positive experience with multimedia might be attributed to the fact that their stories were landing on Page One—and these traditional reporters had been given the royal treatment. The results for these reporters seemed to suggest that, indeed, perhaps text did not triumph over all. But they certainly weren't thinking about how they could tell their stories in different ways—multimedia specialists were doing this work for them.

Some of these reporters were absolutely convinced that interactive experiences could bring more to a story than text alone. Reed Abelson, a health business reporter, explained the benefit of doing multimedia: "I think it's a great way for when people aren't quite getting enough room or space in the story or are reduced to a couple of sentences." Abelson mentioned a story she had written on the lack of research on muscular dystrophy, noting that it was "powerful to have someone talk about that."

Other journalists worked with multimedia journalists on isolated stories but never again thought to propose multimedia treatment for subsequent stories—despite recalling their experience fondly. Julie Creswell, a Sunday business features writer, noted that she had worked on only one major front-page project over the past two years that required multimedia:[26]

I think what we are doing now is putting a lot more data and video and all of these amazing things behind the stories or alongside the stories that enrich them in ways you cannot do in print. Last summer I did a big series, a big story on Simmons, the bedding company. It was amazing to do. It was the first time I really worked with the video team and the data team, and this video series they produced was stunning and added to the story and delved into aspects of story [I didn't. It] touched upon deeper things. It connected the audience in a way the story couldn't quite do.

You were hearing voices of employees, seeing faces of employees, interacting. It gives the stories so much more depth, even more than print, and that's been really fun from my standpoint, growing and trying new things. It's not something I would have expected to have done here, and I'm looking forward to my next project.[27]

But as Creswell told me, this project was geared to be a Page One story. The start of the multimedia project involved a meeting that brought together twenty people in a room to discuss its multimedia potential. That organized attempt at doing a major project may have facilitated her experience. Notably, she had not done any major multimedia or thought about doing any since that project, suggesting that multimedia was not part of her workflow and that it continued to be a top-down initiative.

Nonetheless, some reporters had actually begun to think about interactivity on their own—without the help of multimedia journalists. The majority of them acknowledged that multimedia did mean more work for them. Some of these reporters were like Andrew Martin (see Chapter 2), who reached out to the multimedia staff for help with stories after a good experience on a major story. Understanding the opportunity for interactivity could, indeed, come from journalists in a bottom-up manner, but it rarely did so.

Interest in interactivity from traditional journalists was most pervasive when they were actually able to create interactive projects themselves. Multimedia production became part of what they did, instead of something someone else was doing for them. And its purpose was not duplicative, but rather, in their view, to highlight different aspects of the larger reporting project they had undertaken. In this way, we can see how interactivity may have been less contested for these journalists.

Personal technology columnist David Pogue was one journalist on the business desk who saw himself as benefiting from multimedia—though he argued that multimedia certainly came at a great cost. He starred in a video every week as part of his responsibilities for *The Times* (although it was produced by CNBC). These videos were set at his house, in his living room, and he described them thusly:

> [They're an] illustration of whatever column is that week. . . . I attempt a more entertaining stance. I do accents and characters and have extras and do rudimentary special effects, and sometimes it's more cheesy and funny and looks more ahead than a product review.[28]

But Pogue also described the videos as "a blessing and a curse. It's an exhausting obligation every week. It's lots of prep time." He explained that he had to write a script, which amounted to two columns: "It's something that is added on definitely in terms of workload because in my case the video is not told in the same way as the column at all."

However, Pogue also mentioned the benefits of doing the extra work for the video: "It's a lot of work but it also opens a lot of doors. . . . It's where fans get to know me through videos rather than through written stuff." Pogue was a columnist whose Twitter followers numbered 1.3 million, and his reviews of products were eagerly anticipated. So his belief that multimedia brought him one step closer to being visible to this audience is particularly noteworthy. But he was also careful to point out: "None of this was my idea. None of this was what I pushed for." Still, Pogue's weekly appearance had become part of his routine. In fact, he was in charge of writing the broadcast copy, coming up with the ideas for the segments, and even, at times, getting extras. The multimedia story had become his story.

Other journalists who were able to take ownership over creating multimedia projects also felt that their work was rewarding and even on the cutting edge of what *The Times* offered. They felt empowered as reporters to try new things with their multimedia work. David Carr, a media columnist, also saw multimedia as part of his work. Similarly, his experiments online were also a sign that *The Times* was willing to let journalists apart from multimedia specialists experiment with multi-media. *The Times* let him set up Web video recording equipment in his basement, and he could record multimedia whenever he liked. He noted:

> I wanted to be blogging and doing these almost daily; they don't want that yet—but that fact that I just [asked to film] videos in my basement, and they said, "Okay, Sparky, give it a whirl" [shows that] they are a lot more prone toward beta and experimentation on the Web.[29]

Despite this set-up, and after some initial success, Carr hadn't kept it up. But it was notable that he was thinking about making it part of his routine—even if he hadn't yet made it so. Carr was given the tools to experiment, and he saw that as part of his work, not as more work.

But we should be careful not to assume that only columnists were doing their own multimedia. David Segal, a Sunday features writer, shot his own video when he was on the road for big stories. He had the skill set to edit and shoot, though he admitted that he didn't spend much time either thinking about or planning his videos. He added the following:

> The short answer is I've liked doing it and I've done it. I like shooting and I like editing it. It sort of seems like it is part of the argument of the new dimension of journalism, and I subscribe to that, and I have embraced [it] maybe because I like doing it.[30]

However, Segal wasn't sure whether what he was doing was really having an impact on people visiting the site: "I like doing it, but at the same time it's not clear that it resonates." He mentioned that, when he did a video for a story, the one comment he got was from a *Times* colleague.

Nevertheless, it is interesting to note that these journalists liked the interactive opportunities—in part because their multimedia work centered on projects of their own creation. Segal handed off his project to the production staff for finishing, but he enjoyed the idea that shooting the raw footage was part of his work. Carr got to do his own production in his basement. For them, multimedia was a hands-on activity, rather than one that required constant coordination with a multimedia team to plan stories and shape ideas. This may be one reason why they found it so easy to integrate multimedia work into either their thinking or their regular workflow—it was something they could actually control. These bottom-up initiatives were fairly rare, especially given the frustrations and confusion felt by most traditional journalists about the process. On occasion, though, large-scale projects could emerge from the collaboration of traditional journalists with multimedia journalists without big planning meetings and Pulitzer Prizes as the goal.

Bringing Interactivity and Traditional Media Together

While there weren't many cases of multimedia that started from the traditional reporter hoping to introduce interactivity into his or her story, there were at least a few. And the reporters in these cases didn't see interactivity as a felt imperative, but as a way to enhance their story or even tell it in an entirely new way. For them, interactivity was, indeed, an online value that emerged through the practice of creating content for the Web, and it was something that they thought about from the beginning as they created stories. In my observations, these efforts were generally midsized projects—things that were not aimed at winning Pulitzers but that journalists were still going to be spending a significant chunk of time creating original reporting on. This is what we saw in the case of Andrew Martin's pitches to the video desk for his feature story ideas, many of which involved travel.

One rich example that I saw was the effort of Ron Lieber, a journalist who worked closely with his Web producer, Tanzina Vega, who had been assigned to the personal finance section of the business desk as one of her responsibilities. Lieber, the personal finance columnist, had a positive working relationship with Vega, and together, they had come up with many ways to enhance the blog that accompanied the larger stories he and his team wrote. He also encouraged her to look for opportunities to add video to the site and do smaller projects, like smaller "napkin sketches" that would explain complicated concepts about debit cards and the housing market.

Lieber began advocating in 2009 that, in addition to everyone taking a personal-health day, people should also take a personal-finance day. This would be a day for people to stay home from work and sort out their personal finances. For the 2010 edition, he wanted to offer some form of multimedia. What he had in mind for the story was some sort of checklist that people could use to help them go through the different steps for this "financial tune-up," as it was called. As he realized when thinking about what he'd write, he couldn't fit everything into a single list or column. All the tips would overwhelm readers. Web producer Vega and Lieber began imagining a checklist, something interactive and customizable to give people the chance to figure out the best use of their personal-finance day. In this case, the multimedia component was imagined not only as "added value" but as something that could stand apart from the story itself.

Because they knew that this project had a set date for delivery, Vega and Lieber began planning for the checklist early. The first major meeting called for the checklist was on February 10, 2010—a full six weeks before the checklist and column would be launched. Before that meeting, Lieber and Vega had been talking about the potential features of the checklist, from investments and retirements to loans, credit, planning, and consumer issues. They even started working on a shared Google Documents file about what it would include. The traditional journalist and the Web producer were working together and thinking about combined workflow from the beginning.

At this meeting to really create a bang for the project, Vega brought together people from video; business editor Kevin McKenna, functioning as the Web overseer; Lieber; and Andrew DeVigal, the multimedia editor. DeVigal started off the meeting by asking what Lieber's goals were. This was a useful way to begin the meeting because, as a result, Lieber was not put in the position of thinking up the multimedia treatment himself. Instead, he could leave it to the people who regularly created multimedia to think about the technical aspects, while he helped articulate what other aspects of the story he couldn't convey through text. He began with what he was hoping the checklist would achieve:

> This comes out of a desire to inspire people to take a chunk of time to make a list of things that are undone in their financial life. People who are half-engaged [with this stuff] have a mental list. So if they had eight free hours, and there were ten things they could take care of, this could be an inspiration.

Vega noted another goal: "This is also for people with different levels of financial ability."

Both Vega and Lieber wanted the list to be interactive, but the video editor pushed them to ask what it was that would make this truly interactive beside links, texts, and blog posts. Vega said that she had drawn her inspiration from looking at interactive online checklists for weddings. She thought that, with videos, there might be a way to make the checklist more interactive.

The group ran through a variety of different brainstorming ideas and questions: how to use different colors to indicate the amount of time each task would require; whether the list would be something people could print out or should be designed as something people could come back to online; how to tell users what prerequisites they would need in order to accomplish each particular task; and how to use videos as possible explainers.

The idea of using video in conjunction with a list that people could actually check off took hold. But Lieber said, "There should be something more than just me standing up in front of a video." The video editor assured him that this wouldn't be the case. "We're going to go all James Cameron on you. You'll have an avatar," he joked. The videos would be used sparingly and only for tune-up items that needed more in-depth explanations.

McKenna brought up the need for a community aspect for this presentation. Vega suggested linking to previous blog posts and having the discussion continue there, instead of using the actual multimedia home as the site. Notably, McKenna also talked about using the print version of the column as a way to draw attention to the multimedia.

Following the meeting, Lieber made commitments to work with the video editor to determine how the videos would look, and Vega agreed to work with DeVigal to continue conceptualizing the checklist (with Lieber's content and input). The group collaborated over the next six weeks through more Google Documents that featured the list of what Lieber would be writing and a brainstorming list for the "video treatments." The group also had informal meetings to produce the checklist.

By March 24, 2010, the interactive checklist was ready to go, as was the column. Vega explained that she and another multimedia editor were doing Web coding by hand up until the last minute. But the reward was unusual for a multimedia project: it appeared on the most emailed list.[31] As Vega exclaimed on March 26, 2010, two days later, the multimedia checklist made it up to the number-two "most emailed" story at the newspaper. "That never happens for multimedia . . . ever," she said.

In a subsequent interview with Lieber, he noted that he was also pleased to see the checklist reach the "most emailed" list. He was similarly surprised, but pleased, because of all the hard work that had gone into the checklist.[32]

In this instance, the planning for the multimedia worked through the coordination of a Web producer and a traditional print reporter. The Web producer helped spearhead connections with other parts of the newsroom, but the print reporter was equally invested in creating the multimedia project. Lieber saw the multimedia not just as an add-on, but as possibly "more important than the story itself."[33]

This multimedia checklist showcases, then, how interactivity was becoming an emergent value. It extended the story beyond its original message and beyond its original form, ultimately providing new information. It did involve more work for the traditional reporter. In addition to his column, Lieber had to think about video and what he would choose to feature in the checklist—as well as how to write the content. And it took considerable coordination and collaboration among members of the multimedia team to produce the checklist. But the checklist was ultimately more successful than the story itself, if the "most emailed" list is any indication of success. The column did make the "most emailed" list, but the checklist outranked it. In the end, to Web readers, the checklist was more important than the story.

Notably, to create this product, much informal collaboration had to happen between multimedia and traditional reporters. In this case, from the bottom up, the journalists could take advantage of the fact that there was not necessarily a formalized way about how to create a multimedia checklist, no routine for how to gather this information or produce videos. All of these work products came out of emergent discussions and activities that valued interactivity as part of creating online content.

The Emergence of Interactivity in Online Journalism

Creating interactive projects in the newsroom is not always easy. But when viewed in contrast to immediacy in online journalism, this chapter's focus on interactivity suggests that this value in online journalism may be one way to escape from the overwhelming crush of churn in the 24/7 cycle. Most of the time, online journalism efforts that focus on interactivity are geared toward the long-term story, the feature, the enterprise, the investigation—this is when multimedia can be planned best. In these situations, multimedia journalists see their work as not just additive, but actually a story in and of itself—and the result may, in fact, be worthy of an Emmy. Generally, traditional journalists I observed seemed most pleased with multimedia when they were part of a large, organized project that was geared for Page One and also had multimedia elements, though as we saw with one journalist, this was not always the case. These big projects were the ones that seemed to matter for both multimedia and traditional journalism.

It is when projects are smaller that some of the workflow problems and culture challenges emerge. But significantly, all the journalists working on these projects are not focused on an immediate deadline. They can sit back and focus on the bigger story, away from the more, now, update crush. This may be why many traditional journalists were frustrated by the intrusion of multimedia; the long story was their break from the pressure of online, instant updates. While interactive journalists do work on daily or 24/7 deadlines, especially in the case of breaking news, the interactions I observed with traditional journalists mainly focused around these long-term stories and what these stories would or would not include.

Almost no one doubts that interactivity ought to be part of ny-times.com; they just argue to what extent it ought to affect their work. Interactive journalists have been hired because top-down managers see the merit both editorially and economically of encouraging content that keeps people on the page and plays to the new ways users consume content online. And the "documentary" quality of work, the Emmys, and the Pulitzers all speak to the capacity of *The Times* to create multimedia work that is seen as the standard to meet in the digital age. So, in this way, journalists have accepted the importance of interactivity and see it as a new value of online journalism. The problem is what this means for the routines, patterns, and work processes of journalists, not all of whom see how it fits into their own work practices.

Thus, interactivity remains contested because it challenges basic assessments of worth in a world that still prioritizes print while simultaneously demanding online content. Traditional journalists value the time they have to work on these longer stories, freed from online deadlines. But online journalism still rears into their workflow and work patterns, creating what seems for many to be more work, confusing organization, and crafting an entirely new set of expectations. For those who have found the merits of interactivity, the process of creating this content is, indeed, a departure from their focus on the vaunted print status. But the reward for their efforts is a product that enhances and adds value to their work by creating additional content that they see as complementary, rather than duplicative. And these journalists believe that interactive journalism online is a new form of storytelling and user engagement that enhances the traditional work that they do.

Ironically, all the effort that goes into interactive journalism is still at the mercy of the 24/7 online news cycle. So while the efforts to create interactivity may mesh with the long-term reporting cycle, this says little about the longevity of these efforts in the crush of updating the Web site. For example, a major story could be posted—a Page One story with an extensive interactive graphic. Months might go into making this multimedia story, but a big news day might crowd out the appearance of the graphic in the mix of bigger stories. I saw this happen with Stephanie Rosenbloom's piece that was spoken about at the enterprise meeting, the one about cameras that watch you shop. Despite all the effort that went into it, in the mix of bigger stories, it was gone within a few hours on the Web site.

What happens to these interactive, even Emmy-worthy features? Like their counterparts in text, they live in the small subpages of *The Times*, away from the home page, which generates 50–60 percent of the traffic, according to editors. They are caught up in the churn of daily content. Interactive products, like the longer stories that journalists write, get lost in the 24/7 world of more, now, constant. While readers may find these stories if they go looking, unless interactive features make a splash on the most-read or most-emailed lists, they are likely to be forgotten. The interactive doesn't even have a chance of printed permanence on Page One in this environment.

The Times will have to do more work to understand the consumption habits and engagement patterns of users to make sure that their immense and intensive interactive efforts are indeed worth the manpower they demand for the economic bump that they generate. But economics is not the only question at hand: Just how does this movement toward interactivity impact online news? What does it say about how journalists understand how news ought to be created and consumed?

In some ways, planning for interactivity on the Web can bring out what online journalism may do best: telling stories and giving users control in ways that go beyond the traditional text story. If the future of journalism is what Nisenholtz and Geddes suggest—a world of engagement where users are focused on directing their own experience of content and consuming content in new ways—then multimedia journalism at *The Times* is a way to offer that experience. And the 24/7 crush may be irrelevant if the focus is on getting users to experience interactivity now, today, immediately, rather than on thinking about online journalism as stable and long-term. These online news values may then themselves present conflicting possibilities or complementary ones. What is clear, however, is that interactivity has emerged as an orienting practice, a process that has impacted news routines and set up a new system of worth within the newsroom. Interactivity is part of the new world of online journalism, a new value that shapes how journalism is created and shaped.

Emergent routines, contested news practices, and competing systems of worth in online journalism highlight how new values for journalism are forming in the digital age. We have seen how immediacy presents a contradiction between tradition and the urgent demands of the online reality. But as a felt imperative, it has impacted work routines and order. Even if traditional journalists do not value immediacy as a professional code, immediacy is now *valued* functionally, whether or not emotional value has followed. Interactivity takes a similar path in the newsroom; it has become part of workflow and, albeit in an often contested manner, journalists' work routines. Interactive work gets accolades and support from management, and it offers practical benefits to the newsroom. As interactivity becomes part of news policy, it also becomes an operational news value that orders and orients practices. As we will see in the next chapter, the competing notions of worth around participation, best expressed through journalists' experiences with social media, suggest a new perspective around how journalists may regard their responsibilities to the audience. While participation emerges in reality as an extension of the one-to-many practices of journalism, the idea of bringing ordinary people into the conversation is now a reality of online newswork, albeit a confused and perhaps resisted one.

Chapter 6

Participation, Branding, and the New *New York Times*

Andrew Ross Sorkin, editor of *Dealbook* and columnist, sat hunched over business weekend editor David Joachim's computer.[1] The two were trying to decipher Tweetdeck, the Twitter sharing platform.

"What is it?" Sorkin asked. Joachim explained the advantages of using this site over the main Twitter platform: "You can post the whole URL instead of going to that link shortening thing [Bitly]. And it updates to Facebook automatically."[2]

But Joachim, arguably, was using Twitter pretty poorly at the time. His tweets were composed of links to *New York Times* content, and he only had a few followers, or people who subscribed to his Twitter feed. But he was trying, at least, and doing so without the intervention of the appointed social media editor, Jennifer Preston. And the collaboration between Sorkin and Joachim was informal, rather than the result of something top down. It wasn't going to result in perfect best practices for Twitter use (after all, Twitter itself could update to Facebook, too), but this exchange might have helped Sorkin manage his nearly four hundred thousand followers just a little bit better.

This vignette shows how journalists often taught each other (for better or worse) about social media. And this kind of informal activity had some notable benefits for the newsroom: from the perspectives of branding, revenue, experimentation, and creating relationships with the audience, participation on social media platforms seemed to be a must for the news organization. Like interactivity and immediacy, the value of participation had influenced newswork, albeit in contested ways, on many levels. Significantly, though, participation inside *The Times* certainly did not embody the idea espoused by many Internet theorists about the nature of journalism in the networked public sphere.

When we think about participation from an academic perspective, we think about the social, writeable Web that breaks down boundaries between producers and consumers of traditional media. Users are empowered to make their own content and share it with people they know and don't know (the mantra of YouTube, for instance, is "Broadcast Yourself"). In a social media world, this content produced by users is shareable and spreadable.[3] In fact, that's what we see, for instance, in the generation of memes replicating across the Web: users bring new meaning to these often silly commercials or images, sharing them across Facebook and Twitter.

Participation challenges the traditional norms of journalism by suggesting that anyone, at any time, could become a reporter.[4] News scholar Mark Deuze suggests that journalistic authority is transformed through the "blurring of real or perceived boundaries between makers and users in an increasingly participatory media."[5] By this, he means that traditional journalists and users are now sharing the duties of creating media content, and as such, journalists will have to earn the right to be treated as professionals. Of course, participation has always existed between journalists and their audiences in some form, from letters to the editor to photos bought from ordinary citizens. The public journalism movement of the 1990s and early 2000s sought to bring together journalists and their audiences as part of the story generation and reporting process. However, the participatory Web offers a new dimension to this exchange.

As a result, others imagine a world where journalists and audiences work together via collective intelligence to create collaborative projects. Axel Bruns calls this process *produsage*—and in this pro-am world, distinctions between consumers and producers no longer exist. Together, journalists and audiences work toward the continuous improvement of content in a nearly egalitarian fashion, exemplified by Wikipedia.[6] Internet intellectual and journalism scholar Jeff Jarvis and the London School of Economics' Charlie Beckett both suggest the term *networked journalism*,[7] which "takes into account the collaborative nature of journalism now: professionals and amateurs working together to get the real story, linking to each other across brands and old boundaries to share facts, questions, answers, ideas, perspectives."[8]

But when theory is translated in more practical ways, the utopian ideal can get corrupted. Like the other values we have considered, participation becomes one other possible mechanism of economic survival as newsrooms take advantage of the social Web. Similarly, participation is not always about equal exchange. When journalists heard the message about participation, they translated this as a practical imperative to be on social networks, but they did not, for the most part, take part in a genuine conversation with their audiences. As journalists worked to try to understand participation, there were many hiccups in the road, from resistance in the newsroom to ethical concerns.

There was much at stake for the newspaper to adapt to the new value of participation in the newsroom. Just how much authority would this great newspaper be willing to yield to the supposed new power of the audience? What engagement with the audience was necessary and desirable, and how much of it should journalists do? What were the ethical problems that could result? And could this participation through social media be monetized, in some way? This chapter attempts to get to the core of these questions.

A review of the newsroom's digital social media strategy underscores the top managers' sense of how participation could be monetized; their views suggest a limited vision of the user as anything other than a way to make money. The economic emphasis didn't translate to the editorial side of the newsroom, where top editors failed to consider what participation might add to the conversation. The divisions in the newsroom reveal the variability of the importance journalists placed on making participation part of online news. For some, the newsroom was a welcoming environment for experimentation and learning or an opportunity to try branding and reporting. Others were adamant in their refusals to engage; still others were simply unsure what participation meant in an online newsroom. The tension surrounding ethics, from creating an ethics policy that could last, to avoiding controversy caused by social media, demonstrated just how difficult it was for *Times* journalists to negotiate participation.

In theory, it makes sense to proclaim the dawn of a new age between journalists and audience members. From an aspirational perspective, there is the potential to redistribute the very authority of news production and give new people voices. Yet in practice, this was not so simple—nor necessarily desired or even practical for *The Times*. Rather, what can be seen in the newsroom was a period of transformation, from trying to create a business model to developing an understanding of how to use social media platforms, suggesting the emergent and, at times, contested nature of participation in online journalism.

Who's In the Money?

Even more valuable than a sticky site—the kind loaded with interactive elements—would be a sticky and spreadable site.[9] A spreadable site is one that takes advantage of social content that people can share, comment on, spread across their social networks, augment by adding user-generated content, and even remix—though maybe not all of those things nor all of them at once. A sticky, spreadable site would ideally have the potential to bring in the most money, because visitors would not only stay on the site but also share the site's content with the people who listen to them, read or watch the content they pass along, and perhaps even reshare it. An added benefit is that advertisers know that a participatory audience is a responsive and active audience.

Facebook might have been the ultimate sticky and spreadable site at the time of my research. Facebook was sticky in that users could spend hours and hours scrolling through the site, looking at what their friends were doing, playing games, seeing photos, updating statuses, and the like. But it was also a spreadable site: it served as the vehicle for people to share content about themselves, spread news stories, and comment on each other's profiles. People could post user-generated content, which could then be shared rapidly and broadly across networks.

If it was interactivity—and, to a lesser extent, immediacy—that helped make *Times* content sticky, the next question before *Times* strategists might well have been how to make *Times* content more spreadable. *Times* content, when shared over social networks, talked about on Facebook, commented on, or the like, became spreadable content. And all that interactive content, like the text, was generally spreadable: all the graphics, videos, and slideshows could easily be shared across social networks—and, contrary to the nytimes.com paywall model in place at the time, shared content could be accessed for free—as a way to spread *Times* content even further. The caveat about social media strategy I saw at *The Times* was that it was, in fact, likely to change, and the staff at *The Times* was entirely uncertain about whether any of it would work. But for the period I was there, the strategy revolved around trying to harness the very special audience *The Times* had for its spreadable content.

Martin Nisenholtz, senior vice president for digital operations at *The Times*, noted that one of the questions facing the news organization was whether it, too, could do what Facebook was doing. Speaking to the Wharton School of Business students in 2010, he had this to say:

> By [Facebook spreading itself across the Web], it raises the question of whether Facebook's incredible engagement metrics can now be applied to sites that, today, have implemented only a thin layer of interactivity into their products. I regard this as true for both traditional and non-traditional publishers, with few exceptions.
>
> When Zuckerberg says that "web experiences want to be social," he's not just referring to social sites. He's talking about the need for engagement across the web, including on publishing sites.
>
> ... So in a very direct sense, greater engagement contributes to our emerging business model. This approach is governed by a simple premise: the more engaged our users are with us, the more value we deliver to them, the more likely they will be to pay.[10]

In other words, engagement via social and interactive content, spread by the loyal customer who wants to spend time with *The New York Times* brand and talk about *The New York Times* on social sites, is a survival tactic for *The Times*.

So, if we look at participation from an economic perspective, we see a company that was bound up in branding its reporters and making its content maximally shareable. The top executives were preoccupied, it seemed, with these goals. Engagement was money, whether *The Times* said so directly or not. Consider the following speech from publisher Arthur Ochs Sulzberger, Jr., given at the London School of Economics in November 2011, boasting about a consulting company's report on social media:

> *The New York Times* was ranked Number One as the *most* social company in the United States, based on our social presence. *The Times* scored ahead of powerhouses like Google, Apple, and the Walt Disney Company.
>
> We've put a priority on the utilization of social media. . . . We've had great success building upon our readership that way. We have far more followers on social networks than most other news organizations. The main Facebook page of *The New York Times* has more than 1.7 million fans. And, our main Twitter page has more than 3.8 million followers. That's extraordinary and it doesn't even begin to define our reach since so many of our terrific reporters have their own significant followings on social media. In fact, we have more than 15.8 million followers on Twitter for all *New York Times* accounts. And here is an astounding fact—a *New York Times* story is tweeted every 4 seconds.[11]

What were the implications of all of this? Traffic. Readership. Spreadability. Money. And the best thing about *The Times'* audience, as we will see a bit later, was that it was, as Sulzberger, Jr. noted, "an incredibly enlightened, intelligent and sophisticated group of users who [were] highly engaged with our products"—or more specifically, an audience ideal for marketers.

Was all of this participation implemented with just money in mind? Maybe not. Sulzberger, Jr. did use this speech to talk about *The Times* as a site of democratic conversation. He addressed the moves the news organization was making to include readers. He highlighted the efforts of some of the strongest social media users at *The Times* on Twitter, Facebook, and Tumblr to reach out to audiences in new ways. But when you added up the numbers and potential for expanding *The New York Times'* reach, participation had a strong economic incentive for *The Times.*

The statistics about participation, however, were misleading. First, the @nytimes account on Twitter had 4.5 million followers. A number of key figures (columnists, for the most part) had millions of Twitter followers. David Pogue had 1.4 million Twitter followers; far more people were following his 140-character updates than subscribing to the print paper. Nick Kristof had 1.2 million followers. Other journalists, too, were registering huge numbers of followers. Brian Stelter, media writer, had about 380,000 followers, and David Carr, media columnist, had about 400,000 followers. In contrast, Jill Abramson, executive editor, only had 16,000 followers. In other words, a selection of journalists had most of the followers, while others had a great deal fewer.

Similarly, just bragging about being "the most social" company tells us little about how these journalists were actually using these platforms. A Pew study released in conjunction with The George Washington University looked at the Twitter feeds from thirteen major news organizations and thirteen journalists. The study found that news organizations were much more likely than individual journalists to use the tool to promote their own content. And beyond that, news organizations were far less likely to use Twitter as a reporting tool, or to "curate or recommend information" (2 percent of the time).[12] And a mere 1 percent of those news organization's tweets studied (out of a total of thirty-six hundred) were actually retweets that came from somewhere outside the news organization, such as an individual or another news organization.

Conversely, journalists like Pogue, Carr, Stelter, C. J. Chivers (a war correspondent), and others have developed not only loyal followings but also personal brands. As part of the "*most* social" company, these reporters were helping deliver *Times* content and spread the brand to dedicated readers. Reporters with Twitter accounts and Facebook pages have fans. And the content shared with these fans, on these sites, is both "spreadable" and "sticky." The problem perplexing *The Times* was how to turn these brands into something they could measure and then sell to advertisers. But these loyal fans were certainly an improvement over the aggregate traffic measures online. So while social media editor Jennifer Preston was proud of these journalists who had developed loyal followings, and proud of their audience engagement, an economic motive was also at work. As Jill Abramson, new executive editor of *The Times* as of September 2011, put it in a panel at the annual Austin, Texas, cultural festival South by Southwest, individual *New York Times* journalists on Twitter were "sub-brands" of the news organization.[13]

Preston explained that another aspect of *The Times'* social media strategy was to get readers who were participating on social media sites to come to *The Times* through those social media sites and thereby to develop another type of engaged reader. The newspaper had added a number of Facebook pages where people interested specifically in *Times* content about, say, Broadway or politics or movies could congregate, form communities, and find links back to *Times* content. *The Times* didn't usually ask questions of this audience; instead, someone at *The Times* pushed out a *Times* story, and readers discussed the story among themselves and their friends. The goal, it seems, was to get these readers to come back to *The Times* Web site: this was, in part, a traffic strategy.

However, there was another motivating factor behind the Facebook approach. The hope was that these readers would come to care deeply about *Times* content, enough so that they would become "fans" on Facebook and, as a result, could be mobilized to share content with their non-*Times*-reading friends, thus bringing those friends to the site. And once these readers were on *The Times'* site, the newspaper then made it very easy for them to suggest stories to friends via Facebook (all anyone had to do was click the "Facebook Recommends" link on the bottom of the story). Through this form of social curation—friends suggesting stories to other friends—content would spread naturally.

The Facebook strategy brought together the kind of friend chains that represented what advertisers have, for years, called "quality audiences," or audiences whose demographic profiles made them particularly attractive as consumers. Preston even used the words "quality audience" when talking about *The Times'* Facebook strategy for monetizing this loyal readership. Given the nature of Facebook's ability to chart demographics and traffic patterns, *The Times* knew a lot more about these readers than it ever had before. Facebook fans, and the Facebook Recommends system, were plainly a marketing win.

From the way Sulzberger, Jr., Nisenholtz, and Preston talked, it seemed like *The Times* had a firm digital strategy for social media. However, I think there is also a way in which improvisation (in its elemental form) can be seen at work in the plans they pursued. If improvisation is the process of building new routines out of old ones, we can see this to be the case with this digital strategy. Newspapers needed to come up with some way to make sense of a diminishing regular and predictable consumer base, and now, *The Times'* new strategy, similar to many other newsrooms, was to rely on reader loyalty that flowed through the personal brands of individual reporters.

Past practices dictated that newspapers should try to find audiences marketers would want—wealthy, educated, and otherwise "demographically desirable" people—through traditional methods, like phone surveys or promotions. Now, though, newspapers were still finding these quality audiences, but through such uncharted territories as Facebook groups. And while it was important for *The Times* to find a way to make money online, we need to be critical about the views espoused from the top management about participation. Readers were used for their demographics and their capacity to contribute to reporting, but it is important to question just how much of the rhetoric of Web 2.0 and participation was actually manifested by *Times* digital strategy. From the economic perspective, it seemed to be very little— and perhaps that was entirely logical, given the newspaper's goals.

Interestingly, at no point did I hear from any management figures, who were definitely concerned with the economic impacts of these branding, monetization, and participation proselytizing efforts, any kinds of concerns about *what* these journalists might say. When

I talked to Preston, I did not hear anything about objectivity or even any consideration about how to help reporters develop their informed "voice" to parallel the one that *The Times* so prided itself on in print. She wasn't going to be the "social media police," as she put it. But as we will see, there were very few cases where the audience was anything more than—at best—a reporting source for *Times* journalists, suggesting that Benkler's, Bruns's, and others' aspirations for journalism and participation may not yet be realized (or practical) in reality.

Leave It to the Storytellers?

As much as the drive for participation was rooted in economics, the message about money, thankfully, didn't seem to be the one that journalists were getting. Instead, what journalists heard was that they ought to be participating on social media platforms to connect with audiences in new ways: a very practical rendition of the more theoretical messages of "produsage" and "networked journalism." Just how to participate on these platforms though, was an industry-wide conundrum. Anywhere journalists went to look about how to do reporting in the digital age, from industry blogs to conferences to email newsletters, they would probably be presented with messages about how they should be making the most of their new capacity for interaction with the audience via social networks.

Similarly, news organizations got lots of attention from journoblogs for announcing "social media editors," whose primary purpose was deemed to integrate social media into the newsroom workflow. News organizations had begun to promote participation via social media as a key to their success, like Al Jazeera had done during the Arab Spring. Internet intellectual Jeff Jarvis, a presence in almost all of *The New York Times*' journalists' Twitter feeds that I saw, constantly promoted the idea of participatory engagement.[14] Jay Rosen, another scholar who managed to reach out to journalists, argued that journalists needed to pay much more attention to what audiences were both saying and creating as news producers themselves.[15] The Knight Foundation, the biggest philanthropic funder in journalism, had been pouring millions of dollars into news challenges that rewarded participation, especially projects that enabled citizens to create news. Thus, journalists heard a constant message from industry chatter about the need to participate with the audience—from talk of a Pulitzer for social media to Knight Foundation grants.[16]

Ironically though, not all journalists were getting this message from the top of the editorial food chain at *The Times*. As community editor Vanessa Schneider explained to me, journalists could go all day without engaging in any kind of interaction with readers (even just the basics, from comments to emails or newer tools like Twitter), in part because the institutional buy-in at the top hadn't been made clear:

> If it were [presented as] just a piece of the puzzle, "Yeah I had to answer comments, use Facebook and Twitter [and] it's part of what I do during the day," . . . it won't happen in the company absolutely unless Bill Keller [then executive editor] said "read comments and answer them, go on Twitter and answer [the audience], and promote [their work] on Facebook."
>
> But it takes people away from A1 and at end of day, editors want text and the head print editors that have the final word in how people spend their time.[17]

In other words, in Schneider's view, journalists wouldn't participate on these networks unless there was some sort of institutional force behind the much larger culture of participation journalists were hearing about. Old habits would be too easy to keep if no one in authority was really encouraging change. And despite Preston's efforts, Schneider, her deputy, didn't feel that social media had, at that time, become a regular part of the lives of most reporters in the newsroom.

And as Schneider put it, some of the older, print/text-focused editors saw participatory outlets as a distraction. One editor complained to me about a reporter who had developed a very loyal following on Twitter. In fact, this reporter often broke news on Twitter and then wrote about it for the newspaper. But as the editor told me: "[Reporter X] should be writing more and tweeting less. I'd like to see some more Page One stories out of her." Thus, there were some conflicting messages inside *The Times*: despite the sense in journalism's general professional milieu that social media was supposed to be important, there was still some resistance from top editors who saw social media as an interruption to the more important print product.

Nonetheless, what emerged as particularly interesting from *The Times'* experience with social media was that most journalists didn't need clear messages about social media from the top. The whole idea of participation was simply so new that there were no tried and true ways to think about the process. So there was the capacity for bottom-up trial and error, thanks to the varying institutional support, and plenty of space for experimentation. Some reporters improvised on old routines, using Twitter for news gathering. Other reporters had become brand names, moving beyond bylines to personalities in the social media space. Still others couldn't figure out what all of this meant for them. All of this instability showcased the contested nature of adopting participation as a value of online journalism.

New Participatory Practices Inside the Newsroom

Whenever I asked journalists at *The New York Times* about the "new audience" online, they would generally respond, "You mean Facebook? Twitter?" Then, they would mention a few names of people in the newsroom who were seen as being prolific on these sites, usually some combination of the following journalists: Brian Stelter, David Carr, David Pogue, Rob Mackey (head of *The Lede Blog*), Nick Kristof, Louise Story, and C.J. Chivers. From what I heard in the newsroom, the Web value of participation was an ideal that journalists aspired to, even though many felt quite confused about the actual practicalities of engaging with the audience in new ways. Those who were best at social media were widely regarded as future-oriented, shining stars.

In the 1950s, scholar Warren Breed wrote about the quiet but inescapable socialization of journalists that reinforced certain accepted organizational norms and values.[18] Something similar was happening with participation: as participation became a new value of newswork, journalists influenced each other about its importance, even if many were uncertain about how to make participation work for them. I saw this happening in the newsroom myself. There were Sorkin and Joachim, teaching each other. There were other quick "what should I tweet" conversations in the newsroom. But perhaps my favorite example was the day I watched the reporter Willie Neuman get introduced to Twitter.

Neuman, agriculture and food business beat writer, sat at the back of the tech pod. One result of being so close to the tech team was that he was generally a willing subject for the suggestions of the early adopters around him. For example, he regularly got friendly ribbing for his outdated PalmPilot smartphone, with its antenna held together by duct tape, and eventually took a step up to a better, sleeker Blackberry (though he admitted that even this was still just a shell of what his colleagues had).

After listening to tech journalists Nick Bilton and Jenna Wortham talk about Foursquare one day, Neuman was confused. Bilton and Wortham simply explained to Neuman that the check-in app was a new trend—and didn't elaborate. Instead, they went back to basics with Neuman, or at least "basics" as far as these tech reporters understood it: Twitter. Wortham inquired whether Neuman was on Twitter. Neuman equivocated.[19] He had an account, but he hadn't ever used it.

I listened as Neuman asked, "Why do I want this? What's it for?" Wortham gave a quick response: "You can use it to send out articles." Bilton explained to Neuman that he could "add" people to his Twitter list to see what they were saying. He began instructing Neuman to add *Times* staff members to the list of people Neuman followed. Bilton began calling out names from his own Twitter list for Neuman to add, including other influential media people, like columnists from *Wired* and *The Atlantic*.

Neuman noted, "Carr [media columnist David Carr] is just talking about . . ." with great surprise. I didn't catch what Neuman said, but he was likely surprised that Carr, who tweets about what he ate for breakfast, was tweeting about nothing related to the news.

Bilton then showed Neuman how to retweet. Neuman was confused and asked what retweeting means: "Why would I want to do this?" Bilton explained the concept: "Say you're following me, or liked something I said, you'd retweet me. Then, the next time I saw something you said that I liked, I'd retweet you." Retweeting was one way to help others promote their friends, Bilton explained.

When I spoke to Neuman two months later about social media, he had tried using Twitter, but just briefly. He noted:

> I haven't used it very much. I looked at it for a while, but I have lost interest. I can see what companies were doing with it, and they were mostly just plugging themselves in pretty innocuous ways. Some people use it every time they write a story. And they put it up there. I tried that a couple of times but didn't keep doing it.[20]

This vignette of Neuman's Twitter training, and then his apparent inability to keep up with it, illustrates a number of important themes about participation in *The New York Times'* newsroom. First, Neuman was a willing experimenter—confused but willing to learn about what his more tech-savvy colleagues were doing to increase their Web presence. He was socialized into an ethos of participation. Even when he rejected using Twitter, he was well aware that many of his colleagues were constantly using social media, tweeting "every time they write a story."

Nonetheless, Neuman also posited an important critique of this supposedly participatory forum: the information he was getting was from companies, not from people, and most of it was useless to him. Though he was improvising by trying the new routine of using social media for his work, the old rules were still in place for determining the information sources he would pay attention to—companies, not audiences. So much for his interacting with an audience of ordinary readers.

From another vantage, though, what Bilton and Wortham taught Neuman about social media was illuminating. For these journalists, the primary reason for using Twitter was more about bolstering one's own presence with, say, other *Times* journalists and influential media elites. Talking to readers never came up once during the lesson. And Bilton and Wortham were branded reporters who spent much of their time (as I observed) engaging in dialogue with tech elites over Twitter, exchanges that were nonetheless seen by a fairly large following (Bilton's was then at about one hundred thousand people). Still, for Neuman, the drumbeat of "participation, participation, participation" had now become part of his understanding of working in the digital age, just as it had for many other journalists.

Making Participation Part of Everyday Workflow

Though Neuman didn't know how to make social media part of his workflow, there were certainly other people, beyond just the tech reporters, who had begun to use social media as an extension of their traditional skills in the newsroom. These journalists saw social media as useful for both reporting and audience building (or, more cynically, brand building) and also as a way to communicate with their fellow beat reporters and even some sources. And most of this took place over Twitter, in a public setting where their followers could watch these conversations unfolding in real time.[21]

Journalist Brian Stelter had been heralded for his social media prowess, and examining his workflow gives some sense of the many considerations that were presented to a journalist thinking about using social media as a tool in the newsroom. Stelter was an early adopter of social media in the newsroom. He had presented at the tech-celebration portion of South by Southwest,[22] instructed journalists at Columbia University,[23] and regularly been the subject of articles with headlines like "NYT's Brian Stelter Champions Technology."[24] Influential tech blog *Mashable* called him an "industry leader" in social media.[25] Stelter had some natural advantages: he was one of the youngest reporters in the newsroom, so he had essentially grown up with most of these social media platforms. He had also made his way to *The Times* from the blog he started, *TVNewser*, so his conception of the work required of a reporter included the kind of self-promotion and branding that many journalists had never had to do.

Stelter covered media and television as news (rather than as entertainment) for *The Times*. He was also one of the most prolific reporters at the newspaper, in part because of his Twitter activity. I once heard a Web producer groan when they saw yet another contributing line from him. But his contributing lines were warranted: as he explained to me about an earthquake in California he helped report, he had used Twitter to find out information during the breaking news. "I knew that [the reporter] was far away from the quake," he said. "But I knew people would be on Twitter talking about it. So I got on Twitter and started following what people were saying."[26] Stelter said he was absolutely convinced of Twitter's ability to provide him with news and information from ordinary people—and we can see this as evidence of the preeminent place that participation has in his idea of what constitutes reporting in a new media age.

Watching Brian Stelter work is a bit like watching someone in hyperdrive. He moved from the two stories he was writing to Facebook, to Twitter, to Tumblr, to Google's Gchat IM client, to talking to people around him, to playing with his brand-new iPad. He explained to me as he was working, "Whenever I have a thought, I tweet it." These thoughts were pushed out to his now one hundred thousand–plus followers on Twitter. However, just as I had observed with other reporters, Stelter was most likely to respond on Twitter to people he already knew—such as well-known figures in the news industry or people he covered. The ordinary follower tweeting at him was unlikely to receive a response.

And the "social media police" were unlikely to monitor Stelter, who had his own sense of what he could and could not say. Stelter told me that if he was really concerned with a tweet, he would run it by a friend in *The Times'* corporate communications department. Still, he saw boundaries between his tweets from @BrianStelter as a *New York Times* reporter and @BrianStelter, the individual, and he thought people should be able to distinguish between the two, as well. He explained:

My tweets get more personal and less about work as the day goes on. The lines between personal and professional bleed in social media. Obviously if I tweet something at 2 a.m., it is not about work. If I say something about a movie, I am not *The Times'* movie critic. I think people know that.

This statement suggests the growth of reporters as a personal brand. They are reporters who cover serious topics, but they are also people who become personalities to their followers—people who do more than just cover news, who joke and share photos and the like. The ordinary print reporter in the past would live in the shadow of a byline, but now, reporters have a life beyond the newsroom that they can share with the world.

But *The New York Times*' social media ethics clearly noted that journalists needed to be careful not to editorialize. So while Stelter trusted the public to understand that the movie opinions he offered were just his own views, and that the funny articles he posted on Facebook were just that, *The New York Times* as a whole was still figuring out how to keep people excited about Brian Stelter's tweets while refraining from having them seem like endorsements from *The Times*. So, as we will later see, the lack of "social media police" and the freewheeling nature of Twitter at *The Times* made for some dicey ethical situations.

While I was with Stelter, I also saw how Twitter could play an important role in reporting.[27] Stelter was watching his Twitter feed and noticed some important news: WikiLeaks had posted a video of an American helicopter airstrike on Baghdad that had resulted in the death of two Iraqi journalists working for Reuters.

Stelter, who had been fairly quiet, noticed this development and shouted on the newsroom floor, "WikiLeaks got the video of them being shot and killed. It shows the journalists being killed."

Reuters had been pushing for the release of the video from the US military, but to no avail. This was big news—another leak from the amorphous group known as WikiLeaks. Stelter then asked his editor, Bruce Headlam, in a rushed voice, if this had made the story list for that evening. It had not.[28]

Stelter was the first person at *The Times* to notice this WikiLeaks video—all from monitoring Twitter. His next steps were to call Reuters and to email Elisabeth Bumiller, who covered defense for *The Times*. He then sent her the link to the video and some sample reaction tweets. Bruce Headlam, Stelter's editor and head of the media desk, began alerting other editors to the story.

Stelter rushed me away as I watched him beginning to comb

through the #wikileaks hashtag, searching for hidden gems, sources, and anything else he could get to help Bumiller with the story.[29] In the end, he was credited with a contributing line for his efforts.

Bumiller probably would have found out about the story in another way, perhaps after the Pentagon acknowledged the video, but Stelter found out first online. As he told me, "You can't ignore these things just because they are online. You need to do something about it." Here was a direct case of traditional news-reporting skills being applied in a new context—searching for information on Twitter. These practices were then applied to other existing news norms: the WikiLeaks video was verified by Bumiller, as were other tidbits that Stelter found.

However, participation, even for Stelter, was not about conversation or encouraging user-generated content. Stelter was sharing things with his audience in new ways, and many now had a more personal relationship with this particular reporter, but he rarely talked back to individuals he didn't already know in some capacity, nor did he invite them to respond to him unless he really had a reporting question. In the case of the WikiLeaks story, he was monitoring information on Twitter, using the tool as another reporting source. He was not engaging with individual audience members, but instead, he used their energy to further traditional efforts. So for Stelter, participation had been normalized into his work context, rather than opening up new venues for communication with his audience.

In perhaps a far less dramatic situation than finding out about a WikiLeak, another journalist shared with me how social media has simply made it easier for him to do his work—in part because he could crowd-source his journalism questions. I conducted an interview with another prolific Twitter user, David Pogue, *The New York Times'* tech columnist and author of *The World According to Twitter.* Pogue told me that Twitter was a "wonderful tool" for him as a columnist, noting, "I have [a] big presence on Twitter where there's a lot of give and take." He told me that one of his favorite Twitter memories was when he was having trouble with a column, and his Twitter following helped him:

> CNBC was coming next morning to shoot a video [for his column] and I hadn't prepared and it was 10 pm at night. I finally

had an idea and I needed 4 extras for it. It was too late for my neighbors [to help me], so I went on Twitter and asked for 4 extras to come to my house in Connecticut. 30 people wrote back and volunteered, showed up on time and it was fantastic.[30]

Certainly, this was a new relationship with his audience beyond what print could provide: Pogue was taking advantage of an active fan base (especially as a columnist) to help him do his work. He tried to see if he could crowd-source a reporting problem, and it worked—more evidence of how social media could, in fact, be a site of improvisation in reporting: new routines based on old practices.

If you looked at Pogue's Twitter feed, as often as he was pushing out links to his own columns and drumming up new ideas for blog posts, he was interacting with the audience.[31] What is interesting about Pogue, as compared to so many other journalists, is that he did keep a conversation going with his Twitter followers. These conversations were often in response to posts about his own personal experiences, like streaming movies with his kids. Sharing this with an audience of 1.4 million Twitter followers was a powerful conversation to be having, especially on a non-*Times*-branded platform. The products he was offering—his tweets—were not, as yet, part of traditional news products, and it was still quite messy to figure out how to make sure these fans would get back to *The Times*, rather than just staying on Twitter. Had Pogue become too much of a sub-brand?

But there are also serious critiques that emerge when we think about how journalists are using Twitter, social media, and other forms of user-generated content. My concern was that journalists were simply using social media to further their own ends, rather than taking advantage of an excellent opportunity to get to know their audience better. Their goal simply seemed to be to have help with reporting, to get news out, or to build a public profile. Very little of this actually involved bringing the audience into the newsroom as participants, learning what they might have to say about the news, or taking advantage of this new forum to improve coverage.

On the other hand, are we really to expect that journalists at the most prestigious newspaper in the country should spend most of their time, time that we have seen increasingly eaten up by multimedia demands and more immediate news needs, interacting with the audience? Should journalists be responding to every audience tweet? Is this even possible? How *could* they harness the potential of the user for their work without the relationship being entirely instrumental (e.g., for explicit reporting purposes)? From what we see here, there was no equalizing of journalist and consumer of news. *The Times* was still the giant hub of mainstream media, pushing content out. And as some journalists asked when thinking about their own role in these social networks, how did you balance the authority of being a *Times* reporter with this much more informal network? There were many reasons journalists could find to rethink just how they should understand participation as a value of online journalism.

No Time, No Voice?

Journalists seemed to have a shared definition of participation—being prolific on a social media site. This wasn't, of course, what Web/journalism theorists would hope for journalists to understand about their supposed new relationship with the audience. But theoretical aspirations were left behind in the practice of the newsroom. In the application of participation, what remained contested was not the definition of participation, but what role it would have in their lives—whether journalists were willing to take part and how.

So far, we've only heard about the journalists who seized on Twitter or Facebook or at least encouraged others to do so. But many journalists, all of whom acknowledged that they should somehow engage with this now much more visible audience, didn't wish to invite participation. There were some who couldn't imagine fitting it into their workflow, others who were still sorting out all these new tools, and still others who felt that social media presented some serious ethical quandaries. It's important to hear their voices to remember that social media, even in the "most social" newsroom, was not a given and that participation was very much a contested value.

Journalists who didn't want to engage in social media were quite defensive about their reasons for not engaging online. They couldn't imagine adjusting their workflow to accommodate a new routine. As financial reporter Jennifer Anderson explained to me:

> I have no time for social media. Literally no time. I'm writing a book, I have a job, a baby. I have a Facebook account to share pictures of my kids with my friends. But it's not for a lack for interest—it's for a lack of hours. The time I could be spending on Twitter or Facebook, I could be reporting or sleeping.[32]

Labor reporter Steven Greenhouse agreed. His response to the question of social media use was, "I just spent six months moving from the suburbs to Manhattan."[33] Notably, these journalists felt they *should* be doing something with social media, but they just couldn't imagine how to do it. Nonetheless, as Breed suggests, these journalists had naturalized a workplace norm: the idea that social media—and participation as *The New York Times* has imagined it—was important.[34]

Other reporters didn't see social media as a drain on their time, but they were less convinced that social media was something that could help them. Reporter David Streitfeld put it this way:

> I look at a lot of stuff, but I don't do too much myself. I do not use Twitter professionally. I do not tweet myself, but I do read what other people say. I don't find Twitter helps me covering real estate.
> . . . Social media does not yet play a dramatic role in my journalism for better or worse. I don't know whether this is just my feeling or social media just isn't adaptable to the reporting needs of writing about real estate or maybe a little of both.[35]

Streitfeld was reluctant to make a final declaration about the fate of social media in his own work, suggesting that he was willing to try new practices. But from his words, it is clear that he hadn't quite figured out how to make social media "adaptable" to what he did on a daily basis.

Other journalists had different questions, like what it would mean to suddenly have a relationship with an audience that was more than just as a byline. These journalists were concerned about the new opportunity to broadcast a nonofficial (yet somehow still official) message on social media platforms. They didn't know how, exactly, to communicate in a context that wasn't the traditional, edited story form. Unlike Pogue and Stelter, these journalists held back because they hadn't quite figured out what to do with the precedent that other journalists had set: having an online personality. Journalist Natasha Singer represented how a few journalists felt:

> I am a follower, not a tweeter. I'm using it to see what [is] said. I haven't started tweeting yet, because [I am] trying to figure out what unique thing I add. I see reporters linking to stories or to stories other colleagues have posted and to other things that interest them, but I want to add something, and I want to be more than a listener. I am getting a lot out of following other people, but I haven't figured out my unique contribution.[36]

Her comments reflect the fact that participation did mean, to many reporters, creating a form of personal branding in the newsroom. Singer and other journalists saw their professional roles as authoritative voices, and thus, they reasoned that what they said on these platforms could be just as influential as their stories. So, then, what would they say? And how would they develop the kind of relationship that could make Natasha Singer into a real person with, perhaps, opinions, guidance, and new ideas about the latest information, rather than just someone who pushed out content once a day? This transition, away from the detached journalist, a figure held up as a professional ideal for decades, was hard for many journalists to imagine.[37]

There was no set precedent in the newsroom to form these new relationships with the audience that social media made possible. How Singer will ultimately decide to take her voice online showcases the emergence of participation in the newsroom: journalists are still creating new routines to shape their social media practices. And journalists at *The Times* had few examples to look to; there were just unique personalities like David Pogue and Brian Stelter. So while journalists had long been invited to appear as experts on TV and radio for their commentary, social media presented an unmoderated venue for conversation. And contributions on social media were different: journalists weren't conversing with talk show hosts in a controlled environment anymore. Instead, this new form of contribution came from journalists' own initiatives—and they were still determining what those might be.

Ethical Concerns

The biggest pushback from journalists about participation on social networks related to ethical concerns. After decades of journalists trying to make the case for their role as objective storytellers, many felt that social media outlets left them more exposed to attack for having a bias. Their "friends," sources, the organizations they follow, and more would all be visible to the public. And what they said outside of the story, their unedited tweets or Facebook posts, might provide additional fodder for those looking to demonize their reporting.

One aspect that may have further hindered these journalists' desire to participate was that *The Times* itself was still uncertain about its social media policy. When I asked whether I could offer a link to this policy, or perhaps an appendix, standards editor Phil Corbett responded very nicely:

> While these do reflect our current guidance to the staff, they were intended more as informal, internal memos—they are not publicly available as our Ethical Journalism handbook is [a printed handbook often given to visitors or available as a PDF].
>
> Since these are fast-changing areas, our guidelines are likely to prove fluid and require revision as we go along, so I would rather these memos not be made public as representing "official" *Times* standards.[38]

In short, *The Times* itself used words like "fluid" and acknowledged that, in this uncertain area, the newsroom's views about participation in online journalism were emerging. Unlike the "Ethical Journalism" handbook, a document often used in undergraduate journalism ethics classes, social media guidelines were just too fuzzy to be shared with the public at that moment.

Consider the difference between these social media guidelines and the traditional handbook, which includes a section called "Keeping Our Detachment." The code states flatly that "it is essential that we preserve professional detachment, free of any hint of bias." The code goes so far as to say, "Staff members may see sources informally over a meal or drinks, but they must keep in mind the difference between legitimate business and personal friendship." It warns, "Romantic involvement with a news source would create the appearance and probably the reality of partiality." As my colleague and former CNN White House bureau chief Frank Sesno points out, these in-person exchanges create cozier relationships than would be developed through social media. But this tells us something, both about what the culture of detachment has been at *The Times* and about the potential for a slippery slope. Consider the tradition: "No newsroom or editorial employee may do anything that damages our reputation for strict neutrality in reporting on politics and government." That certainly would seem to leave out a lot of the fun of the chatter on social media platforms.

At first glance, some of the existing social media guidelines seemed that they would answer journalists' questions. But the reality of social media seemed to demand *personality,* or a "unique contribution," as Natasha Singer put it; as such, the code might not have been realistic. These social media standards were not that different from existing standards in *The Times'* editorial guidelines handbook: "Generally a staff member should not say anything on radio, television or the Internet that could not appear under his or her byline in *The Times.*" Staffers were instructed to leave blank their political affiliation on Facebook pages to avoid "casting doubt" on *The Times'* or the reporter's political impartiality (unless they happened to be columnists).

Journalists were also told to be wary of joining groups, despite the fact that these groups could be good sources of information. Joining these groups could suggest that the reporter (and through the reporter *The Times*) was actually affiliated with them. Newsroom reporters were warned to be careful not to recommend or retweet anything that illustrated opinion. As a result, in shaping these guidelines, journalists were relying on improvisation, hoping that there would be clear links to the original sense of ethics. But *The Times* journalists' actual activity across social media platforms bore little resemblance to the original structure of this ethical code.

No one who used these social media platforms prolifically really seemed to follow these guidelines. In the case of Nick Bilton (see Chapter 2), he was clearly tweeting and retweeting his own thoughts and opinions about the new iPad. And joining groups on Facebook could be a great source of information, so it seemed silly to have a reporter avoid joining, say, fans of the GOP. Stelter clearly tweeted his own opinions about movies, restaurants, and the like. So what was a reporter who was uncertain about staying on the safe side supposed to do? The answer, for some, was to simply stay out of the way.

Ed Wyatt, who covers government regulatory efforts from Washington, D.C., put his concerns this way:

> I had a Facebook page that I eliminated because I didn't want it to be used against me. Everything we write [means] someone attacks our motives, and anything that someone can interpret as giving a basis for questioning my objectivity is something that can cause problems. I don't need it and I don't need the grief.
>
> I have a Twitter account, but I generally don't use it. I rarely use it to promote my own stories, and it seems ridiculous because *The Times* has a million or however many readers and I do not have a million readers following me on Twitter. It's just not efficient use of my time.
>
> Maybe it's a naïve 20th-century view, but I don't believe I should be in the business of promoting my own stories. I believe *The New York Times* will promote the stories based on how it displays [them] on the Web page and in the paper.[39]

A number of interesting themes come from Wyatt's response. Journalists have always been accused of bias, but Wyatt saw engaging with the public via social media as just one more way to have his work attacked. Anything taken out of context could remove the distance he tried to have as a reporter. Notably, Wyatt wasn't thinking about how he could include the public in his reporting—he didn't seem to want to; instead, he thought of Twitter and Facebook simply as output. Twitter was a link engine, not conversation.

Other reporters I spoke with shared Wyatt's concern about objectivity. Another reporter similarly noted:

> I don't participate in it. I am happy to go in and look at stuff, but I don't use it this way. At this point it's a conscious decision not to. It's so easy sometimes for [the] kinds of stories I do to be accused of being somehow aligned with certain interests, so rather than Facebook, or even quite frankly LinkedIn, I just don't want to be accused by someone saying you've associated with that person and that's why you like [this] PR firm or advocacy group. That's too hard for me to manage.[40]

These journalists were less concerned about having a conversation with their audience than they were about being subject to attack for their perceived impartiality.

I have, until this point, suggested that theories of the recalibrated journalist/audience relationship were not meshing with the reality of journalistic practice, in part because journalists did not engage with their audience in a more direct way. These journalists were failing to respond to the audience, to engage them in conversation, and to see how they might be able to take part in the news-making process. But the ethical concerns that Wyatt and others brought up are ones that did present some counterpoints to the idea of "networked journalism" or giving up journalistic authority. Soliciting opinions, for instance, might be viewed as asking for endorsements. Replying in the affirmative to a particular link might accidentally put a journalist in the position of defending his or her political neutrality. Thanking someone for a news lead could be similarly dangerous. Conversation with the audience presented an ethical minefield; while most *Times* journalists were not thinking about social media as a site of engagement with the public, if and when they did, these matters of professional ethics could pose many problems.

These reporters' concerns about ethics were not just excuses for staying off social media platforms. In fact, when I was in the news-room, one business journalist's daily use of Twitter got her into serious trouble—and showed the dangers of having Twitter as an extension of "every thought," as Stelter put it. *Times* journalist Hiroko Tabuchi was busy for months covering the fallout of Toyota's terrible PR disaster over sudden acceleration in its cars.[41] She was working overtime—covering the story for New York deadlines but working in her local time zone (Tokyo) as the dispatch reporter at all the press conferences and Toyota events in Japan. As per her usual routine, Tabuchi was keeping her Twitter followers up to date on her reporting activities.

On this occasion, her tweets were about what it was like to be at a Toyota press conference:

- With less than 3 hours sleep, managed to haul myself onto 6 am shinkansen for #Toyota event in Nagoya. We love you Mr. Toyoda!

- ToyotaMan: We're gonna confiscate your mobile phones once we get off the bus. And you must wear our (butt-ugly) yellow Toyota hats. Whaa . . . ?

- Me: Since we're just sitting here waiting to depart, can I go get a coffee?

- ToyotaMan: No.

- Me: I'll be back in just a minute.

- ToyotaMan: No.

- Back! Toyota coffee machine just recalled my coffee, said it failed a taste check so it wd make another cup. I'm dead serious, place is nuts

- Akio Toyoda took very few questions, ignored reporters incl me who tried to ask a follow-up. I'm sorry, but Toyota sucks.[42]

This series of tweets got Tabuchi in more than a bit of trouble at *The Times*. While people inside *The Times* said they spotted her tweets first, they were also picked up on the troublesome *Times* watchdog blog, *NYTPICKER*. Simply put, a reporter should not, according to *New York*

Times social media guidelines I received, "write anything on a blog or a personal Web page that you could not write in *The Times*—don't editorialize."[43] Tabuchi was adding color to her experience and giving readers a real sense of the scene. But she was also adding opinion. And perhaps this opinion was too unprofessional for a *Times* reporter.

The result of Tabuchi sharing her tweets as part of her up-to-the minute reporting was a very public scolding. The public editor, Clark Hoyt, wanted to pull Tabuchi off the story because he thought her reporting was compromised. Inside the newsroom, I heard a defense from editors that Tabuchi was just tired and this had nothing to do with her ability to report the story. Tabuchi, apologetic, said to Hoyt in his weekly column, "The banter on Twitter is often very casual and forces us to economize on words. That can be perilous. But the last thing I'd want is collegial banter and humor to affect perceptions of our coverage." Still, though, according to Hoyt, Tabuchi said she "regards Twitter as an invaluable way to connect with readers and to get sources for stories."[44]

For Tabuchi, participation via social media was a way to extend her reporting beyond the activities of working inside a newsroom. She viewed Twitter as a way to share the experiences of reporting with her followers. And she had incorporated this new approach into her work norms. But the result was unpredictable—the banter itself was a stark contrast to impartiality. Even though Tabuchi wanted to be more than just someone pushing out links, her meltdown with Toyota shows the difficult terrain of navigating between personality and traditional journalism. This ethical minefield was a clear site of negotiating the value of participation in the newsroom.

Rounding Up Participation

Henry Jenkins' work on convergence culture argues that the relationship between producers and consumers is in uncharted territory, because audiences can now so easily create, share, and remix content.[45] The traditional top-down creation of media has been upended as ordinary people can take what they have made and distribute it across the Web. The essence of participatory culture, to theorists like Jenkins and the others I discussed earlier in the chapter, is one in which the industry that formerly had the power to control content can no longer control how, where, when, and by whom the content is used.

Indeed, participation was a new news production value at *The Times*. Journalists felt that participation was both influencing their daily work and increasingly becoming part of what it meant to be a journalist in the digital age. But at *The Times*, participation was *not* the Web 2.0 vision suggested by Jenkins or any of the other theorists discussed at the beginning of this chapter. Instead, participation equaled being present on a social media platform. This was "participating" in the digital age at *The Times*.

This chapter gives an overview of some of the challenges, conflicts, and opportunities that emerged in 2010 at *The New York Times* as participation increasingly became a value of newswork. Journalists understood that interacting with the audience on new platforms was important, so there were opportunities for journalists to teach each other about how to incorporate participation into their daily workflows. Other journalists used social media and citizen participation (albeit in a unidirectional way) to aid their reporting. Showcasing the contested nature of participation, some journalists worried about establishing a unique voice, while others noted the ethical pitfalls that could (and did) emerge.

Journalists, for the most part, seemed fairly ignorant that audiences could quite possibly be citizen contributors to the news-making process. Rather than a shared "mutualisation" of journalism between news organization and audience, as *Guardian* editor Alan Rusbridger spoke about, something different happened at *The Times*.[46] Journalists controlled the conversation, and often, this control meant that they would decide to not even engage in any kind of conversation. Perhaps this was for the better, as it might be impossible for a newspaper on the scale of *The Times* to actually have its reporters busy trying to keep up their reporting duties and also engaging in active daily conversations with readers. In this case, theorists who think about participation may be overly idealistic to suggest that these kinds of relationships can unfold, given the demands of daily news reporting.

Participation was an emergent and, at times, contested value. Journalists did not quite know what to say or how to speak to their new audience or how to make sense of this personal branding mission. The ethics were fuzzy, and they didn't quite make sense to some journalists who tried to have a personality online. Journalists were still figuring out just how much they should pay attention to what their audiences had to say on these new forums. One lesson from this is that, if we do want to consider how we might rethink the journalist-reader relationship, we need to consider the specific goals of the newsroom and journalists in relation to the more theoretical aspirations of user engagement.

What emerges from looking at how journalists engage with social media is that participation is not what journalism theorists say it is or ought to be. For theorists and journalism prognosticators, there is already a stable value called "participation" that should reorder journalism: the audience and the journalist should be in conversation; the authority of the journalist should be meshed with citizen contributions; the one-to-many flow of information should be replaced with a more many-to-many conversation. But for these journalists, the very act of even engaging on participatory platforms was contested. Just joining Twitter was up for debate. Forget having a conversation about the deep advantages of changing journalism and benefiting from user experience; few understood the potential. Even starting to have this conversation was contested.

Yet ultimately, citizen engagement online may help the newspaper survive. Creating shareable content matters economically, and making that content maximally shareable, via Twitter feeds, Facebook pages, or whatever it might be, requires journalist participation. Being on social media platforms may become nonnegotiable, and it may be that participation in practice has a different meaning than it does in theory. In practice, participation may just mean talking to the audience in nontraditional ways, telling stories differently, and creating an online identity that users can recognize. Participation may have little to do with actual conversation, much to the potential dismay of Internet theorists. But nonetheless, some version of participation reordering newswork was emerging in the newsroom of *The Times*, signaling change and underscoring the emergence of new values ordering online journalism in the digital age, just as interactivity and immediacy were.

Chapter 7

Prelude to What?

Whenever I had the occasion to speak with anyone at *The Times* about this project after my departure from the newsroom, at least half would pause and then say, "But wait, *everything* has changed." The other half, by and large, pointed out small but still noticeable differences: that the newspaper's paywall had been put in full motion; that the mobile device apps were continually improving; or that the iPad was now out in full force and now *The Times* could more fully boast of digital, tablet, and print readers. Editors pointed out to me how the ascension of Jill Abramson to executive editor in 2011 signaled a commitment to a new way of thinking. Their proof: Abramson had stepped aside as managing editor for six months to become fully immersed in "the digital operations of *The Times*."[1] Nonetheless, her new second-in-command, Dean Baquet, formerly the Washington bureau chief, was a man fully immersed in thinking about the print, rather than the digital world.

Looking across some of the developments at *The Times*, the trend toward immediacy, interactivity, and participation as regular and, notably, increasingly valued parts of practice became clear. These values, as it were, were becoming "valued"—journalists were increasingly seeing the importance, merit, opportunities, and professional advantages of incorporating them in their work. The emergence of these values was still causing disruption, but perhaps they had become more settled and recognized as *desired* professional aspirations, rather than felt obligations of what it meant to do quality *Times* journalism in the digital age.

I want to give a brief nod to some of the signs of change in the newsroom and *Times*-specific advantages when it comes to tackling the digital age. In this section, I bring together the larger conversation about the values of immediacy, interactivity, and participation to explain why it was so important to talk about them the way I have—as emergent and contested. After seeing these values at work, it becomes much easier to explain the underlying recursive patterns at work.

While I have emphasized how *new* values are changing journalism, it is also important to pause for a moment and recall what remains the same: the constraints upon news that have shaped journalism production from the 1960s and beyond are still influencing newswork. Nonetheless, in the online journalism world of 2010, these core values were changing how journalists thought about their work and how news was produced—and were coming to the forefront of news creation in a way that was dictating the very fabric of journalism. Certainly *The Times* is an exceptional case, and it is worth noting the potential future of the integration of these values in the newsroom, but regardless of the special advantages of *The Times*, there are larger cultural, social, and technological patterns at work reshaping how journalists work, why they work, and what they do.

Participation on social media was perhaps the most obvious marker that something—organization-wide—was changing at *The Times*. *The Times* management eliminated Jennifer Preston's social media editor position. The headline announcing the job change in *The New York Observer* read, "*New York Times* Decides Tweeting Is Not a Job."[2] In the article, Preston declared that the era of social media evangelizing was officially over. And this seemed at least anecdotally true; some Twitter resistors who had previously claimed frustration with the service had joined it. Diana Henriques, an elder statesman of the business desk, had scorned social media when I was in the newsroom. Now, we were exchanging tweets—though part of her tweeting, I surmised, was to promote her book about Bernie Madoff, the financial Ponzi schemer. Another journalist, Tara Siegel Bernard, was pleased to tell me that, after her initial hesitations with Twitter, she was a full convert and had begun using it to help facilitate an online community through the *Bucks* personal finance blog. D.C. business reporter Ed Wyatt, who had been concerned about objectivity over social media, was now a regular presence, tweeting about business news from Washington.

Had *The Times* become even more social? Were journalists actually engaging with people more? Maybe the numbers of Twitter followers were growing, but as I continued to scan through journalists' feeds, I saw only one difference: the people who had simply been pushing out *Times* links were now working more as aggregators of content across the Web. Catherine Rampell, a general economics reporter, had begun sending not only links to the latest serious economic studies from across the Web but also funny jokes about how we spend our money. Participation was still understood as simply joining social media platforms and using them to communicate—though journalists on a more global scale in the newsroom no longer saw social media as strictly business. They had found their voice, as Natasha Singer, a health business writer, had worried about doing. What they had not found, though, was a conversation. The lingering question I have is whether this matters for *The Times*, and for journalism more generally, despite the underlying articulation of professionalism as a *new* value of news by journalism theorists.

Interactivity was continuing to develop inside *The Times* in increasingly significant ways. *The Times'* interactive news desk was already becoming high profile to those outside the journalism world, its journalists actually featured in *New York Magazine*. And though the article appeared shortly before I conducted my research, it's worth noting the evolutionary jumps that outsiders saw taking place inside *The Times* and its capacity to produce multimedia content. The subheading of the article asked, "What are these renegade cybergeeks doing at the New York *Times*? Maybe saving it."

The magazine focused on the capacity of interactivity to create "art . . . or journalism," but also on the importance of interactive journalism as a new business model. Author Emily Nussbaum noted:

> And yet, even as the financial pages wrote the paper's obit, deep within that fancy Renzo Piano palace across from the Port Authority, something hopeful has been going on: a kind of evolution. Each day, peculiar wings and gills poke up on the *Times'* website—video, audio, "drillable" graphics.

Those drillable graphics were the graphics that would lead to engagement—the sticky Web site of advertising opportunity and user-directed experiences. This was editorial and business strategy, new storytelling with a purpose.[3]

When I was in the newsroom, it was far from accepting interactivity as a stable construct guiding journalists' work. However, major projects after I left signaled that there was, indeed, a cultural shift taking place. The newsroom was not making multimedia ancillary or simply creating add-ons to major projects, but actually conceiving of major stories as interactive opportunities, with multimedia their driving centerpiece. The clearest demonstration of this new way of thinking was the pioneering creation "Snowfall: The Avalanche at Tunnel Creek,"[4] which featured long-form storytelling along with 3-D graphics, in what was widely hailed as a revolutionary creation.

"Snow Fall" was called "the future of Web storytelling," a "game changer," and "revolutionary." Moving your mouse literally gave one a 360-degree view of the Cascades Mountains in preavalanche mode; to navigate to various parts of the story, one had to click across a variety of slideshows, audio commentaries, maps, and pictures. Oddly enough, given all the talk of new business models, the story was monetized with just a few small banner ads. This story brought it all together: old media—a richly textured story written by a top narrative journalist—and a stunning (to many industry observers) interactive display that brought text and interactives to a seamless and powerful presentation. This was, as Matt Richtel had said about his own Pulitzer project, "Driven to Distraction," a piece that combined the best of old and new media.

From outside the newsroom, I had less insight into how journalists continued to feel about the tug between print and online, tomorrow and today, but I could watch the changes in the updating pace from my laptop. The Times had, indeed, slowed down the rapid churn of stories; on the East Coast, you would still find major stories from the print paper online for a few hours in the morning. Smaller bits and pieces of the home page were, however, recycled, as op-eds, blog posts, the big photo in the middle of the page, and other items changed with more regularity. Watching the Web site carefully revealed major updates at three-hour intervals, rather than one-hour or thirty-minute intervals, and The Times had started leaving time stamps on almost all major stories, showing when a story had been posted. Presumably, this was a clue to how long a story had been on the home page and when it had last been updated. Either the Web page looked fresh, or it looked stale. *The Times* was crushed between tomorrow's news for today, ASAP news, and lunchtime leftovers. Rivals like *The Guardian* told me that reducing the churn was a major strategic mistake—that "fresh" was essential to keeping an audience.[5]

The presence of live blogs grew stronger—events across the Arab world catapulted the foreign desk's *Lede* blog into a landing page for information about the region, showcasing both *Times* content and content aggregated, curated, and fact-checked from social media.[6] But other Web sites, like Al Jazeera English, were much faster—they were publishing information as it came in with less editing and curation than *The Times'* live blog, a trend that we observed between the iPad live blogs on rival sites and on *The Times*. Journalists continued to provide constant updates for breaking news stories, though the stories the newspaper focused on changed (the 2012 election, rather than the jobs report, for instance).

When I spoke to those in the newsroom, I found that some journalists had embraced the quick speed of the home page—so much so that slowing down the churn seemed to be a terrible idea. One confidant laughed out loud when he explained to me that Abramson wanted a 12 p.m. EST push for new content, as if she had forgotten that *Times* readership was international and that not everyone would be at their desks eating lunch at that time. Another grumbled in frustration that the Web site had slowed down its churn of stories, at least for the moment, to keep them online a bit longer, arguing that this might actually be a great mistake. This journalist had grown so used to the churn that to no longer have the constant, immediate flow of information meant that *The Times* might look stale compared to other news outlets.

Early on-background accounts of these changes, along with the paywall, caused some to surmise that nytimes.com traffic was dipping. The cosmetic brushes to keep the page looking fresh were not working, it seemed to these observers; with a more static home page and limited opportunities to read new stories thanks to the paywall, journalists felt that the lack of churn was actually inhibiting new readership. Hard numbers were, and continue to be, difficult to come by. Immediacy remained contested, and from the outside, it seemed that there continued to be a lack of coherence about how to approach producing news for the constant-deadline online world. Nonetheless, there were many indications that *The Times* was in a good place to face the challenges ahead.

Embracing Change: *The Times* Advantage

As could be expected, uncertainty about the future continued at *The Times* as I finished the final touches on this manuscript. One journalist told me, "I'm not sure I really like all of these changes. I don't know if they [the management] know what they are doing." But the organization's not knowing what to expect—or what to do—was part of what I think made *The Times* an exciting place to watch the future of news unfold. *The Times*, a giant organization, was functioning as a real-world laboratory for the future of news, continuing to refine, adapt, and change. The organization was tolerating ambiguity. Scholar David Stark argues that, in fact, an organization's very capacity to allow for internal uncertainty to exist means that it is more likely to be able to adapt to rapid change.[7] And this may be why *The Times* continues to look like it will be successful.

In fact, when people talked about the future of news, they noted that only the strong would survive: *The New York Times, The Wall Street Journal, USA Today,* and *The Washington Post.* As Jeffery Cole of the Center for the Digital Future at USC Annenberg noted, "It's likely that only four major daily newspapers with global reach will continue in print."[8] One of those, was, of course, *The Times.* People in the newsroom talked about functioning in beta mode, much like a start-up in Silicon Valley. In fact, the newspaper even implemented a public beta site for the newsroom to start testing apps and new ideas "without disrupting nytimes.com."[9] If ideas didn't work, someone tried something new. A lack of hierarchy among new positions, perhaps uncomfortable to some, enabled experimentation. No clear mandate about social media left people to proceed at their own pace. And there were other institutional advantages that simply came with the size, legacy, and influence of *The Times*.

Some prognosticators of the future of news put *The Times* in a "category of one." As C.W. Anderson, Emily Bell, and Clay Shirky note in their tome *Post-Industrial Journalism*, they chose not to focus on *The Times* because it is a distinct case that "has so many added advantages that suggest its continued capacity to change, grow, and survive":

> In the last generation, the Times has gone from being a great daily paper, in competition with several other such papers, to being a cultural institution of unique and global importance, even as those papers—the Washington Post, Chicago Tribune, Los Angeles Times, Miami Herald, among others—have shrunk their coverage and their ambitions. This puts the Times in a category of one. Any sentence that begins "Let's take the New York Times as an example . . ." is thus liable to explain or describe little about the rest of the landscape.
>
> The Times newsroom is a source of much interesting experimentation—data visualizations, novel partnerships, integration of blogs—and we have talked to many of our friends and colleagues there in an effort to learn from their experiences and make recommendations for other news organizations. However, because the Times is in a category of one, the choices its management can make, and the outcomes of those choices, are not illustrative or predictive for most other news organizations, large or small, old or new.[10]

And indeed, *The Times* has advantages that other news organizations do not: a brand name; an international presence; an ostensibly committed publisher dedicated to public service; a fairly insulated stock ownership structure; and, despite the grumbling, a newsroom committed to embracing change. This is an incredibly different picture from the newsrooms observed in David Ryfe's recent account of regional dailies in the United States, which kept trying to institute a myriad of changes, from digital to cultural, that simply wouldn't stick. Ryfe's outlook for their future was dismal.[11]

The Times had high-profile symbols that seemed to demonstrate a commitment to a future built on experimentation and change. It was one of only four newsrooms in the United States to have a committed R&D lab *inside* the newsroom (the others include *The Washington Post, The Boston Globe,* and NPR*).* Here, not only are people developing touch-screen tables for news and infographics for 3D TVs, but they are also working on figuring out how to measure an incredibly valuable metric: the power of sharing content socially.[12] And as we saw with the iPad Twitter counter in Chapter 2, small innovations from this lab feed back into the newsroom.

The Times has built a pool of people who like working at *The Times* and who happen to be at the cutting edge of the tech world. These individuals, who spend time working on the most exciting parts of the Web site, regularly turn down offers from Amazon, Google, Facebook, and the like. As one interactive graphics journalist wooed by Google told me about why she stayed at *The Times,* "I just like journalism." And as *The Times* begins to further engage with the tech community through events such as hack days and support of the tech/journalism collaboration Hacks and Hackers, it is likely that this infusion of tech talent and experimentation will continue to strengthen the newsroom, even if most people in the organization have no idea who these people are—or what their titles might mean. *The Times* has even begun to solicit offers from tech start-ups for free space inside *The Times* newsroom for "four month partnerships" in the hopes of a "mutually beneficial relationship."[13]

For all of its past, present, and future financial troubles, *The Times* has the chance to remain a stalwart institution that is likely to survive in the digital future. Its Web site alone, with such massive traffic, suggests a stability that other institutions do not have. The commitment that *The Times* has poured into making the site sticky and spreadable is a strategy shared by the biggest sites on the Web. And *The Times'* strong brand means that it is able to retain talent that other newspapers cannot.

With so much uncertainty around digital change at the newspaper, so many new developments, and so much possible technological change, what emerges as lasting from this project? I think we can make sense of this newsroom through the lens of how immediacy, interactivity, and participation were fundamentally reorienting what it meant to do work inside a newsroom. These new values of newswork—born of the online journalism era—have already had a profound influence inside *The Times*. As values that describe the very nature of online communication, their influence will remain a marked change, even while their implementation and their impact on news production may look different years from now. These values were coming of age as I began my research at *The Times*, and I expect them to be an underlying framework for doing newswork in the digital age.

Nonetheless, I want to caution readers to remember that I looked at one particular moment in the history of this august institution. From this work, I have shed some light on the ways the newsroom was grappling with the dominant Web values of the time, as well as on the newsroom's attempt to tackle the economic challenges besetting the entire news industry. This is only one moment for news and just five months in the history of a newspaper established in 1851, but it is nonetheless particularly revealing for what it shows: ultimately, the survival of *The Times* will likely depend on journalists' being able to incorporate these larger Web values into their work process. My story captures a period when this integration was still unresolved.

Why Values Matter

Throughout this book, I've talked about "emergent values" and "contested values." Why does it matter to talk about immediacy, interactivity, and participation? Why consider them values? To reiterate, values come out of routines, internal and external constraints, professional practices, and cultural and social norms and assumptions. This is a sociologically grounded vision of values, rather than a philosophical one. In this book, I have used the term *emergent* because it describes how values are socially constructed by the people who are creating and shaping news content and production in the digital age. *All* values are, to some degree, contested, but in the case of *The New York Times* in 2010, very basic notions of journalism were being renegotiated for a world that had a 24/7 Web enabled; a potentially active audience assembled; and computing powers sophisticated enough to handle a broad array of digital presentations of sound, graphics, interactives, and multimedia.

Thus, signaling these values as "contested" suggests that the newsroom is a site of struggle over their meaning in a particularly unstable time, where there is no specific dominant interpretation of what they mean.

We can also think about the way that values order social knowledge, but the process is recursive; the values themselves are created through and by human action. So to break this down a bit more, these values were both ordering how people thought about what they did and, at the same time, being created by the very people helping to define them. This is what ultimately makes for the point of tension throughout the book, that journalists are caught in a position of redefining online journalism without necessarily knowing what the outcome will be, while *at the same time* responding to what they feel creates the routines, practices, and external and internal pressures of doing work with online journalism.

Immediacy, then, takes on a temporary definition as ASAP journalism in the online world, but it holds on to the legacy of "aged news" at the same time. It is understood as "fresh," as rapid motion, as churn. Ultimately, this may not be the more enduring meaning of immediacy in the digital age or what will become the commonly held dominant understanding—but that doesn't matter; in some form, the very need to respond in some way to the dismantling of deadlines across media and platforms reorders social knowledge. As a result, immediacy in online news is distinctly influencing the way journalists do their work. There is felt demand to do work on the ASAP schedule, yet because immediacy is still emerging as a value that orders how journalists think about what they do, and why they do it, journalists are caught between the print world and the online world.

To most journalists, interactivity is translated as multimedia, though as I have illustrated, interactivity is more than just storytelling; it is also a way to think about user-computer interaction. Most journalists, though, are focused on the story, so it's understandable that they use this term and talk about interactivity in this way. For traditional journalists, multimedia is tangible—they can see the results. It has been set out there by internal pressures inside the newsroom. As Warren Breed and others have argued, these newsroom policies can, in fact, create news values (he argues that news *becomes* a value).[14] On the other hand, journalists are engaged in figuring out what interactivity means to them, how they will incorporate it into their work, and how new journalists who embrace a different vision for news become part of the newsroom. They are simultaneously being shaped by and shaping what interactivity will mean for *The Times*.

Participation was a particularly intriguing value to observe as it was negotiated at *The Times*. To those not directly affiliated with news production—and even some who were, like Alan Rudsbridger, who preached about the "mutualisation" of the audience from his pulpit as editor of *The Guardian*—participation was a new value of journalism. To these strong voices in the future of journalism, participation belonged in the pantheon of journalism aspirations, much like objectivity. To these industry and academic contributors, participation was a normative and professional practice of journalism that resulted in either an exchange between audience and producer or, more radically, the audience as producer of news.

Yet, when this wider discourse was filtered into *The Times*, it was chopped up into utilitarian terms: How should journalists handle the fact that there is a visible audience? The first answer was simply to get on these platforms, and "participation" was a buzzword for simply being on social media. *Times* journalists had constructed what participation meant to them: it certainly meant engaging on these platforms, but what they were unsure of was whether doing so was significant and whether it ought to reorder how they did their work. This was the pressure point: simply being on the platforms to engage. But the pressures from outside the newsroom, and even inside the newsroom, suggested a larger turn toward embracing at least being *on* a social network. Whether the more normatively defined value of participation would take hold at *The Times* remained unclear—and whether it ought to take hold remains another question about the nature of authority at *The Times*.

Ultimately, though, these three values—immediacy, interactivity, and participation—were changing online journalism in ways we can see throughout the text. They were altering how journalists did their jobs and what they thought about them. They were changing professional norms and expectations of how journalism was supposed to look, how journalists were supposed to act, and when and how news was supposed to be created. A new set of realities shaped and molded by the recursive exchange between social practices and accumulating social knowledge recalibrated what was happing inside *The Times* newsroom. What happened inside *The Times* may be different, a case of one, but the larger forces of online change as seen through the adoption of immediacy, interactivity, and participation should be found throughout newsrooms in the digital age. Nonetheless, amid the change, I want to pause to recall that, while these values show change, there are many things that remain constant about news production from past to present to future.

What Remains the Same?

What then, can we say is lasting about this era of news production? If you ask Herbert Gans, as I have, he will tell you that all newsrooms are the same, even today, in this time when many newsrooms are at varying points in their acceptance of new technology. In fact, in the preface to the 2004 reissue of his 1979 classic, Gans writes, "I doubt that a restudy of the four news organizations [NBC, CBS, *Newsweek*, and *Time*] would require significant changes in the conclusions." He goes on to note:

> Source power, audience power, and efficiency remain the major explanations of why the news comes out as it does. . . . Perhaps the audience has become more important, for soft news is there to hold and enlarge the audience as well as the advertisers that sell to them. Efficiency also has higher priority, not only because of the more intense pursuit of the audience but also because of the higher profit demands from news firms and Wall Street.[15]

Is he right?

I have not set out to reevaluate these constraints, but to consider what more we might say about the processes and patterns influencing newswork, because the conditions have changed so dramatically. Even the industrial process of actually *making* the news product has changed drastically since Gans wrote his book. The distribution methods are notably distinct. Nonetheless, many of the routines and practices of news production observed in the golden era of news ethnography remain constant, and it is worth noting how they continue to function in the newsroom.

Journalists need content to fill their news outlets. The cycle of production depends upon creating this content. Managing a regular flow of news through predictable routines makes it easier to know when to expect news for various platforms and how much to expect. Event-driven news and scheduled stories are still the easiest kinds of stories to predict: journalists have a regular rhythm they follow for every big story, and scheduled stories (like the monthly jobs report story featured in Chapter 4) ensure that enough content will exist to fill the needs of the newsroom. The more efficient the process, the better the use of human and economic resources will be, and also the more likely that there won't be hiccups that leave the news organization without needed coverage. However, the pressures of new technology in the digital age—the radical changes that emerge from a networked society—demand that we look at the new values that inform news production.

One limitation that I faced throughout this book was my inability to truly comment on whether the relationship with sources had changed in an immediate, interactive, and participatory world. My agreement with *The Times* prohibited disclosure of confidential or proprietary information learned during the course of my research, including details about sources. What I can say is that the stuff of journalism movies— quiet lunches with insiders, surprise phone calls, carefully crafted relationships, and the like—is still a mainstay of journalism at *The Times*. One change, though, may be the new proliferation of untraditional sources, like Twitter feeds. But as we saw with the Reuters Iraq shooting story that Stelter learned about via Twitter, fellow reporter Elisabeth Bumiller still needed the Pentagon to confirm the veracity of the video. Increasingly, journalists are turning to nontraditional sources through social media, but I wonder if this is just another extension of reaching out to the vox populi through more tech-savvy means.

Audiences still influence news production, perhaps even more now than before. Audiences are, after all, the key to unlocking the economic mystery, but at *The Times*, there has not been a distinct turn toward soft or tabloid news. However, as media scholar C.W. Anderson points out, though journalists are able to both know more about their audiences from all sorts of online metrics data and conceivably reach out to these audiences via participatory forums, what they may actually be able to understand from all of these inputs is likely an incomplete picture.[16] The audience seems knowable, even personalizable, but it is also quantifiable, and many of these quantifiable metrics are imprecise and often unclear. Readers have become clicks per mille, pageviews, and other metrics that can be sold to advertisers. Are journalists writing for the people they know on Facebook or for these clicks? The audience, as we have seen in the discussion of participation, still remains distant from journalists' own understanding of whom they write for. The conversation is still generally one-to-many. Should the people formally known as the audience become more involved in news production, or does *The New York Times* remain a site of curation, albeit with a little more personality?

Similarly, old arguments about journalists creating norms for each other to follow are still quite true. Breed advanced this argument in 1955, and scholars since then have provided further suggestions that this is the case over ensuing years.[17] Consider, for example, the case in the late 1980s of A. Kent MacDougall, who admitted to being a socialist at *The Wall Street Journal*—a shocker given the norms of that newsroom.[18] From objectivity to political persuasion, the newsroom is a place where journalists socialize each other about what it means to be a professional. We could see this happening in many instances throughout this book, from some journalists trying to get each other to understand the demands of the immediate newsroom, to others groaning about multimedia, to others teaching each other social media platforms.

Additionally, these older ethnographies argue that economics often structure newswork. Edward J. Epstein offers the strongest ethnographic framing for this, interpreting how all decisions in a newsroom are made with economics in mind.[19] And as Gans recalls, *Time* magazine, even in the halcyon days of the 1960s, still had layoffs due to budget cuts. Similarly, when speaking about news values, it is important to recognize the importance of the underlying social and economic structures at play. Some scholars, like Robert McChesney and Ben Bagdikian, argue that economics drive coverage and news policy[20]—and might argue that immediacy, interactivity, and participation could all be seen through the economic lens of newsroom survival.

As we saw at *The Times*, though, only some of the people, some of the time, were concerned about economics. My time in the newsroom suggests a strong (but not bulletproof) buffer between business and editorial. But I do see how immediacy, interactivity, and participation, as growing values of newswork, can partially be explained through economics. The focus on immediacy *elsewhere* suggests that more new content leads to an uptick in traffic and reader engagement. There is a financial incentive to be fresh, but at *The Times*, a place free of big-screen monitors with traffic data, journalists felt that immediacy meant ASAP, because the Internet was ASAP. Management did not talk about immediacy as an associated economic benefit.

However, management was quite vocal about the economic incentives behind interactivity and participation—engagement and branding, sticky and spreadable content. These economic realities were not expressed by journalists, but I do want to acknowledge the potential for subtle publisher encouragement to adopt these values to keep the newsroom solvent. Nevertheless, on a day-to-day level, journalists at *The Times* are so far removed from economic concerns that they spend little time thinking about the state of their industry. It's still about the story to most journalists, at least at *The Times*.

One underlying tension is the position of journalists' agency in their capacity to negotiate the overarching patterns and routines of newswork. Previous ethnographers argued that the newsroom could be reduced to a factory assembly line: "The selection and production processes have been likened to a funnel, with many stories being placed on the assembly line."[21] And if we take the newsroom at face value, journalists are still plugging away, day by day, minute by minute, trying to get their work out to feed a machine constantly hungry for news. But the tensions at play in digital change in the newsroom seem to suggest that journalists are engaged in an active process of negotiating what their job means in the information age—and their agency and buy-in matters, perhaps more now than ever.

What Is Different?

So if the fundamental processes of newswork are the same, from source pressure to audience pressure to content demands, what is different? And what is lasting? Part of the challenge left to future ethnographers is to see just what processes and practices emerge to define journalism in the Web era. However, what is enduring about my contribution is the importance of trying to understand the role of changing technology in newswork as it is becoming fully incorporated into the work of formerly print-only journalists, the rise of the social Web, and the incorporation of our networked communication ecology at the nation's paper of record.

The values I've identified come directly out of the social experience of online journalism and new media at the time I wrote this book. I bridged social and theoretical understandings of online journalism by anchoring my argument in past and present journalism studies literature and studies about new media and technology. And it has been my job as an ethnographer to see how these emergent values were crucial in shaping culture, behavior, and attitudes in my study site, *The New York Times*. These values themselves may be temporal; however, there's some argument for saying that they will not shift. As one Web programmer/journalist told me over Twitter, arguing that these values were here to stay, "Tools change, Principles remain the same."[22]

I see immediacy as a great opportunity for newswork. Immediacy has always been a core value of newswork, but it is revolutionary for online journalism because of the rise of the networked society and the possibility of 24/7 ASAP news. The advent of near-instant communication made possible by the rise of broadband and wireless technology means that information can be spread instantly. The complex flows of finance, politics, and media have been fundamentally altered. If information has always been valued in part by how quickly it has reached people, then we are likely at a pivotal moment with the Web, as so many have argued. Immediacy is shaped by technology itself, as well as by our expectations of technology in a networked society. But immediacy is also built into Web architecture: the faster the speed of Web technology, the more immediate Web sites must be in responding to audience demand. Immediacy has become a fundamental dictate for how to create content for the Web.

In newsrooms, immediacy emerged as a contested value, in part because it was still being negotiated in practice. Journalists did not know what to make of what seemed like an imperative to be responsive to the networked society. Immediacy highlighted the contradictions in a newsroom that was, on one hand, trying to remain tied to more than 160 years of daily print news production while, on the other hand, attempting to respond to the felt demand for new content on the Web all the time. One of the most difficult things about working in this newsroom was the lack of order and routines to deal with the demands of content. One can see the possibility for limitless content for a 24/7 world: churnalism, hamsterization, the news cyclone—names to describe the condition keep coming. Journalists were still improvising how they could order their work routines. Some of their tactics included writing B matter ahead of time to get the story out as quickly as possible, then sitting down for a brutal day of constant updates. Others included a seemingly haphazard approach to pushing content on the Web site. The home page editors had some sense for their own way to manage the day, but the influx of news for potentially immediate output was so intense that they could often barely leave their desks.

For *The New York Times*, one of the outstanding questions will be how to resolve the cognitive dissonance between setting a news agenda through the five or six most important stories of the day and setting a news agenda that changes every few minutes, or every few hours, or at the pace and according to the whims of the home page editor. How will an agenda be set when most people read the newspaper online? How will the newspaper retain its authoritative curation powers if it must respond to the ASAP pressure? This remained a lingering challenge—and opportunity—for the newspaper during the time of my research.

Immediacy is not just a value embedded in news practice; it is also a constraint. As Livingston and Bennett point out, immediacy limits the ability of journalists to do adequate sourcing if they're constantly under the gun, racing to chase after event-driven news.[23] We saw that Graham Bowley only had the time to talk to official sources when writing the first few drafts of his earnings report on Goldman Sachs (see chapter 34)—and in reality, we don't know how many of the clicks that are counted represent people coming back to see the fuller story with richer analysis that contains reporting from nonofficial sources. Similarly, immediacy puts pressure on journalists to produce content right away, rather than taking time to think carefully about news judgment. We saw the mistakes made when journalists rushed to put up the unemployment numbers, and only a journalist with fresh eyes noticed that the trend was actually good for the US economy, rather than bad, as the first few drafts of the story asserted (see Chapter 4). The felt pressure to keep pushing out more content on the Web site meant that journalists were pushing out news that might, at other times, be considered far less relevant, less worthy of prominence on the Web. The result, perhaps, was that readers might be getting lower-quality news.

In some ways, though, immediacy, when balanced properly against reporting depth, can be a great asset in the newsroom. Any newsroom that can convey information to a network hungry for instant news may be likely to succeed in the digital age. Immediacy may actually help news judgment. With fewer journalists in the newsroom and less time to respond to events, journalists may be equipped to make better choices about where to focus their attention. Similarly, a good understanding of immediacy can help journalists bolster their roles as authoritative storytellers.

By being able to put rapidly changing events into context—say, for instance, verifying the content appearing in a Twitter stream—or by providing larger narratives for other user-generated content, journalists can continue to uphold their roles as distillers of what can seem like an overwhelming flow of information. Immediacy may present an opportunity for journalists to be more responsive to the needs of their audiences. Immediacy, in some ways, may seem like a product of the environmental conditions for producing newswork; however, it is also a motivating force and guiding action that influences newswork. In this way, it is an orienting value for news production in the digital age.

Interactivity also works as a value that both guides and constrains practice. The definition of interactivity emerges from a fundamental understanding of how the Web has been built. Interactivity existed even in the days when the Web was little more than hyperlinks. The basic understanding was that the Internet was built for user direction and control, responsive to a built environment. Web architecture has increasingly taken advantage of the capacity of interactivity through front- and back-end development. Incorporated into our contemporary experience of the Web is an environment that is rich with video, audio, vibrant photography, interactive graphics, and more. Interactivity allows the user to manipulate rich content, and the underlying framework for this value is a core principle of Web design and user experience.

But interactivity also creates new constraints for the newsroom. Journalists now have to reckon with trying to understand what it means to do storytelling across multiple platforms. This requires traditional print journalists to think hard about what they are doing and to question whether their way of telling the story is the best way to get the news across. Maybe interactivity is more work, but ultimately, it will be better for the news consumer, as journalists begin to think more about the experience of audiences consuming news on the Web. And certainly, it was confusing for *Times* journalists to figure out how to mediate among all the new people in the newsroom who were there to make interactive products, from Web producers, to multimedia designers, to the interactive news team. This did, indeed, create a messy situation for traditional journalists not used to navigating in this environment. But perhaps the biggest constraint upon newsrooms is the felt need to create interactive stories: with so few people able to tell these types of stories, newsrooms are now in the position of needing to fill an entirely new type of online content demand.

However, interactivity also creates new forms of opportunity for newsrooms. As interactivity strengthens as an online journalism value, journalists, it is hoped, will choose the best way to tell stories. Readers will have the opportunity to navigate beyond an initial article; ideally, they will be able to take a deep dive to explore major events and investigations. This potential for new kinds of storytelling creates a new vocabulary for news, one where images, videos, and graphics are given parity with the written word.

And finally, participation as part of online journalism seems to embody the core of Web 2.0. The Web has become a platform for a social, shared experience of content. The possibility of being connected to anyone at any time is here. But more than that, participation invites user creation: people are invited to talk back—the Web architecture is a writeable, shareable space. Yohai Benkler argues that mass media faces a new challenge when people can participate in networked modes of communication.[24] The hub-and-spoke model is no more! Yet, this seemingly promising value actually brings with it some new constraints for newswork.

Participation-related constraints in the newsroom are probably the result of confusion. On one hand, journalists heard messages from the industry about the need to bring users into the conversation. At a time of declining revenue and circulation, it may have seemed like inviting readers to become producers of content was a wise choice. But at *The Times*, people did not have a sense for what this meant, and we saw confusion about everything from ethics to envisioning what it might mean to have a voice on these platforms.

So what would a participatory newsroom at *The Times* look like? Could it be one that wasn't exploiting people just because they were going to share content? In my ideal world, this newsroom would be one where more than just one editor would be assigned the job of community editing, with the role of aggregating and creating community conversation. Instead of pushing out questions and articles on Facebook, someone would actually answer questions and guide conversation on these platforms—and respond to comments, as well. The @nytimes Twitter handle would respond to people's comments about *Times* articles. *The Times* would surrender some control over its demands for user-generated content, which would not inhabit a place where everything is put neatly into a considered, attractive format. Instead, some of this content would not be highly produced multimedia, but just the result of public aggregation and acknowledged as such.

What would become of the folks who have decided to become brands and build household names? Perhaps some of the expectations regarding their reporting could be curtailed as they carried out reporting and opining through Twitter or shorter online posts, rather than their being expected to produce the same output. After all, as we saw, only a few journalists have been able to reach truly branded status. Perhaps it's best to encourage them to take the time to engage in conversation. We have started to see some targeted efforts that involve bringing audiences in for targeted reporting projects, such as *Huffington Post*'s OfftheBus campaign, which dispatched more than seventeen hundred "citizen journalists" to help the Web site cover the 2008 election.[25] Twelve thousand people eventually signed up to participate, according to head of the project, Amanda Michel. A single citizen report from this effort—the one relaying then-candidate Obama's comment that "It's not surprising, then, they get bitter, they cling to guns or religion or antipathy for people who aren't like them"—"ignited a media firestorm," to use Michel's words. A modified approach was taken for the 2012 election. More could be done like this, especially with *The Times* leading the charge. The potential to reshape politics through mainstream news organizations working with a distributed network is huge. And this may be the idealized form of networked journalism.

Forecasting Away the Future

What's next for *The Times*? What's next for journalism? In the great debate over the future of news, what does this book tell us to be wary of or excited about?

When Edward Diamond wrote his account of "The New *New York Times*" in what he called the "multimedia era" of 1995, he forecast in his epilogue the dawn of a new information age that would change *The Times*. But his focus was on personnel, and he suggested that *The Times* would move away from its trend, at the time, of trying to capture soft news and back toward trying to keep its stoic authority. Truthfully, though, he had no real insights to help us think about the newspaper in the digital age—in part because the paper didn't even have a Web site then.

As I write this, there are dozens of prognosticators in the "future of news" camp. Some big names come to mind: Jeff Jarvis, Jay Rosen, Clay Shirky, David Carr, Emily Bell, Jenny 8. Lee, the Knight Foundation, and others who have taken a shot at redefining what news ought to mean. One can find them in the *Columbia Journalism Review* (Dean Starkman, for example). Others can be found in *Nieman Journalism Lab,* where columns and posts offer the best and worst of the state of the news in transition. I've contributed to this site. The major debates concern whether traditional newsrooms will continue to survive, in what form, and who will pay. There's a lot of puffery and hubris and some serious attempts to plan for the future. These voices are very much concerned with just what role our newly empowered audience might play in the growing ecosystem of news and information. Though the economic model takes center stage in these debates, part of unraveling the puzzle means teasing out what counts as journalism.

There's an abbreviated history to the recent reexamination of journalism. First, we considered whether bloggers were journalists (now bloggers often work for newsrooms or mainstream outlets), and then organizations like the Knight Foundation invited the audience to create citizen journalism products (and funded them), and now crowd-mapping outlets and social media platforms are proving to be viable sources of news in new ways. We may have entered an era of "news and information," when traditional journalists must argue their case that they should still be regarded as authoritative storytellers.[26] This is where *The Times* may be able to retain a foothold.

The Times is, and will strive to be, a unique case in American journalism. It began in 1851 with the explicit purpose of serving an elite readership, a paper that would write above the penny presses of the day. And it has been, for decades, the general-interest newspaper of record, especially since it expanded its national terrain and section coverage between 1979 and 1980. Though print readership is clearly on the decline, when I was working on this book, the business staff was happy to point to a picture that had been taken of President Obama sitting on Air Force One, reading a print copy of *The Times'* business section.[27] *The Times* reaches the media elite, as well as a stable online audience, and in this huge reach, it has tremendous influence.

If I had to guess, I would posit that *The Times'* role as a paper of the media elite is unlikely to change, at least for a while. If *The Times* shrinks in size, as it is likely to do if it cannot keep its profit model sustainable, my bet is that the core of its reporting—international and political—will be saved at all costs. After all, *The Times* ownership has decided to keep the Baghdad bureau running at a cost of over $3 million a year.[28] This coverage is what makes *The Times* special—the unique content that it brings from all over the nation and world. Certainly, the Associated Press has more bureaus (over two hundred) all over the world providing breaking news, but *The Times*' aspiration is for its second-day coverage to provide the context to help readers make sense of both far-flung and war-torn regions of the world and an American political and media system stuffed to overflowing with hyperbole.

But the moment that *The Times* joins the chorus of other news organizations and loses its key ability to differentiate content is the moment that the paper starts to lose its brand value. What *The Times* has now is its authority, and this authority is the core of a brand recognized across the world. Sure, Yahoo! News and *The Daily Mail* are ahead of *The Times* in online news traffic. And that's okay, because these readers, for now, are not *The Times*' audience. *The Times* is not a wire service nor a tabloid, and it is unlikely to ever have the kind of staff or desire to really supply this kind of news.

For all of the focus on immediacy, *The Times* still tries to wrap context around what is happening. When *The Times* doesn't, its news becomes news that can be found anywhere—commodity news—and the only reason to come back to *The Times* is habit. The great danger for this newsroom is falling subject to the rat race of the hypercompetitive world of the Web—doing stories because other people are doing them, moving as fast as everyone else, pushing out the same content, and failing to offer a distinct product that speaks with a unique, clear, authoritative voice of news coverage. I would say the same would likely be true for any news organization that might abandon its key strengths.

Just as *The Times* must retain its distinctly authoritative brand, it must also continue to develop a relationship with its audience. So far, we've seen what seems like an almost creepy approach from top management to thinking about how to harness audience power. And from journalists, we've seen how participation is not about true conversation, as much as visibility on social networks. But as we grow into an increasingly more social Web (which some argue is Web 3.0),[29] *The*

Times is going to have to rethink its relationship with this audience. The newspaper is going to have to balance its desire for control over the brand with the need to have genuine, personal relationships with readers. And somehow, this has to be scalable for an audience of thirty million, so this relationship can feel authentic to each member. This is a tricky proposition. As I've suggested, the mechanism for doing so may be letting the reins of control over content quality go a bit to allow for increased user engagement. Similarly, journalists might mobilize their readers to help them pick up the slack for some of the reporting that may no longer be prioritized by staff at the newspaper.

In this fairly desperate environment for news, many newsrooms have become obsessed with using algorithms and metrics as guides for editorial and business decision making. The worst thing that could happen to *The Times* would be for it to start to take metrics into account for its daily decision making. When I was in the newsroom, metrics for individual story performance (and even the site itself) were quite opaque. Journalists were aware if they were on the most-emailed list, but they also knew that the list wasn't particularly accurate. Bloggers got some information about traffic: they knew who had the top blogs for the week. But actual numbers for stories were rarely released. The reason for this, as explained to me by Kevin McKenna, the business editor charged with Web operations, was that no one should feel that the number of people reading their story would somehow equate to the impact that their story might have.[30]

And beyond that, daily metrics were a poor judge of stories that had a much longer shelf life online—one example I was given was a series on water quality, which kept gaining new visitors over a long period, rather than in a single day's spike. Concern with metrics might prompt *The Times* to forget that its content is lasting, especially the expansive packages it builds around particular social issues, from how we deal with technology, to the Great Recession, to the reasons Wall Street led us to the economic crisis[31]—these are projects that last beyond the daily news cycle. Metrics might distort the incentive to produce such packages if the payoffs are not immediate. Letting editorial judgment be compromised by metrics, or even influenced by them, would signal a sharp turn at *The Times*, where so far the newsroom has been strictly shielded from commercial imperatives. In fact, it would be a complete cultural shift.

We are in the middle of what Kuhn might describe as a paradigm shift, a period when there are questions that are "sufficiently open-ended to leave all sorts of problems for the redefined group of practitioners to resolve."[32] The questions are many, from the practical to the more theoretical. How will newsrooms make money? What organizational form should they take? What should journalists be responsible for? What kinds of stories should be told? And then, from a more theoretical perspective, we should now wonder: What is the place of the traditional journalist in this new news ecology? What do new information flows mean for the production and creation of news? How has networked communication changed the role of mainstream news models? Who is the audience? What is new? What is old?

My intervention has been to try to understand how a sociocultural revolution has influenced newswork. These values I've talked about come from journalism but also from society, and they have fundamentally reshaped the ways that we experience and engage with our daily practices more generally. In fact, some even argue that new technology has reshaped and rewired the very patterns of our brains.[33] Increasing evidence points to a demand for immediate, on-demand content, as I have noted—and we may actually be growing even more impatient, because we are so used to getting what we want, when we want it, online.[34] The richness of immersive and participatory experiences leaves some wondering whether people are spending too much of their lives online, rather than offline.[35]

Journalists are in a conflicted place about how to adjust to the information age. The speed of information is only getting faster, and our lives are only growing more social. Similarly, the capacity for displaying information, content, games, and more on the Web is only getting more sophisticated. Journalists reckon with immediacy, torn between a world that seems to demand instant satisfaction and their own professional legacy of considered decision making and more than 160 years of a single, daily product. Interactivity suggests a whole new capacity for telling stories in an immersive Web environment. And the rise of the audience, perhaps not as an equal, but as a group that does now have the capability to talk back, has certainly made journalists aware that they can no longer hide behind the mask of "mass media" and must instead find some way to engage readers. News practices, news values, and journalism are contested, and what lies beyond is a new paradigm for news in the information age. And the economic question will loom large: all thirty million readers of nytimes.com still cannot finance the entire functioning of the news-gathering operation at *The New York Times*. And that's for the fifth-largest news site in the world and largest online newspaper site in the U.S.

The takeaway is that, in times of change, like the one chronicled here, nothing is certain, and there are many existing problems that journalism will have to solve. Taking on the challenges of preparing for the digital future requires addressing the demands of immediacy, interactivity, and participation, even if these are ephemeral and transitional points along the way to a much more stable place for journalism in the Web-, mobile-, and ICT-dominated world. Taking note of these changes gives us a historic groundwork that can assist us with understanding what comes next. The stakes were high for the future of *The New York Times* in 2010, as the newspaper looked to retain its authority in a world with an increasingly unpredictable information and economic environment. How, at the end of the day, do you tell the world what the most important stories are if you are a global news organization and there is no true end of the day in a 24/7 information environment? How do you create content that engages people in a way that goes beyond the traditional story but still insures that news content is just as compelling as the interactive content they might find on Facebook or YouTube? And how do you take advantage of the ever-increasing number of people who are able to share their voices and opinions about content? These are the essential questions for *The New York Times* as it leaps into the future. Past practices will only provide so much guidance; ingenuity, talent, quality, and luck will be necessary for the newspaper's survival.

Methods

I gained access to *The Times* through a confluence of lucky events. First and foremost, Martin Nisenholtz had been a student of my advisor, Larry Gross, at the University of Pennsylvania, and he was able to issue a command from the top to let me in to the newsroom. Second, Kevin McKenna, one of the heads of *CyberTimes*, who was now a deputy business editor, remembered Pablo Boczkowski's 1998 fieldwork and understood what I was trying to accomplish. Finally, I was able to meet *Business Day* editor Larry Ingrassia at a Society of American Business Editors and Writers get-together at Columbia University to explain my study. His college roommate at Yale had done a newsroom ethnography for his dissertation. My own project began as a doctoral dissertation for the University of Southern California's Annenberg School for Communication and Journalism.

In order to secure access to the newspaper, I worked with *New York Times* lawyers to hammer out an agreement that would keep the newsroom confident that I would not leak any information about breaking news or new developments in *The Times'* business strategy. As a result, I agreed both to focus my research away from delicate subjects like sourcing and to avoid inquiry about *The Times'* business model. In subsequent conversations, I agreed to devote most of my attention to the business desk (instead of observing, say, daily news meetings on the national desk, as well). To insure that I had not revealed any information that could jeopardize source relations, and to help check for factual accuracy, I gave McKenna the right to review my dissertation manuscript. Others were given the opportunity to review the manuscript if they were profiled extensively (such as Andrew Martin, Nick Bilton, and Graham Bowley). None of the field anecdotes have changed since this time, though the framing of the argument has. This means that *The Times* was given the right to review the initial dissertation for compliance to our original agreement and for any factual errors they saw in this draft, but I did not make any changes to the argument in the initial dissertation. However, this version has substantially revised the argument for the work.

To comply with the Institutional Review Board (IRB), I was able to secure an agreement with USC that required a verbal agreement, followed up by an information sheet. The IRB said that I was able to use names with consent. My purpose in the newsroom was explained with an introductory email to the entire Business Day staff and a clear note that no one had to participate unless they wanted to. Only one journalist, Louise Story, declined to participate, and I did not include any direct quotes or specific observations of her from my time there— and she was comfortable with this arrangement (and requested to be named as not participating). While I was unable to blast the entire business staff with the information sheet all at once, I provided information sheets to those I observed and interviewed. In some cases, it was simply not possible to provide every single person with the IRB information sheet—such as top editors in Page One or people whom I met casually in the newsroom. Nonetheless, it was well communicated to the newsroom staff that I was a visitor working according to traditional journalism rules (on-the-record, off-the-record, on background) who would use the information first for a dissertation and then for other academic publishing, including this book or additional articles. I was able to confirm with USC that my work met the standards they expected from this kind of IRB research and have sent this confirmation to the publisher.

To protect my research subjects in this difficult time for journalism, I was very careful to explain the purposes of the project and its outcomes to the best of my ability to each and every journalist with whom I worked closely. Journalists agreed to be named, unless they decided to go "on background" for specific comments. When journalists said negative things about the newspaper, I omitted their names unless they specifically requested otherwise. I also scrubbed the dates from the book, as either emails, news events, or assorted markers, and journalists could be identified as speaking to me by those dates. However, upon request, I can provide field dates to academics who request this information.

As for the actual process of information gathering and information processing, my research began the second week in January 2010. I entered the newsroom with the intention to spend three days a week at *The Times*, but after a week or two, I quickly began going nearly every day. After this short period of observing meetings and introducing myself to both the business desk and the newsroom more generally, I began soliciting journalists for what I called "shadowing." This meant that I would spend a day with a specific journalist, from the time they came into the office generally until the time they left or they asked me to give them the space to focus on a task that generally would not yield more information for me (e.g., writing the final draft of an article). These journalists let me watch them do everything—I was privy to their emails, their IM conversations, their phone conversations, and so on. One might wonder how I could understand what kind of phone conversations they were having, but all text-based journalists I observed now take their notes on Microsoft Word, so I was able to see the other side of the conversation. I was also able to observe interoffice communication through IM. I am thankful for their generosity. I benefited from working with a subject population that understood the need to gather as much information as possible and understood how this information could become public knowledge.

Ultimately, I shadowed thirty-six people throughout my five months in the newsroom, from text-focused "traditional" reporters on the business desk, to home page editors, to Web producers. After two months in the newsroom, I began conducting interviews with a protocol I had developed. Ultimately, I interviewed eighty-one people, from Bill Keller, executive editor, to the youngest journalist on the business desk, Javier Hernandez. These interviews were not limited to the business desk but included discussions with people all across the newsroom hierarchy, focusing particularly on those thinking about digital strategy, investigations, and changes in the newsroom.

In between shadowing and interviewing, I generally attended three newsroom meetings a day—the Business Day morning meeting and the two Business Day afternoon meetings. I also attended Web "turnover meetings" and morning Web meetings on occasion, though as I detail, they were quite short and had little impact on the ultimate decision making of the home page editor. I also attended approximately one month's worth of Page One meetings across my time in the newsroom.

I had an excellent "campout" spot in the newsroom to observe and overhear conversation. My little "desk" was a small, round, one-person table located in the middle of the Business Day newsroom, quite close to the pod that included all the top editors and directly next to the financial reporters. As such, I could listen to editors and reporters talking to each other about stories. One critique often harvested about newsroom ethnography is that ethnographers never leave the newsroom to watch people report. In this case, most business reporters did work from their desks in New York, save for in-person source meetings. The event-driven news could be observed from the newsroom, as I detail. Since I often couldn't watch source meetings, I did, in fact, miss these quiet lunches. However, I was often invited to sit in on more casual meetings, and *The Times* business staff regularly brought in CEOs and government officials to provide off-the-record commentary about their specialties. I was welcome to attend these meetings. As you saw in chapter 2, I was also invited to sit in on conference calls and the like on occasion.

In addition, I visited the *International Herald Tribune* (*IHT*) in Paris for a week, and after my research at *The Times*, I was able to visit the *IHT* in Asia. This material does not appear in this text, but it did yield rich information about the twenty-four-hour business news cycle, print and online convergence, interactivity without resources, and other valuable information.

Traditional ethnographic methods guided my research. Journalists were not at all surprised to see me with a notebook in hand, jotting down as much conversation as possible. I had small field notebooks on hand with me, and thanks to my training as a journalist, I was able to capture direct quotes verbatim throughout the course of the day. Each day would yield approximately ten pages' worth of single-spaced field notes, replete with full conversations, which I, in turn, typed and transcribed onto Google documents. For each interview, I sat with my laptop and directly transcribed the conversations onto Google Documents.

Each weekend, I took the plethora of field notes and started to code the notes using the methods first outlined by Glaser and Strauss. I relied on the constant comparative method to go through my notes. I first looked for key codes, and then I looked more broadly for concepts and then finally for themes, which ultimately guided my analysis. In the initial version of this manuscript, there was more detail about business news decision making, but in this manuscript, the focus ultimately came to be on the themes most closely related to print and online news in the digital age. In the first weeks, I found it difficult to find recurring codes, but then I quickly was able to see common threads throughout the course of each day as I became more immersed in the newsroom.

I relied on a backdrop of theory about news ethnography and the larger culture of the Web as I began my research. I had read contemporary and historic ethnographies before beginning my work, and I reread them as I began my analysis. I also immersed myself in literature about the culture of the Web in 2010 as I began to consider the role of the information technology world at large. In this way, I used the grounded theory method to move from my data to a larger work that drew on extant theory to produce this book's text.

Notes

1. Shaffer, "Viracon Glass."

2. The continuous news desk is a group of editors and reporters at *The Times* dedicated to writing breaking news for the Web. A desk at *The Times* refers to a cluster of journalists grouped according to a common theme or section of the newspaper, e.g., the business desk or the national desk.

3. Gerry Mullany, personal communication with author, Apr. 5, 2010.

4. Susan Edgerley, personal communication with author, May 11, 2010.

5. Auletta, "Inheritance."

6. Hagan, "Bleeding 'Times' Blood."

7. Foer, "Source of the Trouble"; M. Carlson, *On the Condition of Anonymity.*

8. Swanson, "Battle for the Newsroom."

9. Talese, *Kingdom and the Power,* 9.

10. Tifft and Jones, *Trust.*

11. McGowan, *Gray Lady Down.*

12. Deuze, "What Is Journalism?" 449.

13. Stephens, "History of Newspapers."

14. For most of this story, please see the review offered by the classic textbook on media history: Emery, Emery, and Roberts, *Press and America.*

15. Jackaway, *Media at War.*

16. Spence and Quinn, "Information Ethics"; Karlsson, "Immediacy of Online News."

17. Karlsson, "Immediacy of Online News," 286.

18. Starkman, "Hamster Wheel."

19. Starkman, "Hamster Wheel."

20. Lasar, "Has the Internet 'Hamsterized' Journalism?"; Waldman, *Information Needs of Communities.*

21. Lasar, "Has the Internet 'Hamsterized' Journalism?"

247

22. Belopotosky et al., "Fed Chairman's Life."

23. de Sola Pool, *Technologies of Freedom*, 217.

24. Bucy, "Interactivity in Society," 374.

25. Garrett, "Elements of User Experience."

26. Steensen, "What's Stopping Them?" 882.

27. Domingo, "Interactivity in the Daily Routines," 680.

28. Chung, "Interactive Features of Online Newspapers"; Colson and Heinderyckx, "Do Online Journalists Belong"; O'Sullivan, "Delivering Ireland"; Quandt, "Old and New Routines."

29. Micheline Maynard, personal communication, May 17, 2010.

30. Twitter screen grab, Jan. 17, 2013, https://twitter.com/nytkeller

31. Rosen, "People Formerly Known."

32. Benkler, *Wealth of Networks*, 255.

33. Benton, "Clay Shirky."

34. Lewis, "From Journalism to Information," 311; Lewis, "Tension between Professional Control."

35. Jarvis, "Networked Journalism."

36. Sonderman, "Problem with Retweets."

37. "Facebook for Reporting and Storytelling."

38. "KDMC Presentations."

39. Ingram, "Should There Be a Pulitzer Prize."

40. Silverman, "Profiles in Courage."

41. "People Formerly Known."

42. State of the News Media, 2012.

43. Cottle, "New(s) Times," 19.

44. Breed, "Social Control in the Newsroom"; White, "Gate Keeper."

45. Tuchman, "Objectivity"; Tuchman, "Making News by Doing Work"; Tuchman, *Making News*.

46. Epstein, *News from Nowhere*; Schlesinger, *Putting "Reality" Together*; Fishman, *Manufacturing the News*; Sigal, *Reporters and Officials*.

47. Klinenberg, "Convergence."

48. Ryfe, *Can Journalism Survive?*

49. Anderson, *Rebuilding the News*, 4.

Chapter 1

1. Esch, "Martin Nisenholtz Resigns."

2. Author's field notes, Apr. 12, 2010.

3. Jenny Anderson, personal communication with author, Mar. 3, 2010.

4. Carr, "Fissures Are Growing."

5. Starr, "Goodbye to the Age."

6. Downie and Schudson, "Reconstruction of American Journalism"; Pickard, Stearns, and Aaron, *Saving the News*.

7. Edmonds, Guskin, and Rosenstiel, "Newspapers."

8. Doctor, *Newsonomics.*

9. Arango, "Fall in Newspaper Sales."

10. Jones, *Losing the News.*

11. Anderson, Bell, and Shirky, *Post-Industrial Journalism,* 2.

12. Dorroh, "Statehouse Exodus."

13. M. Carlson, "Where Once Stood Titans."

14. Richman and James, "Seattle P-I to Publish Last Edition."

15. Carr, "Newspaper Barons Resurface."

16. Carr, "At Flagging Tribune."

17. Theim, "Save the Times-Picayune!"

18. Schiller, "Letter to Readers."

19. Tenore, "How Paywalls Affect Social Media."

20. Pew Research Center, "Newspapers stabilizing but still threatened," http://stateofthemedia.org/2013/newspapers-stabilizing-but-still-threatened/.

21. Chittum, "Anti-Paywall Dead-Enders."

22. Usher, "Less of Less."

23. Ahuja, "ProPublica, Storify."

24. Matter, http://matter.vc/, April 2, 2013.

25. Lewis, "Journalism Innovation and Participation."

26. Usher and Lewis, "Lessons from #MozFest."

27. Anderson, Bell, and Shirky, *Post-Industrial Journalism,* 23.

28. Beckett, "Continuing Digital Transformation."

29. Hirschorn, "End Times."

30. Mnookin, "Kingdom and the Paywall."

31. Heim, "Why Did the Company Just Lose?"

32. Buttry, "Don't Believe Anyone."

33. Newspaper Guild of New York, "In Silence, Times Guild."

34. Haughney, "New York Times Seeks Buyouts."

35. Smolkin, "Challenging Times."

36. Beckett, "Continuing Digital Transformation."

37. Boczkowski, *Digitizing the News.*

38. Susan Jacobson, personal communication with author, Jan. 24, 2013.

39. Rich Meislen, personal communication with author, May 7, 2010.

40. Bernard Gwertzman, personal communication with author, May 17, 2010.

41. Boczkowski, *Digitizing the News.*

42. John Haskins, personal communication with author, Apr. 23, 2010.

43. Boczkowski, *Digitizing the News.*

44. Jim Roberts, personal communication with author, Apr. 6, 2010.

45. Susan Edgerley, personal communication with author, Apr. 2, 2010.

46. Len Apcar, personal communication with author, May 10, 2010.

47. Bill Keller, personal communication with author, May 7, 2010.

48. Jonathan Landman, personal communication with author, May 3, 2010.

49. Author's field notes, January 20, 2010.

50. Keller, personal communication with author, May 7, 2010.

51. Keller, personal communication with author, May 7, 2010

52. Perez-Pena, "Jonathan Landman Culture Editor."

53. Keller, personal communication with author, May 7, 2010.

Chapter 2

1. Prior, "Foreclosures in 2011."

2. Newport, "Americans Rate Computer Industry Best."

3. Michelstein and Boczkowski, "Between Tradition and Change," 562.

4. This larger public discourse can be traced through TV, print, and online coverage. Goldman stories got an outpouring of comments from the public on *The Times'* Web site and other news sites.

5. Derivatives are securities whose values are determined based on one or more underlying assets, and they are traded according to expectations of future prices. Collateralized debt obligations are investment-grade securities backed by pools of bonds, loans, and other assets.

6. Net revenue is the amount of income a company collects. Net earnings are revenue minus expenses, or the money earned after costs are removed.

7. This reference suggests a potential audience not of big-time investors, but of people who are small-time investors in the stock market. The reference, then, suggests an audience who would be investing in Goldman Sachs.

8. A story that might get copy edited over and over would be a planned Page One scoop, for instance.

9. Bowley, "Strong Year for Goldman."

10. An interchange fee is the fee that credit card companies charge merchants for using credit cards to accept payment. Often, these fees are passed on to consumers in the form of higher prices.

11. *New York Times Bits* (blog), introduction, http://bits.blogs.nytimes.com/, January, 27, 2010.

12. Garber, "The New York Times R&D Lab"; Danny K, "Augmented Reflection Mirror."

13. Bilton, *I Live in the Future.*

14. During my tenure at *The Times*, Grobart and other staffers took on new positions. Grobart moved to the home section, and Goel became the enterprise editor.

15. A vertical at *The Times* refers to a particular area of coverage that is oriented around a particular niche audience. Some of these verticals include energy and environment, technology, *DealBook*, personal technology, small business, Your Money (personal finance), and media. These also have their own associated blogs.

16. Carr, "Savior in the Form"; Chmielewski and Pham, "Apple's Rumored Tablet."

17. A liveblog is a stream of very short blog posts that is intended to provide instant updates as an event is happening. At *The Times*, a liveblog is also expected to provide analysis.

18. Stone, "Three Reasons Why."

19. Bilton, "Three Reasons Why."

20. Stone, "Three Reasons Why"; Bilton, "Get Your Non-Apple News"; Bilton, "Blogosphere Reacts to the iPad"; Bilton, "Google Adds More Social"; Bilton, "Monitoring Twitter's iPad Commentary"; *New York Times Bits* (blog), introduction.

Chapter 3

1. B. A. Williams and Delli Carpini, "Real Ethical Concerns."

2. "Americans Spend More Time."

3. Larry Ingrassia, personal communication with author, May 3, 2010.

4. Brian Stelter, personal communication with author, Apr. 5, 2010.

5. Greenhouse, "Unpaid Intern"; author's field notes, Apr. 3, 2010.

6. Feuer, "Snapshot of the World."

7. Jim Roberts, personal communication with author, May 4, 2010.

8. Huff, "Arthur Sulzberger, Jr."

9. Bill Keller, personal communication with author, May 7, 2010.

10. Chan, "Voices That Dominate Wall Street."

11. Hakim and Rashbaum, "Paterson Is Said."

12. Author's field notes, Mar. 4, 2010.

13. Barboza, "Market Defies Fear."

14. Author's field notes, Feb. 3, 2010.

15. Author's field notes, May 4, 2010.

16. "Tick-tock" is newsroom language for a timeline-type story that attempts to recount events in the order they happened.

17. Author's field notes, May 4, 2010.

18. Berke had changed jobs.

19. These deadlines are somewhat flexible and depend on a story's significance. Later, I address the print deadlines for the different editions, but story text and page layout must be completed before these absolute page deadlines. In the event of a developing story, like a presidential election, deadlines may be extended.

20. Johnson, "More with Dementia Wander."

21. Story and Morgenson, "SEC Accuses Goldman."

22. Author's field notes, Apr. 16, 2010.

23. The second national edition goes to Atlanta; Boston; Concord, California; Los Angeles; Seattle; and Springfield, Virginia.

24. Keith Leighty, personal communication with author, Oct. 4, 2010.

25. Author's field notes, Mar. 11, 2010.

26. Author's field notes, Mar. 2, 2010.

27. Roberts, personal communication with author, Apr. 16, 2010.

28. A separate home page producer mans the "global" edition of nytimes.com, which can be accessed by www.iht.com or http://global.nytimes.com/?iht

29. Hernandez, "What Makes Gillibrand Scary to Rivals?"

30. Urbina, "Toll Mounts"; author's field notes, Apr. 5, 2010.

31. Author's field notes, Apr. 5, 2010.

32. Author's field notes, Apr. 1, 2010.

33. Author's field notes, Mar. 1, 2010.

34. Mark Getzfred, personal communication with author, May 5, 2010.

35. Author's field notes, Feb. 10, 2010.

36. Mark Getzfred, personal communication with author, Jan. 13, 2010.

37. Author's field notes, Apr. 13, 2010.

Chapter 4

1. Author's field notes, Mar. 8, 2010.

2. B. Meier, "High Cost."

3. Barry Meier, personal communication with author, Apr. 5, 2010.

4. Author's field notes, Apr. 19, 2010.

5. Kamer, "Nick Denton's 'State of Gawker 2012.'"

6. Author's field notes, Mar. 4, 2010.

7. "Hard news" is news that deals with serious or formal topics.

8. Goodman and Hernandez, "Jobless Rates Hold Steady."

9. Ed Wyatt, personal communication with author, May 10, 2010.

10. Jad Mouawad, personal communication, Mar. 24, 2010.

11. Senior reporter, personal communication with author, Jan. 20, 2010.

12. Author's field notes, Feb. 12, 2010.

13. Diana B. Henriques, personal communication with author, Jan. 21, 2010.

14. Author's field notes, Apr. 13, 2010.

15. Hakim and Rashbaum, "Spitzer Is Linked."

16. Morgenson and Story, "Clients Worried."

17. In the past, putting up exclusive documents was simply not possible. Now, thanks to the Web, journalists often put up documents that they have collected from their investigative efforts as further proof of their reporting.

Chapter 5

1. Author's field notes, Apr. 12, 2010.

2. Dance, Jackson, and Pilhofer, "Gauging Your Distraction."

3. Moss, "Burger That Shattered Her Life."

4. Bucy, "Interactivity in Society," 374.

5. Meridian Web Design, "Make It Sticky."

6. University of Michigan Journalism Jobs and Internships, "News Application Developer" (job posting), (April 13, 2013).

7. Author's field notes, Apr. 14, 2010.

8. Author's field notes, Apr. 14, 2010.

9. Aron Pilhofer, personal communication with author, Dec. 11, 2010.

10. Andrew DeVigal, personal communication with author, Apr. 20, 2010.

11. Pilhofer, personal communication with author, Dec. 11, 2010.

12. Dance, Pilhofer, Lehren, and Damens,"Faces of the Dead."

13. "Closer Look at the Destruction."

14. "Assessing the Damage."

15. Clark, "El Mundo Wowed Me."

16. "Haiti: 360."

17. Author's field notes, Apr. 16, 2010.

18. Lawson, "*New York Times* 'TimesCast.'"

19. Hoyt, "Danger of Always Being On."

20. Author's field notes, Apr. 20, 2010.

21. Jane Bornemeier, personal communication with author, Apr. 8, 2010.

22. Damon Darlin, personal communication with author, Apr. 21, 2010.

23. Author's field notes, Apr. 20, 2010.

24. Author's field notes, May 5, 2010.

25. Rosenbloom, "In Bid to Sway Sales."

26. Creswell, "Profits for Buyout Firms."

27. Julie Creswell, personal communication with author, Apr. 1, 2010.

28. David Pogue, personal communication with author, May 13, 2010.

29. David Carr, personal communication with author, Apr. 5, 2010.

30. David Segal, personal communication with author, Apr. 1, 2010.

31. Wise, Lieber, and Vega. "31 Steps."

32. Ron Lieber, personal communication with author, Apr. 8, 2010.

33. Author's field notes, Feb. 10, 2010.

Chapter 6

1. Author's field notes, Jan. 14, 2011. At the time, Twitter could also automatically update to Facebook. Similarly, now Twitter can shorten links for you. But the spreading of knowledge, correct or incorrect, suggests a commitment to sharing ideas about participation.

2. Twitter bought Tweetdeck for $40 million in Mar. 2011 and now includes the ability to shrink links as one of its features.

3. Jenkins, "If It Doesn't Spread."

4. Gillmor, *We the Media*, xxiii.

5. Deuze, "Convergence Culture," 243.

6. Bruns, *Blogs, Wikipedia, Second Life*, 2.

7. Beckett, *Supermedia*.

8. Jarvis, "Networked Journalism."

9. Jenkins, "If It Doesn't Spread."

10. Tartakoff, "NYT's Nisenholtz's Speech."

11. Beckett, "Continuing Digital Transformation."

12. Holcomb, Gross, and Mitchell, "How Traditional Media Outlets."

13. Brian Stelter, Twitter post, Mar. 12, 2012 (https://twitter.com/#!/brianstelter/status/179244348528005120).

14. Jarvis, "Public Parts."

15. Rosen, "What I Think I Know."

16. Ingram, "Should There Be a Pulitzer Prize."

17. Vanessa Schneider, personal communication with author, Apr. 9, 2010.

18. Breed, "Social Control in the Newsroom," 328.

19. Author's field notes, Feb. 3, 2010.

20. Willie Neuman, personal communication with author, Apr. 19, 2010.

21. Author's field notes, Apr. 5, 2010.

22. SMWG, "New York Times Media Reporter."

23. Krochmal, "Advanced Social Media."

24. Goodridge, "NYT's Brian Stelter."

25. J. Diamond, "3 More Industry Leaders."

26. Brian Stelter, quoted in author's field notes, Apr. 5, 2010.

27. Bumiller, "Video Shows U.S. Killing."

28. If you watch *Page One*, the documentary, it seems like the WikiLeaks story all broke on one day. In fact, however, the WikiLeaks story featured in the movie came after this breaking news. See Cohen and Stelter, "Iraq Video Brings Notice."

29. Bumiller, "Video Shows U.S. Killing."

30. Pogue, personal communication with author, May 13, 2010.

31. David Pogue, Twitter feed, http://twitter.com/#!/Pogue, April 13, 2010.

32. Anderson, personal communication with author, Mar. 3, 2010.

33. Steve Greenhouse, personal communication with author, Feb. 5, 2010.

34. Breed, "Social Control in the Newsroom," 328.

35. David Streitfeld, personal communication with author, May 3, 2010.

36. Natasha Singer, personal communication with author, Mar. 11, 2010.

37. Schudson, *Discovering the News*.

38. Phil Corbett, email message to author, Oct. 28, 2010.

39. Wyatt, personal communication with author, May 10, 2010.

40. Reed Abelson, personal communication with author, Apr. 19, 2010.

41. In a distinction perhaps only meaningful to *The Times*, Tabuchi is technically on contract and not officially "staff."

42. "NYT Tokyo-Based Business Reporter."

43. Phil Corbett, email message to author, Oct. 26, 2010.

44. Hoyt, "Danger of Always Being On."

45. Jenkins, *Convergence Culture*, 131.

46. Confino and Judge-Brown, "Living Our Values," 8.

Chapter 7

1. Turner, "Jill Abramson Steps Away."

2. Stoeffel, " New York Times Decides."

3. Nussbaum, "New Journalism."

4. Branch, "Snowfall."

5. Wolfgang Blau, personal communication with author, Oct. 23, 2013.

6. Mackey, "Twitter Transformed."

7. Stark, *Sense of Dissonance.*

8. Center for the Digital Future, "Digital Turning Point."

9. Ives, "New York Times Plans Public Beta."

10. Anderson, Bell, and Shirky, *Post-Industrial Journalism,* 17.

11. Ryfe, *Can Journalism Survive?*

12. Author's field notes, Feb. 29, 2012.

13. Roberts, "New York Times Contest."

14. Breed, "Social Control in the Newsroom."

15. Gans, *Deciding What's News,* xix.

16. Anderson, "Between Creative and Quantified Audiences."

17. Breed, "Social Control in the Newsroom."

18. Reese, "News Paradigm."

19. Epstein, *News from Nowhere.*

20. McChesney, "Problem of Journalism"; Bagdikian, *New Media Monopoly.*

21. Gans, *Deciding What's News,* 109.

22. Pippin Lee, Twitter communication with author, Feb. 14, 2012 (https://twitter.com/#!/PippinLee/status/169469292776132610).

23. Livingston and Bennett, "Gatekeeping, Indexing."

24. Benkler, *Wealth of Networks,* chap. 7.

25. Michel, "Get Off the Bus."

26. Lewis, "Tension between Professional Control."

27. White House, P052209PS-0007, May 22, 2009 (digital image) (http://www.flickr.com/photos/whitehouse/3582767967/in/set-72157618986791573).

28. Mnookin, "*New York Times'* Lonely War."

29. Wharton School at the University of Pennsylvania, "Web 3.0: 'Social Waves.'"

30. Kevin McKenna, personal communication with author, May 14, 2010.

31. Richtel, Scelfo, Parker-Pope, and Connelly, "Your Brain on Computers"; Stravato, "With No Job"; Morgenson and Story, "House Advantage."

32. Kuhn, *Structure of Scientific Revolutions,* 10.

33. Richtel, "Attached to Technology."

34. Parker-Pope, "Ugly Toll of Technology."

35. Turkle, *Alone Together,* 1.

Bibliography

Access Digital. "New York Times Media Reporter Brian Stelter on Social Media and Journalism, More." *Access Point* (blog), March 14, 2011. http://blog.accesspr.com/2011/03/new-york-times-media-reporter-brian-stelter-on-social-media-and-journalism-more-video/.

Ahuja, Masuma. "ProPublica, Storify, and the Top 5 Cool New Media Startups That Are Changing the Game." *Policymic*, 2012. http://www.policymic.com/articles/ 3953/propublica-storify-and-the-top-5-cool-new-media-startups-that-are-changing-the-game.

Anderson, C. W. "Between Creative and Quantified Audiences: Web Metrics and Changing Patterns of Newswork in Local U.S. Newsrooms." *Journalism: Theory, Practice, Criticism* 12, no. 5 (2011): 550–66. doi: 10.1177/1464884911402451.

Anderson, C. W. *Rebuilding the News: Metropolitan Journalism in the Digital Age.* Philadelphia: Temple University Press, 2013.

Anderson, C. W., Emily Bell, and Clay Shirky. *Post-Industrial Journalism: Adapting to the Present.* Columbia Journalism School: Tow Center for Digitial Journalism, 2012. http://towcenter.org/research/post-industrial-journalism/.

Arango, Tim. "Fall in Newspaper Sales Accelerates to Pass 7%." *New York Times*, April 27, 2009. http://www.nytimes.com/2009/04/28/business/media/28paper.html.

Arizona State University Walter Cronkite School of Journalism and Mass Communication. "Undergraduate Programs." http://cronkite.asu.edu/undergrad/index.php., April 13, 2013.

"Assessing the Damage in Haiti." *New York Times*, January 18, 2010. http://www.nytimes.com/interactive/2010/01/18/world/americas/0118-haiti-assess-maps.html#tab=0.

Auletta, Ken. "The Inheritance: Can Arthur Sulzberger, Jr., Save the Times—and Himself?" *New Yorker*, December 19, 2005. http://www.newyorker.com/archive/2005/12/19/051219fa_fact.

Bagdikian, Ben H. *The New Media Monopoly.* Boston: Beacon Press, 2004.

Bantz, Charles R., Suzanne McCorkle, and Roberta C. Baade. "The News Factory." *Communication Research* 7, no. 1. (1980): 45–68. doi: 10.1177/ 0093650280 00700103.

Barboza, David. "Market Defies Fear of Real Estate Bubble in China." *New York Times*, March 4, 2010. http://www.nytimes.com/2010/03/05/business/global/ 05yuan.html.

Barnhurst, Kevin G., and John Nerone. *The Form of News: A History*. New York: Guilford Press, 2001.

Barnhurst, Kevin G., and John Nerone. "The Form of News: Thoughts on the Newspaper as Environment." Media Ecology Association, 2002. http://ww.media-ecology.org/publications/MEA_proceedings/v3/Barnhurst-Nerone03.pdf.

Beckett, Charlie. "The Continuing Digital Transformation of *The New York Times* by Arthur Sulzberger." *Polis Blog* (blog), November 1, 2011. http://blogs.lse. ac.uk/polis/2011/11/ 01/the-continuing-digital-transformation-of-the-new-york-times-by-arthur-sulzberger/.

Beckett, Charlie. *Supermedia: Saving Journalism So It Can Save the World*. Malden, MA: Blackwell, 2008.

Belopotosky, Danielle, Sewell Chan, Eric Owles, and Ben Werschkul. "A Fed Chairman's Life." *New York Times*, May 15, 2010. http://www.nytimes.com/interactive/2010/05/ 14/business/16ben-timeline.html?ref=business.

Benkler, Yochai. *The Wealth of Networks: How Social Production Transforms Markets and Freedom*. New Haven: Yale University Press, 2006.

Bennett, W. Lance. *News: The Politics of Illusion*. New York: Longman, 2001.

Bennett, W. Lance, Regina G. Lawrence, and Steven Livingston. *When the Press Fails: Political Power and the News Media from Iraq to Katrina*. Chicago: University of Chicago Press, 2007.

Benton, Joshua. "Clay Shirky: 'Let a Thousand Flowers Bloom to Replace Newspapers; Don't Build a Paywall around a Public Good." *Nieman Journalism Lab*, September 23, 2009. HYPERLINK "http://www.niemanlab.org/2009/09/ clay-shirky-let-a-thousand-flowers-bloom-to-replace-newspapers-dont-build-a-paywall-around-a-public-good/" http://www.niemanlab.org/2009/09/clay-shirky-let-a-thousand-flowers-bloom-to-replace-newspapers-dont-build-a-paywall-around-a-public-good/.

Berliner, Paul. *Thinking in Jazz: The Infinite Art of Improvisation*. Chicago: University of Chicago Press, 1994.

Bigge, Lauren. "Journalism Schools Embrace a Multimedia Education." *In Vocus* (blog), August 27, 2009. http://www.vocus.com/invocus/media-blog/journalism-schools-embrace-a-multimedia-education/.

Bilton, Nick. "The Blogosphere Reacts to the iPad. Bits. *New York Times Bits* (blog), January 27, 2010. http://bits.blogs.nytimes.com/2010/01/27/reaction-from-the-technology-blogosphere/.

Bilton, Nick. "Get Your Non-Apple News." *New York Times Bits* (blog), January 27, 2010. http://bits.blogs.nytimes.com/2010/01/27/get-your-non-apple-news/.

Bilton, Nick. "Google Adds More Social to Search. *New York Times Bits* (blog), January 27, 2010. http://bits.blogs.nytimes.com/2010/01/27/google-adds-more-social-to-search.

Bilton, Nick. *I Live in the Future and Here's How It Works: Why Your World, Work and Brain Are Being Creatively Disrupted.* New York: Crown Business, 2010.

Bilton, Nick. "Monitoring Twitter's iPad Commentary." *New York Times Bits* (blog), January 27, 2010. http://bits.blogs.nytimes.com/2010/01/27/chart-monitoring-twitters-ipad-commentary.

Bilton, Nick. "Three Reasons Why the iPad Will Kill Amazon's Kindle." *New York Times Bits* (blog), January 27, 2010. http://bits.blogs.nytimes.com/2010/01/27/three-reasons-why-the-ipad-will-kill-amazons-kindle/.

"Bits Blog Introduction." *New York Times Bits blog* (blog), January 27, 2010. http://bits.blogs.nytimes.com/.

Boczkowski, Pablo J. *Digitizing the News: Innovation in Online Newspapers.* Boston: Massachusetts Institute of Technology, 2005.

Boczkowski, Pablo J. *News at Work: Imitation in an Age of Information Abundance.* Chicago: University of Chicago Press, 2010.

Boczkowski, Pablo J. "The Process of Adopting Multimedia and Interactivity in Three Different Online Newsrooms," *Journal of Communication* 54, no. 2 (2004): 197–230. doi: 10.1111/j.1460–2466.2004.tb02624.x.

Boczkowski, Pablo J. "Rethinking Hard and Soft News Production: From Common Ground to Divergent Paths." *Journal of Communication* 59, no. 1 (2009): 98–116. doi: 10.1111/j.1460–2466.2008.01406.x.

Boczkowski, Pablo J., and Jose A. Ferris, "Multiple Media, Convergent Processes, and Divergent Products: Organizational Innovation in Digital Media Production at a European Firm." *Annals of the American Academy of Political and Social Science* 597, no. 1 (2005): 32–47. doi: 10.1177/0002716204270067.

Bowley, Graham. "Strong Year for Goldman, as It Trims Bonus Pool." *New York Times*, January 21, 2010. http://www.nytimes.com/2010/01/22/business/22goldman.html.

Branch, John. "Snowfall: The Avalanche at Tunnel Creek." *New York Times*, December 20, 2012. http://www.nytimes.com/projects/2012/snow-fall/#/?part=tunnel-creek.

Breed, Warren. "Social Control in the Newsroom: A Functional Analysis." *Social Forces* 33, no. 4 (May 1955): 326–35. doi: 10.2307.2573002.

Bruns, Axel. *Blogs, Wikipedia, Second Life, and Beyond: From Production to Produsage.* New York: Peter Lang Publishing, 2008.

Bucy, Erik P. "Interactivity in Society: Locating an Elusive Concept." *Information Society: An International Journal* 20, no. 5 (2004): 373–83. doi: 10.1080/01972240490508063.

Bumiller, Elisabeth. "Video Shows U.S. Killing of Reuters Employees." *New York Times*, April 5, 2010. http://www. Nytimes.com/2010/04/06/world/middleeast/06baghdad.html?scp=1&sq=WikiLeaks&st=nyt.

Buttry, Steve. "Don't Believe Anyone Who Tells You Paywalls (or Any Aspect of News-Biz Revenues) Are a Settled Matter." *Buttry Diary* (blog), December 5, 2012.

http://stevebuttry.wordpress.com/2012/12/05/dont-believe-anyone-who-tells-you-paywalls-or-any-aspect-of-news-biz-revenues-are-a-settled-matter/.

Carlson, Matt. *On the Condition of Anonymity: Unnamed Sources and the Battle for Journalism.* Chicago: University of Illinois Press, 2011.

Carlson, Matt. "Where Once Stood Titans:' Second-Order Paradigm Repair and the Vanishing US Newspaper." *Journalism* 13, no. 3 (August 2012): 267–83. doi: 10.1177/1464884911421574.

Carlson, Nicholas. "'A Bridge Too Far:' AOL Requires Patch Editors to Drum Up Ad Sales Leads." *Business Insider*, September 23, 2011. http://www.businessinsider.com/aol-requires-patch-editors-to-drum-up-ad-sales-leads-2011-9.

Carr, David. "At Flagging Tribune, Tales of a Bankrupt Culture." *New York Times*, October 5, 2010. http://www.nytimes.com/2010/10/06/business/media/06tribune.html?_r=1&src= tptw& pagewanted=all.

Carr, David. "The Fissures Are Growing for Papers." *New York Times*, July 8, 2012. http://www.nytimes.com/2012/07/09/business/media/newspapers-are-running-out-of-time-to-adapt-to-digital-future.html?_r=3&src=dayp.

Carr, David. "Newspaper Barons Resurface." *New York Times*, April 8, 2012. http://www.nytimes.com/2012/04/09/business/media/the-return-of-the-newspaper-barons.html?_r=1&pagewanted=all.

Carr, David. "A Savior in the Form of an Apple Tablet." *New York Times*, January 3, 2010. http://www.nytimes.com/2010/01/04/business/media/04carr.html.

Center for the Digital Future, USC Annenberg School. "Is America at a Digital Turning Point?" December 14, 2011. http://annenberg.usc.edu/News%20 and%20Events/News/ 111214CDF.aspx.

Chan, Sewell. "Voices That Dominate Wall Street Take a Meeker Tone on Capitol Hill." *New York Times*, January 13, 2010. http://www.nytimes.com/2010/01/14/business/14 panel.html.

Chittum, Ryan. "Anti-Paywall Dead-Enders." *Columbia Journalism Review*, December 3, 2012. http://www.cjr.org/the_audit/zombie_lies_of_the_anti-paywal. php?page=all.

Chmielewski, Dawn C., and Alex Pham. "Apple's Rumored Tablet May Write Next Chapter in Publishing." *Los Angeles Times*, January 25, 2010. http://articles.latimes.com/2010/jan/25/business/la-fi-ct-apple25–2010jan25.

Chung, Deborah S. "Interactive Features of Online Newspapers: Identifying Patterns and Predicting Use of Engaged Readers." *Journal of Computer-Mediated Communication* 13, no. 3 (April 29, 2008): 658–79. doi: 10.1111/j.1083–-6101.2008.00414.x .

Clark, Tracy Boyer. "El Mundo Wowed Me with Their Haiti Multimedia Coverage." *Innovative Interactivity*, January 26, 2010. http://www.innovativeinteractivity. com/2010/01/26/el-mundo-haiti-coverage/.

"A Closer Look at the Destruction in Haiti." *New York Times*, January 17, 2010. http://www.nytimes.com/interactive/2010/01/13/world/20100113-haiti-close-ups.html.

Cohen, Noam, and Brian Stelter. "Iraq Video Brings Notice to a Web Site." *New York*

Times, April 6, 2010. http://www.nytimes.com/2010/04/07/world/07wikileaks.html?_r=2.

Colson, Vinciane, and Francois Heinderyckx. "Do Online Journalists Belong in the Newsroom? A Belgian Case of Convergence." In Paterson and Domingo, *Making Online News* (2008), 143–54.

Columbia Journalism School Tow Center for Digital Journalism. "Introduction: The Transformation of American Journalism is Unavoidable," November 26, 2012.

Confino, Jo, and Hannah Judge-Brown. "Living Our Values: Sustainability Report." *The Guardian* and *The Observer*, December 2009. http://www.guardian.co.uk/sustainability/report-mutualisation-citizen-journalism.

Cottle, Simon. "Ethnography and Journalism: New(s) Departures in the Field." *Sociology Compass* 1, no. 1 (2007): 1–16.

Cottle, Simon. "New(s) Times: Towards a 'Second Wave' of News Ethnography." *Communications: The European Journal of Communication Research* 25 (2000): 19–41.

Creswell, Julie. "Profits for Buyout Firms as Company Debt Soared." *New York Times*, October 4, 2009. http://www.nytimes.com/2009/10/05/business/economy/05simmons.html? pagewanted=all.

Crouse, Timothy. *The Boys on the Bus*. New York: Ballantine Books, 1973.

Dance, Gabriel, Tom Jackson, and Aron Pilhofer. "Gauging Your Distraction." *New York Times*, August 4, 2009. http://www.nytimes.com/interactive/2009/07/19/technology/20090719-driving-game.htm.

Dance, Gabriel, Aron Pilhofer, Andy Lehren, and Jeff Damens. "Faces of the Dead." *New York Times*, 2012. http://www.nytimes.com/interactive/us/faces-of-the-dead.html#/copes_gregory_t.

Danny K. "New York Times' Augmented Reflection Mirror." *Bangstyle* (blog), December 9, 2011. http://www.bangstyle.com/2011/12/new-york-times-augmented-reflection-mirror/.

De Sola Pool, Ithiel. *Technologies of Freedom*. Cambridge: Harvard University Press, 1983.

Deuze, Mark. "Convergence Culture in the Creative Industries," *International Journal of Cultural Studies* 10, no. 243 (2007): 243–63. doi: 10.1177/1367877907076793.

Deuze, Mark. *Media Work*. Cambridge: Polity Press, 2007.

Deuze, Mark. "The Web and Its Journalisms: Considering the Consequences of Different Types of News Media Online." *New Media and Society* 5, no. 2 (2003): 203–30. doi: 10.1177/1461444803005002004.

Deuze, Mark. "What Is Journalism? Professional Identity and Ideology of Journalists Reconsidered." *Journalism* 6, no. 4 (2005): 442–64. doi: 10.1177/1464884905056815.

Dewey, John. *Theory of Valuation*. Chicago: University of Chicago Press, 1939.

Diamond, Edwin. *Behind the Times: Inside the New "New York Times."* New York: Villard Books, 1994.

Diamond, Jennifer. "3 More Industry Leaders Join the Mashable Media Summit." *Mashable* (blog), October 10, 2011. http://mashable.com/2011/10/10/industry-leaders-mashable-media-summit/.

Doctor, Ken. *Newsonomics: Twelve New Trends That Will Shape the News You Get.* New York: St. Martin's Press, 2010.

Domingo, David. "Interactivity in the Daily Routines of Online Newsrooms: Dealing with an Uncomfortable Myth." *Journal of Computer-Mediated Communication* 13, no. 3 (April 29, 2008): 680–704. doi: 10.1111/j.1083–6101.2008.00415.x.

Dorroh, Jennifer. "Statehouse Exodus." *American Journalism Review* (April/May 2009). http://www.ajr.org/article.asp?id=4721.

Dougherty, Connor. "Outlook Brightens for Jobless." *Wall Street Journal*, March 6, 2010. http://online.wsj.com/article/SB10001424052748703915204575103172403936754.html.

Downie, Leonard, Jr., and Michael Schudson. "The Reconstruction of American Journalism." *Columbia Journalism Review*, October 19, 2009. http://www.cjr.org/reconstruction/the reconstruction_of_american.php?page=all.

Durkheim, Emile. *The Division of Labor in Society.* New York: Free Press, 1984.

Edmonds, Rick, Emily Guskin, and Tim Rosenstiel. "Newspapers: Missed the 2010 Media Rally." *Pew Research Center's Project for Excellence in Journalism: The State of the News Media 2011*, March 14, 2011. http://stateofthemedia.org/2011/newspapers-essay/.

Eliasoph, Nina. "Routines and the Making of Oppositional News." *Critical Studies in Mass Communications* 5, no. 4 (1988): 313–34. doi: 10.1080/15295038809366719.

Emery, Michael, Edwin Emery, and Nancy Roberts. *The Press and America: An Interpretive History of the Mass Media.* 9th ed. New York: Pearson, 2000.

Epstein, Edward J. *News from Nowhere: Television and the News.* New York: Random House, 1973.

Esch, Janis. "Martin Nisenholtz Resigns from NYT Position." *Third Age.com*, November 7, 2011. http://www.thirdage.com/news/martin-nisenholtz-resigns-from-nyt-position_11-07–2011.

Estrin, James. "One in 8 Million Wins an Emmy." *New York Times*, September 29, 2010. http://lens.blogs.nytimes.com/2010/09/29/one-in-8-million-wins-an-emmy/.

Ettema, James S., and Theodore L. Glasser. *Custodians of Conscience: Investigative Journalism and Public Virtue.* New York: Columbian University Press, 1998.

"Facebook for Reporting and Storytelling," Poynter Institute. http://www.newsu.org/facebook-reporting, May 16, 2012.

Faulkner, Robert R. "Shedding Culture." In *Art from Start to Finish: Jazz, Painting, Writing and Other Improvisations*, ed. Howard Saul Becker, Robert R. Faulkner and Barbara Kirshenblatt-Gimblett. Chicago: University of Chicago Press, 2006.

Feiler, Bruce. "Should You Google at Dinner?" *New York Times*, December 10, 2010. http://www.nytimes.com/2010/12/12/fashion/12THISLIFE.html?pagewanted=all

Feuer, Alan. "A Snapshot of the World at 4 P.M." *New York Times*, July 1, 2009. http://www.nytimes.com/2009/07/02/nyregion/02rooms.html?_r=4&scp=1&sq=news%20meet ing%20room&st=cse.

Fishman, Mark. *Manufacturing the News*. Austin: University of Texas Press, 1980.

Foer, Franklin. "The Source of the Trouble." *New York*, May 21, 2005. http://nymag.com/nymetro/news/media/features/9226/.

Gans, Herbert J. *Deciding What's News: A Study of CBS Evening News, NBC Nightly News, Newsweek, and Time*. Evanston: Northwestern University Press, 1979.

Garber, Megan. "The New York Times' R&D Lab has built a tool that explores the life stories take in the social space." Nieman Journalism Lab, April 22, 2011. "http://www.niemanlab.org/2011/04/the-new-york-times-rd-lab-has-built-a-tool-that-explores-the-life-stories-take-in-the-social-space/"

Garrett, Jesse James. "The Elements of User Experience." *jjg.net*, March 30, 2000. http://www.jjg.net/elements/pdf/elements.pdf.

Gillmor, Dan. *We the Media: Grassroots Journalism By the People, For the People*. Sebastopol, CA: O'Reilly Media, 2006.

Gitlin, Todd. *Media Unlimited, Revised Edition: How the Torrent of Images and Sounds Overwhelms Our Lives*. New York: Henry Holt and Company, 2007.

Gleick, James. *The Information*. New York: Pantheon Books, 2011.

Golding, Peter, and Philip Elliot. *Making the News*. London and New York: Longman, 1979.

Goodman, Peter S., and Javier C. Hernandez. "Jobless Rates Hold Steady, Raising Hopes of Recovery." *New York Times*, March 5, 2010. http://www.nytimes.com/2010/02/06/business/economy/06jobs.html.

Goodridge, Courtney. "NYT's Brian Stelter Champions Technology." *Hill News*, September 21, 2011. http://www.thehillnews.org/?p=2915.

Greenhouse, Steven. "The Unpaid Intern, Legal or Not." *New York Times*, April 2, 2010. http://www.nytimes.com/2010/04/03/business/03intern.html?pagewanted=all&_r=2&.

Haar, James. *Essays on Italian Poetry and Music in the Renaissance, 1350–1600*. Berkeley: University of California Press, 1986.

Hagan, Joe. "Bleeding 'Times' Blood." *New York*, October 13, 2008. http://nymag.com/news/media/51015/index5.html.

"Haiti: 360," CNN. January 17, 2010. http://www.cnn.com/interactive/2010/01/world/ haiti.360/index.html.

Hakim, Danny, and William K. Rashbaum. "Paterson Is Said to Have Ordered Calls in Abuse Case." *New York Times*, March 1, 2010. http://www.nytimes.com/2010/03/12/nyregion/ 02paterson.html.

Hakim, Danny, and William K. Rashbaum. "Spitzer Is Linked to Prostitution Ring." *New York Times*, March 10, 2008. http://www.nytimes.com/2008/03/10/nyregion/10cnd-spitzer.html?pagewanted=all.

Harlow, Summer. "Change in Social Media Editors at USA Today, New York Times," *Journalism in the Americas blog* (blog), Knight Center for Journalism in the

Americas, University of Texas, Austin, December 10, 2010. http://knightcenter. utexas.edu/blog/changes-social-media-editors-usa-today-new-york-times.

Haughney, Christine. "New York Times Seeks Buyouts from 30 in Newsroom." *New York Times*, December 3, 2012. http://mediadecoder.blogs.nytimes. com/2012/12/03/new-york-times-seeks-buyouts-from-30-newsroom-managers/.

Heim, Anna. "Why Did the New York Times Company Just Lose Its CEO?" *Next Web*, December 16, 2011. http://thenextweb.com/media/2011/12/16/why-did-the-new-york-times-company-just-lose-its-ceo/.

Henrikson, Teemu. "Reuters Appoints Social Media Editor." *editorsweblog.org* (blog), World Editors Forum, July 7, 2011. http://www.editorsweblog.org/ web_20/2011/07/reuters_ appoints_social_media_editor.php.

Hernandez, Raymond. "What Makes Gillibrand Scary to Rivals?" *New York Times*, April 2, 2010. http://www.nytimes.com/2010/04/03/nyregion/03gillibrand. html.

Hindman, Matthew. *The Myth of Digital Democracy*. Princeton: Princeton University Press, 2009.

Hirschorn, Michael. "End Times." *Atlantic*, January/February 2009. http://www. theatlantic.com/magazine/archive/2009/01/end-times/7220/.

Hoelzle, Urs. "The Google Gospel of Speed." *Think Quarterly* http://www.think-withgoogle.com/quarterly/speed/the-google-gospel-of-speed-urs-hoelzle. html, January 2012.

Holcomb, Jesse, Kim Gross, and Amy Mitchell. "How Mainstream Media Outlets Use Twitter." Journalism.org: Pew Research Center's Project for Excellence in Journalism, November 14, 2011. http://www.journalism.org/analysis_report/ how_mainstream_media_outlets_ use_twitter?src=prc-headline.

Howard, Phil N. *The Digital Origins of Dictatorship and Democracy: Information Technology and Political Islam*. Oxford: Oxford University Press, 2010.

Hoyt, Clark. "The Danger of Always Being On." *New York Times*, April 10, 2010. http://www.nytimes.com/2010/04/11/opinion/11pubed.html.

Huff, Steve. "Arthur Sulzberger Jr. Admits the Inevitable." *New York Observer*, September 8, 2010. http://www.observer.com/2010/daily-transom/arthur-sulzberger-jr-admits-inevitable.

Ingram, Matthew. "Is More Real-Time Information a Dream Or a Nightmare?" *GigaOM* (blog), October 7, 2011. http://gigaom.com/2011/10/07/is-more-real-time-information-a-dream-or-a-nightmare/.

Ingram, Matthew. "Should There Be a Pulitzer Prize for Twitter Reporting?" *GigaOM*, November 30, 2011. http://gigaom.com/2011/11/30/should-there-be-a-pulitzer-prize-for-twitter-reporting/.

Ives, Nat. "New York Times Plans Public Beta Site for Its Experiments." *Ad Age Mediaworks*, June 15, 2010. http://adage.com/article/mediaworks/york-times-plans-public-beta-site-experiments/144452/.

Jackaway, Gwyneth L. *Media at War: Radio's Challenge to the Newspapers, 1924–1939*. Westport, CT: Praeger, 1995.

Jarvis, Jeff. "Networked Journalism." *Buzz Machine* (blog), July 5, 2006. http://www.buzzmachine.com/2006/07/05/networked-journalism/.

Jarvis, Jeff. "Public Parts," *Buzz Machine* (blog). August 1, 2011. http://www.buzzmachine.com/publicparts/.

Jenkins, Henry. *Convergence Culture: Where Old and New Media Collide.* New York: New York University Press, 2006.

Jenkins, Henry. "If It Doesn't Spread It's Dead (Part Two): Sticky and Spreadable—Two Paradigms." *Confessions of an Acafan* (blog), February 13, 2009. http://henryjenkins.org/2009/02/if_it_doesnt_spread_its_dead_p_1.html.

Johnson, Kirk. "More with Dementia Wander from Home." *New York Times*, May 4, 2010. http://www.nytimes.com/2010/05/05/us/05search.html?pagewanted=all.

Jones, Alex S. *Losing the News: The Future of the News That Feeds Democracy.* Oxford: Oxford University Press, 2009.

Kamer, Foster. "Nick Denton's 'State of Gawker 2012' Memo: 'Relentless and Cynical Traffic-Trawling Is Bad for the Soul." *New York Observer*, January 5, 2012. http://www.observer.com/2012/01/leaked-gawker-memo-01052011/.

Karlsson, Michael. "The Immediacy of Online News, the Visibility of Journalistic Processes and a Restructuring of Journalistic Authority." *Journalism* 12, no. 3 (April 2011): 279–95. doi: 10.1177/1464884910388223.

Klinenberg, Eric. "Convergence: News Production in a Digital Age." *ANNALS of the American Academy of Political and Social Science* 597 (2005): 48–64. doi: 10.1177/0002716204270346.

Klinenberg, Eric. *Heat Wave: A Social Autopsy of Disaster in Chicago.* Chicago: University of Chicago Press, 2002.

Knight Digital Media Center. "KDMC Presentations." http://multimedia.journalism.berkeley.edu/presentations/cat/social. Accessed November 17, 2011.

Kopper, Gerd, Albrecht Kolthoff, and A. Czepek, "Research Review: Online JournalismA Report On Current and Continue Research and Major Questions in the International Discussion." *Journalism Studies* 1, no. 3 (2000): 499–512.

Krochmal, Mo. "Advanced Social Media with @Sree and @brianstelter." *Krochmal's posterous* (blog), May 15, 2011. http://krochmal.posterous.com/advanced-social-media-with-sree-and-brianstel.

Krugman, Paul. *The Return of Depression Economics and the Crisis of 2008.* New York: W. W. Norton & Company, 2009.

Kuhn, Thomas S. *The Structure of Scientific Revolutions.* Chicago: University of Chicago Press, 1970.

Lasar, Matthew. "Has the Internet 'Hamsterized' Journalism?" *Ars Technica*, June 2011. http://arstechnica.com/web/news/2011/06/has-the-internet-hamsterized-journalism.ars.

Lawson, Richard. "*New York Times* 'TimesCast': Desire under the Big Red Stairs." *Gawker*, March 22, 2010. http://gawker.com/5499445/new-york-times-TimesCast-desire-under-the-big-red-stairs.

Lawson-Borders, Gracie. *Media Organizations and Convergence: Case Studies of Media Convergence Pioneers.* Mahwah, NJ: Lawrence Erlbaum, 2006.

Lewis, Seth C. "From Journalism to Information: The Transformation of the Knight Foundation and News Innovation." *Mass Communication and Society* 15, no. 3 (2012): 309–34. doi: 10.1080/15205436.2011.611607.

Lewis, Seth C. "Journalism Innovation and Participation: An Analysis of the Knight News Challenge." *International Journal of Communication* 5 (2011): 1623–48. doi: 1932–8036/20111623.

Lewis, Seth C. "The Tension between Professional Control and Open Participation: Journalism and Its Boundaries." *Information, Communication and Society* 15, no. 6 (2012): 836–66. doi: 10.1080/1369118X.2012.674150.

Livingston, Steven, and W. Lance Bennett. "Gatekeeping, Indexing, and Live-Event News: Is Technology Altering the Construction of News?" *Political Communication* 20, no. 4 (2003): 363–80. doi: 10.1080/10584600390244121.

Mackey, Robert. "Twitter Transformed into a Barometer of Anxiety as Egypt Waited for Election Results." *New York Times: The Lede* (blog), June 25, 2012. http://thelede.blogs.nytimes.com/2012/06/25/twitter-transformed-into-a-barometer-of-anxiety-and-exasperation-as-egypt-waited-for-the-name-of-its-new-president/.

Mangan, Katherine. "Stop the Presses: Revamped Journalism Courses Attract Hordes of Students." *Chronicle of Higher Education*, September 21, 2009. http://chronicle.com/article/Stop-the-Presses-Revamped/48497/.

McAdams, Mindy. *Flash Journalism: How to Create Multimedia News Packages.* New York: Focal Press, 2005.

McChesney, Robert W. "The Problem of Journalism: A Political Economic Contribution to an Explanation of the Crisis in Contemporary US Journalism." *Journalism Studies* 4, no. 3 (2003): 299–329. doi: 10.1080/1461670032000099688.

McGowan, William. *Gray Lady Down: What the Decline and Fall of the "New York Times" Means for America.* New York: Encounter Books, 2010.

Meier, Barry. "The High Cost of Failing Artificial Hips." *New York Times*, December 27, 2011. http://www.nytimes.com/2011/12/28/business/the-high-cost-of-failing-artificial-hips.html?_r=2&pagewanted=all

Meier, Klaus. "Innovations in Central European Newsrooms." *Journalism Practice* 1, no. 1 (2007): 4–19. doi: 10.1080/17512780601078803.

Meridian Web Design. "Make It Sticky. Make 'Em Stick." Meridian Design, 2003. http://www.meridiandesign.net/ASS2003/stickyelements.html.

Michel, Amanda. "Get Off the Bus." *Columbia Journalism Review*, March–April 2009. http://www.cjr.org/feature/get_off_the_bus.php?page=all.

Michelstein, Eugenia, and Pablo J. Boczkowski. "Between Tradition and Change: A Review of Recent Research on Online News Production." *Journalism* 10, no.5 (October 2009): 562–86. doi: 10.1177/1464884909106533.

Michelstein, Eugenia, and Pablo J. Boczkowski. "Tradition and Transformation in Online News Production and Consumption." In *The Oxford Handbook of Internet Studies*, ed. William Dutton. Oxford: Oxford University Press, forthcoming.

Mnookin, Seth. "The Kingdom and the Paywall." *New York Magazine*, July 24, 2011. http://nymag.com/news/media/new-york-times-2011-8/.

Mnookin, Seth. "*The New York Times'* Lonely War." *Vanity Fair*, December 2008. http://www.vanityfair.com/politics/features/2008/12/nytimes200812.

Morgenson, Gretchen, and Louise Story. "Clients Worried about Goldman's Dueling Goals." *New York Times*, May 18, 2010. http://www.nytimes.com/2010/05/19/business/ 19client.html?pagewanted=all.

Morgenson, Gretchen, and Louis Story. "House Advantage." *New York Times*, Business Series http://topics.nytimes.com/top/news/business/series/house_advantage_series/index.html (accessed March 8, 2012).

Morton, John. "40 Years of Death in the Afternoon." *American Journalism Review* (November 1991). http://www.ajr.org/article.asp?id=73.

Morville, Peter, and Louis Rosenfeld. *Information Architecture for the World Wide Web*. Sebastapol, CA: O'Reilly Books, 1998.

Moss, Michael. "The Burger That Shattered Her Life." *New York Times*, October 3, 2009. http://www.nytimes.com/2009/10/04/health/04meat.html?_r=2.

Myers, Steve. "Americans Spend Just a Fraction of Online Time with News Compared to Social Media." *Poynter*, September 14, 2011. http://www.poynter.org/latest-news/mediawire/145736/americans-spend-just-a-fraction-of-online-time-with-news-compared-to-social-media/.

Neuman, W. Russell. *The Future of the Mass Audience*. Cambridge: Cambridge University Press, 1991.

Neuman, William. "Goodbye Food Pyramid, Hello Dinner Plate." *New York Times*, May 27, 2011. http://www.nytimes.com/2011/05/28/health/nutrition/28plate.html?_r=1.

Newport, Frank. "Americans Rate Computer Industry Best, Federal Gov't Worst." *Gallup*, August 29, 2011. http://www.gallup.com/poll/149216/Americans-Rate-Computer-Industry-Best-Federal-Gov-Worst.aspx.

Newspaper Guild of New York. "In Silence, Times Guild Sends a Loud Message." March 2011. http://www.nyguild.org/guild-protest-at-times-editors-meeting.html.

The New York Times. "Ethical Journalism: A Handbook of Values and Practices for the News and Editorial Departments." September 2004. http://www.nytco.com/pdf/NYT_Ethical_ Journalism_0904.pdf.

Nielsen, Jakob. *Designing Web Usability: The Practice of Simplicity*. Boston: New Riders, 1999.

Nussbaum, Emily. "The New Journalism: Goosing the Grey Lady." *New York Magazine*, January 11, 2009. http://nymag.com/news/features/all-new/53344/.

"NYT Tokyo-Based Business Reporter Hiroko Tabuchi Tweets Her Verdict: 'Toyota Sucks!'" *NYT Picker* (blog), March 30, 2010. http://www.nytpick.com/2010/03/nyt-tokyo-based-business-reporter.html.

O'Reilly, Tim. "What Is Web 2.0: Design Patterns and Business Models for the Next Generation of Software." *O'Reilly*, September 30, 2005. http://oreilly.com/web2/archive/what-is-web-20.html.

O'Sullivan, John. "Delivering Ireland: Journalism's Search for a Role Online." *International Communication Gazette* 67, no. 1 (2005): 45–68. doi: 10.1177/0016549205049178.

Pardee, Thomas. "Finding the Sweet Spot for Journalism and Social Media." *Ad Age MediaWorks*, December 14, 2010. http://adage.com/article/mediaworks/finding-journalism-s-social-media-sweet-spot/147632/.

Parker-Pope, Tara. "An Ugly Toll of Technology: Impatience and Forgetfulness." *New York Times*, June 6, 2010. http://www.nytimes.com/2010/06/07/technology/07brainside.html.

Paterson, Chris, and David Domingo, eds. *Making Online News: The Ethnography of New Media Production.* New York: Peter Lang Publishing, 2008.

Paterson, Chris, and David Domingo, eds. *Making Online News: The Ethnography of New Media Production.* 2nd ed. New York: Peter Lang Publishing, 2011.

"The People Formerly Known as the Audience." *Economist*, July 7, 2011. http://www.economist.com/node/18904124.

Perez-Pena, Richard. "Times Names Jonathon Landman Culture Editor." *New York Times*, September 16, 2009. http://www.nytimes.com/2009/09/16/business/media/16times.html.

Peters, Jeremy W. "Some Newspapers, Tracking Readers Online, Shift Coverage." *New York Times*, September 5, 2010. http://www.nytimes.com/2010/09/06/business/media/06track.html?_r=1.

Pew Research Center for the People and the Press. "Americans Spend More Time Following the News." September 12, 2010. http://www.people-press.org/2010/09/12/americans-spending-more-time-following-the-news/.

Pew Research Center's Project for Excellence in Journalism, "The Changing Newsroom: What Is Being Gained and What Is Being Lost in American's Daily Newspaper?" *Journalism.org*, July 21, 2008. http://www.journalism.org/files/PEJ- the%20Changing%20Newspaper%20Newsroom%20FINAL%20DRAFT-NOEMBARGO-PDF.pdf.

Pew Research Center's Project for Excellence in Journalism. "The State of the News Media. 2013. Newspapers Stabilizing but Still Threatened." July 18, 2013. http://www.stateofthemedia.org/2013/.

Phelps, Andrew. "A Post-Mortem with Raju Narisetti: 'I Would Have Actually Tried to Move Faster." *Nieman Journalism Lab*, January 23, 2012. http://www.niemanlab.org/2010/01/a-post-mortem-with-raju-narisetti-i-would-have-actually-tried-to-move-faster/.

Pickard, Victor, Josh Stearns, and Craig Aaron. *Saving the News: Towards a National Journalism Strategy.* Washington, DC: Free Press, 2009. http://www.freepress.net/files/saving_the_news.pdf.

Pogue, David. *The World According to Twitter.* New York: Black Dog & Leventhal Publishers, 2009.

Prior, Jon. "Foreclosures in 2011 Break Last Year's Record: RealtyTrac." *Housing Wire,* January 12, 2011. http://www.housingwire.com/2011/01/12/foreclosures-reach-record-high-in-2010-realtytrac.

Quandt, Thorsten. "Old and New Routines in German Online Newsrooms." In Paterson and Domingo, *Making Online News* (2008), 77–97.

Reese, Stephen. "The News Paradigm and the Ideology of Objectivity: A Socialist at the Wall Street Journal." *Critical Studies in Mass Communication* 7, no. 4 (1990): 390–409. doi: 10.1080/15295039009360187.

Richman, Dan, and Andrea James. "Seattle P-I to Publish Last Edition Tuesday." *Seattle Post-Intelligencer*, March 16, 2009. http://www.seattlepi.com/business/article/Seattle-P-I-to-publish-last-edition-Tuesday-1302597.phpFirefoxHTML%5CShell%5COpen%5CCommand.

Richtel, Matt. "Attached to Technology and Paying a Price." *New York Times*, June 6, 2010. http://www.nytimes.com/2010/06/07/technology/07brain.html?_r=3.

Richtel, Matt, Julie Scelfo, Tara Parker-Pope, and Marjorie Connelly. "Your Brain on Computers." *New York Times*, Times Series, June 6, 2010. http://topics.nytimes.com/top/features/timestopics/series/your_brain_on_computers/index.html.

Roberts, Jeff John. "New York Times Contest Brings Tech Startups into Its Headquarters." *paidContent*, January 29, 2013. http://paidcontent.org/2013/01/29/new-york-times-contest-brings-tech-start-ups-into-its-headquarters/.

Robinson, Susan. "The Mission of the J-Blog: Recapturing Journalistic Authority Online." *Journalism* 7, no. 1 (February 2006): 65–83. doi: 10.1177/1464884906059428.

Rosen, Jay. "Bloggers v. Journalists Is Over." *Press Think* (blog), January 21, 2005. http://archive.pressthink.org/2005/01/21/berk_essy.html.

Rosen, Jay. "The People Formerly Known as the Audience." *Huffington Post*, June 30, 2006. http://www.huffingtonpost.com/jay-rosen/the-people-formerly-known_1_b_24113.html.

Rosen, Jay. "The Twisted Psychology of Bloggers vs. Journalists: My Talk at South by Southwest." *Press Think* (blog), March 12, 2011. http://pressthink.org/2011/03/the-psychology-of-bloggers-vs-journalists-my-talk-at-south-by-southwest/.

Rosen, Jay. "What I Think I Know about Journalism." *Press Think* (blog), April 26, 2011. http://pressthink.org/2011/04/what-i-think-i-know-about-journalism/.

Rosenbloom, Stephanie. "In Bid to Sway Sales, Cameras Track Shoppers." *New York Times*, March 19, 2010. http://www.nytimes.com/interactive/2010/03/20/business/surveillance-videos.html?ref=business.

Rosenbloom, Stephanie. "The New Touch-Face of Vending Machines." *New York Times*, May 26, 2010. http://www.nytimes.com/2010/05/26/business/26vending.html.

Ryfe, David Michael. *Can Journalism Survive? An Inside Look in American Newsrooms*. Malden, MA: Polity Press, 2012.

Ryfe, David Michael. "Guest Editor's Introduction: New Institutionalism and the News." *Political Communication* 23, no. 2 (2006): 135–44. doi: 10.1080/10584600600728109.

Ryfe, David Michael. "Structure, Agency and Change in an American Newsroom." *Journalism* 10, no. 5 (October 2009): 665–83. doi: 10.1177/1464884909106538.

Salmon, Felix. "Whither the M&A Scoop?" *Reuters* (blog), August 15, 2011. http://blogs.reuters.com/felix-salmon/2011/08/15/whither-the-ma-scoop/.

Schiller, Vivian. "A Letter to Readers about TimesSelect." *New York Times*, September, 18, 2007. http://www.nytimes.com/ref/membercenter/lettertoreaders.html/.

Schlesinger, Philip. *Putting "Reality" Together: BBC News.* London: Constable, 1978.

Schudson, Michael. *Discovering the News: A Social History of American Newspapers.* New York: Basic Books, 1978.

Schudson, Michael. *The Sociology of News.* New York: W. W. Norton and Company, 2011.

Schudson, Michael. "The Sociology of News Production." *Media Culture and Society* 11, no. 3 (1989): 263–82.

Shaffer, Christine. "Viracon Glass Helps New York Times Building Shine." *Green Building Pro,* May 2, 2011. http://www.greenbuildingpro.com/articles/57-features/3062-viracon-glass-helps-new-york-times-building-shine.

Shirky, Clay. *Here Comes Everybody: The Power of Organizing without Organizations.* New York: Penguin Books, 2008.

Sigal, Leon V. *Reporters and Officials: The Organization and Politics of Newsmaking.* Lexington, MA: D. C. Heath, 1973.

Silverman, Craig. "Profiles in Courage: Social Media Editors at Big Media Outlets." *MediaShift* (blog), PBS, November 19, 2009. http://www.pbs.org/mediashift/2009/11/profiles-in-courage-social-media-editors-at-big-media-outlets323.html.

Singer, Jane B. "Strange Bedfellows: The Diffusion of Convergence in Four News Organizations." *Journalism Studies* 5, no. 1 (2004): 3–18. doi: 10.1080/1461670032000174701.

Singer, Jane B. "Who Are These Guys? The Online Challenge to the Notion of Journalistic Professionalism." *Journalism* 4, no. 3 (2003): 139–64. doi: 10.1177/146488490342001.

Smolkin, Rachel. "Challenging Times." *American Journalism Review* (February-March 2007). http://www.ajr.org/article.asp?id=4262.

Sonderman, Jeff. "The Problem with Retweets and How Journalists Can Solve It," *Poynter* (blog), November 8, 2011. http://www.poynter.org/category/latest-news/media-lab/social-media/.

Spence, E. H., and A. Quinn. "Information Ethics as a Guide for New Media." *Journal of Mass Media Ethics* 23, no.4 (2008): 264–79. doi: 10.1080/089005208020889.

Stark, David. *The Sense of Dissonance: Accounts of Worth in Economic Life.* Princeton: Princeton University Press, 2009. http://press.princeton.edu/titles/9070.html.

Starkman, Dean. "The Hamster Wheel: Why Running as Fast as We Can Is Getting Us Nowhere." *Columbia Journalism Review,* SeptemberOctober, 2010. http://www.cjr.org/cover_story/the_hamster_wheel.php?page=all.

Starr, Paul. *The Creation of the Media: Political Origins of Modern Communications.* New York: Basic Books, 2004.

Starr, Paul. "Goodbye to the Age of Newspapers (Hello to a New Era of Corruption)." *New Republic,* March 4, 2009. http://www.tnr.com/article/goodbye-the-age-newspapers-hello-new-era-corruption.

Steensen, Steen. "What's Stopping Them: Towards a Grounded Theory of Innovation in Online Journalism." *Journalism Studies* 10 (2009): 821–36. doi: 10.1080/14616700902975087.

Stephens, Mitchell. *A History of News*. 3rd ed. New York: Oxford University Press, 2007.

Stephens, Mitchell. "History of Newspapers." *Collier's Encyclopedia*. http://www.nyu.edu/classes/stephens/Collier's%20page.htm. Accessed March 12, 2012.

Stoeffel, Kat. "New York Times Decides Tweeting Is Not a Job." *New York Observer*, December 9, 2010. http://www.observer.com/2010/12/emnew-york-timesem-decides-tweeting-is-not-a-job/.

Stone, Brad. "Three Reasons Why the iPad Won't Kill Amazon's Kindle." *New York Times Bits* (blog), January 27, 2010. http://bits.blogs.nytimes.com/2010/01/27/three-reasons-the-ipad-wont-kill-amazons-kindle/.

Story, Louise, and Gretchen Morgenson. "S.E.C. Accuses Goldman of Fraud in Housing Deal." *New York Times*, April 16, 2010. http://www.nytimes.com/2010/04/17/business/17goldman.html.

Stravato, Michael. "With No Job, a Family Struggles." *New York Times*, November 11, 2009 (audio slideshow, 3:15). http://www.nytimes.com/interactive/2009/11/11/us/20091111_FAMILIES2_AUDIOSS/index.html.

Sundar, S. Shyam, Sriram Kalyanaraman, and Justin Brown. "Explicating Web Site Interactivity: Impression-Formation Effects in Political Campaign Sites." *Communication Research* 30, no.1 (2003): 30–59. doi: 10.1177/0093650202239025.

Swanson, Carl. "The Battle for the Newsroom." *New York*, May 26, 2003. http://nymag.com/nymetro/news/media/features/n_8722/index1.html.

Talese, Gay. *The Kingdom and the Power*. New York: Random House, 1969.

Tartakoff, Joseph. "NYT's Nisenholtz's Speech: The Importance of Engagement." *paidContent.org*, April 30, 2010. http://paidcontent.org/article/419-nyts-nisenholtzs-speech-the-importance-of-engagement/.

Tenore, Mallary Jean. "How Paywalls Affect Social Media Efforts at Five News Sites." *Poynter*, March 7, 2012. http://www.poynter.org/latest-news/top-stories/165625/how-6-news-sites-combine-paywalls-and-social-media-efforts/.

Terranova, Tiziana. *Network Culture: Politics for the Information Age*. London: Pluto Press, 2004.

Theim, Rebecca. "Save the Times-Picayune!" *Change.org*. http://www.change.org/petitions/save-the-times-picayune, May 2012.

Tifft, Susan E. and Alex S. Jones. *The Trust: The Private and Powerful Family behind the "New York Times."* Boston: Little Brown, 1999.

Tuchman, Gaye. *Making News: A Study in the Construction of Reality*. New York: Free Press, 1978.

Tuchman, Gaye. "Making News by Doing Work: Routinizing the Unexpected." *American Journal of Sociology* 79, no.1 (July 1973): 110–31. http://www.jstor.org/stable/2776714.

Tuchman, Gaye. "Objectivity as a Strategic Ritual." *American Journal of Sociology* 77 (1972): 660–80.

Turkle, Sherry. *Alone Together: Why We Expect More from Technology and Less from Each Other*. New York: Basic Books, 2011.

Turner, Zeke. "Jill Abramson Steps Away from Managing Editor Role to Focus on the Times Digital Operations." *New York Observer*, May 19, 2010. http://www.observer.com/2010/05/jill-abramson-steps-away-from-managing-editor-role-to-focus-on-the-emtimesem-digital-operations/.

University of Michigan. Journalism Jobs and Internships. "News Application Developer/Journalist at the *Milwaukee Journal Sentinel*." April 3, 2012. http://memphisjourjobs.com/2012/04/03/news-application-developerjournalist-at-the-milwaukee-journal-sentinel/.

Urbina, Ian. "Toll Mounts in West Virginia Coal Mine Explosion." *New York Times*, April 5, 2010. http://www.nytimes.com/2010/04/06/us/06westvirginia.html.

Usher, Nikki. "Less of Less: FCC-Commissioned Report Finds a 'Surprisingly Small Audience for Local News Traffic." *Nieman Learning Lab*, June 15, 2011. http://www.niemanlab.org/2011 /06/ less-of-less-fcc-commissioned-report-finds-a-surprisingly-small-audience-for-local-news-traffic/.

Usher, Nikki. "What Impact Is SEO Having on Journalists? Reports from the Field." *Nieman Learning Lab* (blog), September 23, 2010. http://www.niemanlab.org/2010/09/what-impact-is-seo-having-on-journalists-reports-from-the-field/.

Usher, Nikki. "Will the Last Reporter Please Turn Out the Lights. Professional Journalists—Hands Off! Citizen Journalism as Civic Responsibility." In *Will The Last Reporter Please Turn Out the Lights? The Collapse of Journalism and What Can Be Done to Fix It*, ed. Robert McChesney and Victor Pickard. New York: New Press, 2011.

Usher, Nikki, and Seth C. Lewis. "Lessons from #Mozfest: How the Knight and Mozilla Foundations Are Thinking about Open Source." *Nieman Learning Lab*, November 16, 2011. http://www.niemanlab.org/2011/11/lessons-from-mozfest-how-the-knight-and-mozilla-foundations-are-thinking-about-open-source/.

Usher, Nikki, and Patti Riley. "The *Christian Science Monitor* and Change: Keeping the Values of a Print Daily in a Web-First World." Paper presented at the National Communication Association, San Francisco, CA, November 2010.

Van Natta, Don, Jr., Jo Becker, and Graham Bowley. "Tabloid Hack Attack on Royals, and Beyond." *New York Times Magazine*, September 1, 2010. http://www.nytimes.com/2010/09/05/magazine/05hacking-t.html?pagewanted=all.

Waldman, Steve, and Working Group on Information Needs of Communities. *The Information Needs of Communications*. Federal Communications Commission, July 2011. www.fcc.gov/Infoneedsreport.

Wharton School at the University of Pennsylvania. "Web 3.0: The 'Social Wave' and How It Disrupts the Internet." July 6, 2011. http://knowledge.wharton.upenn.edu/article.cfm?articleid=2808.

White, David Manning, "The Gate Keeper." *Journalism Quarterly* 27 (1950): 383–90.

Williams, Andy, Clair Wardle, and Karin Wahl-Jorgensen, "Have They Got News for Us?" *Journalism Practice*, 5, no. 1 (2011): 85–99. doi: 10.1080/17512781003670031.

Williams, Bruce A., and Michael X. Delli Carpini, "Real Ethical Concerns and Fake News: *The Daily Show* and the Challenge of the New Media Environment." In *The Stewart/Colbert Effect: Essays on the Real Impacts of Fake News*, ed. Amarnath Amarsingam. Jefferson, NC: McFarland & Co., 2011.

Winder, Rob. "Maximizing Multimedia in Online News." *Media Helping Media*, August 17, 2011. http://www.mediahelpingmedia.org/training-resources/on line-journalism/370-maximising-multimedia-in-online-news-.

Wise, Zach, Ron Lieber, and Tanzina Vega. "31 Steps to a Financial Tune-up." *New York Times*, March 24, 2010. http://www.nytimes.com/interactive/2010/03/24/ your-money/financial-tuneup-checklist.html.

Wodtke, Christina. *Information Architecture: Blueprints for the Web*. Boston: New Riders, 2003.

Wodtke, Christina, and Austin Govella. *Information Architecture: Blue Prints for the Web*. 2nd ed. Berkley: New Riders, 2009.

Index